Life and _____

making sense of it

A thought-provoking spiritual perspective on our lives

Francis O'Neill

Pat

It has been great knowing you and being inside in helping to bring this book to fruition.

Thank you for your much valued review, comments and support — I'm really grateful to you.

Frankie

29/04/2016

Praise for Life and Death: Making Sense of It

This book has the potential to change the world view of its readers. It offers a broad yet very detailed sweep across the whole spectrum of the subject matter, which makes the book wide-ranging and inclusive.

I am pretty cynical when it comes to believing in the supernatural in any form, but I found myself having to stop short and really think about the possibility of life after death here. I particularly liked how it touches on the fact that people who believe in life after death are happier than those who don't. Food for thought, indeed.

This is a very individual and readable book which is written from the heart, and which reaches out with great warmth to its readers.

Joanne Harrington, professional editor
(via PublishNation UK)

Life and Death: Making Sense of It

ISBN: 978-0-9934626-1-0 (Paperback)

Cover image (with modification): 'Game over' by Sinisa Botas.

Printed by Lightning Source

Life and Death: Making Sense of It is the first book in a series of planned books by the author. Other titles to include:
The Soul Agenda | **The Spiritual Roadmap** | **Fringe Benefits Denied**.
For updates on these titles please visit LifeandDeaththeBook.com or the publisher website.

 Some Inspiration Publications
SomeInspiration.com
Cotswolds, UK

Acknowledgements

Firstly, a very personal thank you and gratitude to the mediums and authors, Alan and Andrea Grieveson, for the exchanges we've had on spiritual matters over the years, and for the knowledge they helped me to acquire on three of my previous lives. I write about these lives in *The Soul Question* chapter. I'm also very grateful to Andrea for her answers to the questionnaire in *The Other Side* chapter. Her input has helped enormously to add value to that particular chapter.

I'd like to also thank the medium, Colin Fry (now on the *Other Side*), for permitting me to use his one-to-one reading example for the *Fringe Benefits* chapter.

Books have played a very important part in my life and journey. I owe a huge gratitude of thanks to all of the writers whose works have tested, or helped to influence, the direction and metal of my beliefs – and subsequently helped my own writing. These are the writers of books across a spectrum of topics from the sciences and psychology out to the fringes, the spiritual and downright esoteric. A number of these wonderful souls get a mention, or more, in the following pages.

I also thank Wikipedia. What a fabulous resource, and one that I have made full use of over the years. How fortunate for those of us across the world who have access to such a knowledge bank and educational *game-changer* at our fingertips.

Dedication

This book is dedicated to my mother, and also to my partner, Annie.

To my mother, Margaret, not only for the obvious of bringing me into this world but for all the love and support she gave me as a child and young adult. And particularly – in context with this work – her tireless help on getting me to improve on my reading, writing and spelling all those years ago. Thank you mother, I'm so grateful to be able to apply the skills you helped me with, in this way.

And to Annie, with whom I have laughed, argued, cried and travelled for a good chunk of this journey. It is in great measure down to her love and belief in me that has helped me to stay focused and grounded while writing this work. On that score, she has also been instrumental in helping to edit a good part of this book – thank you sweetheart.

CONTENTS

Introduction -- **1**

    The book's content in brief --- 2

    Writing this book -- 3

    A guide for beginners and seasoned travellers----------------------- 13

    Notes & references --- 15

Chapter 1 The Good Life -- **16**

    The Good Life Milestones --- 17

    What a life... --- 21

    A big missing component --- 23

    Getting a handle on things --- 25

    Where to next--- 27

    Notes & references --- 28

Chapter 2 Are You Ready for This? -------------------------- **29**

    It's coming... the elephant in our lives ----------------------------- 29

    Another big burning question--- 33

    Father Christmas – a rite of passage --------------------------------- 38

    Soul Journey Start -- 42

    Life and Death Questions--- 44

    Remembering where we are -- 51

    Notes & references --- 58

Chapter 3 Fringe Benefits --- **59**

    Ten reasons why I believe in the afterlife -------------------------- 60

    The Paranormal -- 63

    Ghosts and Poltergeists -- 73

    Possible explanations for ghostly paranormal events--------------- 90

    Near-Death Experience (NDE) -- 98

    Children's recall of previous lives ----------------------------------- 109

    Past Life Regression (PLR) -- 118

    Communications through Psychics and Mediums ----------------- 128

    Notes & references --- 135

Chapter 4 Out of the Garden ------------------------------------ **140**

    The apes aren't building cars or measuring the stars ------------- 141

    Living in innocence --- 142

    Leaving the Garden --- 144

Life – who'd have thought it? --- 148
The Missing Links-- 149
The Awakening --- 153
Why the sudden change?--- 158
Intelligence and consciousness-- 163
Of Sludge and Slime -- 167
Notes & references -- 171

Chapter 5 The Soul Question ----------------------------------- **174**
The Soul and Christian teachings ------------------------------------- 175
Being told of past lives--- 184
There is meaning to life -- 189
The Soul Point-- 191
Vehicles of the Soul -- 194
Does an ant have a Soul? --- 205
Reincarnation and the Soul --- 207
Karma – the law of balance -- 213
Notes & references --- 221

Chapter 6 The Other Side -------------------------------------- **225**
Starting from This Side--- 226
Hell, Fire and Damnation – avoiding the dark side-------------------- 238
Moving to the Other Side--- 246
Time out --- 256
Arriving at the Other Side-- 257
The Other Side as seen through mediums ------------------------------ 262
So where is the Other Side? -- 269
Returning to Earth for another life ----------------------------------- 272
The Other Side in summary --- 273
Notes & references --- 276

Chapter 7 Life and Death: Making sense of it-------------- **278**
Quenching our spiritual thirst -- 280
The Soul on another physical journey --------------------------------- 285
Urgency from a Buddhist perspective--------------------------------- 290
Getting the bigger picture -- 291
Mark this… -- 293
What if… --- 294
Notes & references --- 296

Appendix: Six months to live ------------------------------------ **298**

Bibliography --- **304**

Index --- **311**

About The Author -- **316**

📖 BONUS ONLINE CONTENT

Where displayed indicates associated articles that can be found online by visiting the book's website: **LifeandDeaththeBook.com**

INTRODUCTION

What is life all about and what happens when we die? Does it all just end there, at that point, or do we go to somewhere else, to what is often called the *Other Side*? If we do go to the Other Side what is it like when we get there? More importantly what is the point of it all? Is there actually a point to our lives or is it simply the outpouring of what we call nature and evolution – needing no willing participation on our part?

This book examines and proposes answers to these questions, and more... It proposes an overriding vision intended to aid a better understanding of life and death. This is presented from a spiritual and evolutionary perspective, that ultimately includes all of life, not just ourselves.

> Our new Constitution is now established, and has an appearance that promises permanency; but in this world nothing can be said to be certain, except death and taxes.
>
> Benjamin Franklin, a Founding Father of the USA[1]

Apart from *taxes* all of us face death, whether we want to or not. I think it fair to say that it is really beholden upon us to make sense of what this life process is about while there is time to do so. I would go a lot further too, and say that when we come to entertain, and, even further, come to accept the possibility of there being life after death, then it is absolutely imperative that we begin to make sense of life during our time. Not only is this important in order to better understand who we are, why we are here on this journey and adventure, but also to consider that how we live this life could well affect what happens to us after we die. The two states could be inextricably linked together. Indeed I would suggest they most certainly are.

In context, we need, in our busy lives, to be able to take time out to explore the matters and issues behind life in order to gain clarity and wisdom. Preferably this needs to be done under our own steam. It is okay to allow ourselves to be guided by cultural and conventional wisdom, but in order to arrive at our own take on things we would be advised to also explore the less conventional route too. This book, one of many such books I hope you will be exploring, or may have already explored, does offer the *less conventional* in abundance – so you've come to a good place to help you meet this need.

The book's content in brief

To give you a flavour of what is to come, let us look briefly at what each chapter is offering:

The book kicks off with *The Good Life* chapter, which contemplates, *if we are secure, with all or most of our sociocultural, material needs and ambitions being met, are we living the good life.* I've started here because, I believe, for a great many of us, achieving the good life, as we commonly perceive it, is what we interpret life as being all about. So are we *living the dream* or perhaps living in a dream, if we see it this way?

In *Are you ready for this?* I raise the serious matter of death, and later head into asking a series of ten questions linked to it. I'd say, from a spiritual perspective, these are imperative questions. You can decide if you think they are. These questions serve to set things up to give focus for the book.

Faith in there being an afterlife is important but what a growing number of us need is evidence, whether circumstantial, anecdotal or via research, that may help convince us our chances of surviving death are better than fifty-fifty. In the *Fringe Benefits* chapter I draw on a range of such evidence to suggest our chances of survival may indeed be a great deal better than fifty-fifty.

The *Out of the Garden* chapter broadly explores the evolution of consciousness. It asks if there is more going on with life than the product of blind evolution; if there is indeed a plan, an intelligence, an intention operating behind it? In context it considers what might have happened, around fifty thousand years ago, that made us humans what we are today.

Do we have a soul? Given that we do, what is it, what does it look like, and where is it? In *The Soul Question*, this exploration is conducted in context with Christian and esoteric beliefs, and also draws on Eastern traditions of karma and reincarnation.

What is, and where is, *The Other Side* that we speak of? Is it for real? For a number of people who have had a NDE, or, who are practicing mediums, or psychic, the Other Side definitely exists. This chapter looks at some of the growing evidence for believing in it. It explores what and where it is, what it is like being there and how it arguably fits into our situation here.

After all that has been covered in the book, the concluding *Life and Death: Making sense of it* chapter asks if we have made any sense of life and death from what we have explored. It also considers how we may move forward with what we may have discovered.

The *Six Months to Live* appendix leaves us with some thoughts on what we might consider doing now to get our spiritual act together and be able to say, on the Other Side, we made some headway in our time on the earth.

Writing this book

Let me tell you a bit about my writing this book. I should kick off by saying this book represents the outcome of years of exploration, learning and contemplation. I began drafting a book of this nature during the Nineties when I started to resource ideas and make copious notes for it. However the book you are holding isn't that book. This book has taken on a form of its own and I have sometimes wondered who was writing it. What I mean is that I've had a sense of being pushed along with this. Almost all of what I had written previously fell by the wayside, although it still provided nourishment, *grist to the mill,* for the general direction in which the present work has headed.

Making sense of life and death is, on the face of it, a tall order but I've come to rest in the knowledge that it is equally important to speak up, or *report back,* as I prefer to see it, when one has something to say on such important matters.[2] You can, and no doubt will, make up your own mind regarding how valuable what I have to say is to you. It is important that you do. All I would ask, particularly if you are new to the information presented, that you give it all serious consideration. The following pages focus on providing insight and clarification on what life and death is, as I have come to understand it. If I have a further agenda it is this: that it is my intention to remind you of, and, if need be, awaken you to, the adventure you are already on. It is, more than anything, that of finding and regaining your soul. Okay one can just as easily say it is about climbing an inner mountain, finding one's higher self, seeking higher consciousness or nirvana, being on a quest for the Holy Grail. It makes little difference in essence. The book offers an overview and starting point by which to set sail on such a voyage while having a clearer destination in mind. Hopefully it will help inspire you to grasp this wonderful moment while you are here, and here now.

What has contributed to my writing the book

It may also help to share some of my own background experience. This is experience that brought me to begin questioning my beliefs regarding what life is about. When I think back my interest to understand life and death began in earnest during the Seventies, but actually the process started much earlier, way back to when I began to question my religious upbringing.

Given my Irish roots, being raised as a Roman Catholic may come as no surprise. My family moved to England, from County Waterford, when I was less than two-years-old. At that time my father was mostly away at sea in the Merchant Navy, and meanwhile my mother took to housekeeping for a group of priests, at a presbytery, in Leicestershire. You could say I became inducted into

Catholicism in more ways than one. Growing up it was normal practice for the family (which later included my three sisters) to attend church regularly on Sundays and *Holy Days of Obligation*; and probably every three weeks or so we would also attend *Confession* to seek forgiveness for our sins. To add to this mix, I also attended a Roman Catholic school (Corpus Christi SM in Leicester) for my secondary education. So, as you can gather, I had back then every opportunity for turning into a good Catholic and indeed I was heading that way.

It was while I was in my first year of secondary education that I became most inspired with my faith. I got completely sold on my religion, and, at that time, I seriously – as any eleven-year-old child could be serious – had designs on becoming a priest when I grew up. After talking to my mother, and the local priest, about it, I decided I would begin this quest by serving on the altar of my local church. I recall pressuring my mother to get the necessary vestments made for me – for which, regretfully, she made financial sacrifices in order for me to do so.

I say *regretfully* as, to cut a long story short, my altar boy excursion didn't work out. Within three months I discovered it was not for me. I wasn't as committed as I thought I was. I also found I needed more help with serving the mass, and in Latin, than I recall I was being offered at the time. Things culminated in one very embarrassing mass where I was the only altar boy available and I made a pig's ear of it to put it mildly. This experience provided what was to be the first big chink in my proposed priesthood plan. Outside, peer group pressure also played a part in this. I was in the school first eleven football team for my year (and also involved in athletics), and admittedly I was getting more fun out of sports than my religion. It wasn't all that long after ending my altar boy career, some months, that I opened a second chink in my plan; I decided to pull out of attending regular catechism on Sundays. I was by now becoming restless and rebellious against what I was being expected to learn by rote, and after being ticked-off a number of times by one of the nuns – for not doing my studies, and speaking out of turn – I decided to move on. I hasten to add it was not the nun's fault that I decided upon this action, rather, on reflection, I was looking for any excuse to drop out.

Depending on one's viewpoint, fortunately or unfortunately for me, my Christian faith came in for serious questioning starting from that period – possibly for all the wrong reasons. The priesthood plan was shelved. My decisions had left me with an underlying sense of failure too. I felt I had let myself and the family down. I was still, after all, a member of a devout Roman Catholic family. Even so a month or two down the road, having now near disconnected from going to church altogether, I could be found doing a paper-round on Sunday mornings instead – and no doubt sporting black marks all over my soul.[3] This was much to the chagrin of my father who, while away at sea during most of my rebellion, had, as I recall, held my mother responsible for not keeping a tighter rein on me.

But it wasn't just my learning issues and rebellion that had sparked my questioning. Around that time I got talking to a man I met on a park bench. Well let me say here that it wasn't quite such a *no-no* for children to speak to strangers back then – we're talking the late Fifties. What might have been considered odd, especially with regard to the direction of our conversation, was that this person was from the Church of England, a protestant no less, and, although it was never verbalised publicly, folk attending the C of E were considered to be, *not of the true faith* by us Catholics. So talking to a person with supposedly inferior beliefs, and touching on religion to boot, was breaking unspoken rules and not really on.

As I recall I quizzed him on his sadness and he told me something of his story. It transpired he had been the organist for his local church, and had played there consistently for the last thirty-three years. But then tragedy struck. Not long before I met him he had sadly lost his wife, and then shortly afterwards had suffered a stroke which left him disabled in one arm. He was clearly in pain and very unhappy – still grieving at his huge loss. I remember asking him if he was angry with God and he told me he was. He couldn't play the organ anymore due to his stroke, and had decided to leave his church – with the upshot being that now, from his perspective, no one seemingly cared whether he lived or died. He was asking why God could have done this to him, after all the service he had given to the Church. Back then I had no answer. He was in a miserable state and hearing his story had only aided and abetted my decision to drop out of attending catechism and further question my faith.

It was all very sad and I commiserated as much as a child could do. I saw him once again before we went separate ways. His plight however had carried a message that was probably ripe for me to hear. It was this that led me, some years later, to descend into hell, as some might see it, by becoming, what I'd describe as a fully signed-up atheist and existentialist, with attitude.

The matter, of what I now believed in, however, was still raw. My growing perspective had to make sense, provide arguments (to myself as much as anyone) against the influences of my upbringing, and I was driven to better understand *existence*, more as a means to counter religious argument than anything more profound. This led to my asking questions about life and death in the broader sense – which in turn took me on a quest into reading up on topics notably involving philosophy, psychology and animal behaviour. Once I got started I developed quite a thirst for it. This was in my twenties. I was seeking to fully endorse my new found beliefs, and I have to say I was getting well into my version of existentialism by that point. It was a godless meaningless world I existed in for the most part. That is not to say I was unhappy in it though as it was providing the drive, the passion to read, to study and explore. Besides I was now feeling fully vindicated in my decision to leave my religion behind. Subsequently I could find nothing in my explorations, discussions and challenges with others to dissuade me from that position. At least it was looking that way…

From Freud to Jung – a turning point

One cannot read up on psychology in the general and philosophical sense without taking stock of Sigmund Freud's view on the psyche. The sexual orientation of Freud's model to explain the workings of the psyche and behaviour made complete sense to my take on life. However, taking interest in Freud eventually led me to hearing of one of his close buddies. Initially I was more than a bit sceptical of all this talk of *archetypes* and *mandalas*; and even worse, talk of *alchemy* – he had to be out there with the fairies. I thus avoided looking into his views for quite some time. But as I eventually came to read more books with references to this psychiatrist I decided to get hold of one of his books – and what better than one about the man himself. I came by *Memories, Dreams, Reflections*. This is an autobiography of Carl G Jung (by his friend and biographer, Aniela Jaffé)[4] and this, with resistance on my part, somehow sparked my interest. Well I know what the "somehow" was. The manner in which it was written was open, refreshing and honest. Jung had also wrestled with his Christian upbringing, being the son of a pastor, and if nothing else this caught my attention and imagination to read on...

Whereas Freud spoke of the psyche being as an iceberg floating in the dangerous seas of the unconscious, Jung viewed the psyche more as an island jutting out of the sea. From his perspective each one of us is like an island that, underneath the waves, joins up with other islands on the seabed. Jung was proposing that at this deep unconscious level our psyches are as a collective whole, all linked together – hence his concept of the *Collective unconscious*. It is via this collective unconscious that we may tap into material and experience from something deeper and more ancient than our individual selves may muster. Jung linked his archetypes – universal motifs such as *the tree of life, the great mother, the child, the shadow, the trickster* and many more – to this concept. These motifs are expressed through our art, our dreams, myths and our religions. Understanding the collective unconscious then helps to link us to something larger, more universal that can percolate up through our lives. It opens a doorway into other possibilities in consciousness, in intuition, and allows the *symbolical* and the *meaningful* to become not just valid to our understanding but to be considered at the very root of our existence.

I was kicking against this. On more than one occasion I shelved the book, almost threw it away, but I came to admit to myself that I liked the eloquence of his argument, and particularly his concept of *the collective*. It was logical, optimistic and had immediate appeal. The notion that we could be *all in this together* struck an important chord. The difference in Freud and Jung's perspectives on the psyche gave me a big clue too that they were like chalk and cheese in their worldviews. Jung was interested in such matters as the paranormal, parapsychology and the occult. It was all part of what he was open to and exploring – and it tied in with the unusual, the paranormal, the magical, the spiritual, the profound, also *being possible* within his overarching collective unconscious concept. Freud, on the other hand, was a complete sceptic regarding such matters – a narrative I was well used to expounding myself. He and Jung were polarised with regard to the matter of what happens at death – with Jung being more open to survival and the notion of our having a soul.

One idea and one acceptance led to another and, to put it mildly, Jung's book did more than spark my interest. Rather, by the end of it, it had helped me to begin a 180-degree turn from the direction in which I was travelling. It had helped me to begin that turn with gusto and excitement. It started me on a new path no less. It was like a homecoming for me, a quenching of a thirst, and I began to look into his theories on archetypes and yes, even alchemy. Later I got hold of a number of his Collected Works to study more on these topics in depth. His autobiography also introduced me to the Chinese oracle, the I Ching (ye jing), which I have consulted ever since on various important personal matters. Also Jung's idea of *synchronicity* interested me greatly – and to some degree tied in with my later interest in astrology. This was all sparked off as a direct result of reading his autobiography. A door had creaked open to my considering I may truly have been missing some vital component in what I had hitherto believed.

Following exploration of Jung's ideas I began to consider things differently, to focus on a more positive questioning, in search of the spiritually oriented view of life. I might just mention another work that also gave me a bit of a broadside on my old direction of travel at around this time. This was Lyall Watson's book, *Supernature*,[5] a birthday present, from one of my sisters. Oh my, doors were creaking open alright. In Jung I'd found a psychiatrist talking seriously of what could otherwise be called *fringe* interests, and now here was Watson, a life scientist, treating a whole raft of hitherto taboo subjects – that I had also previously rubbished with venom – with some serious respect and articulation.

Pursuing a growing interest in the I Ching took me almost inevitably into looking at Eastern philosophy and religion – involving reading up on Confucius, Lao Tzu, Zen, Buddhism, Sufism and Hinduism. My world was opening up to spiritual possibilities. I must tell you that it was an absolutely fantastic voyage of discovery for me at that time – a time when I was also immersed in running archaeological excavations mostly on Roman or earlier Prehistoric sites – and insights, and connections were coming on almost daily. Now, for instance, I better understood Neolithic and Bronze Age burials, a returning to the earth womb – to be reborn. They held powerful spiritual beliefs, that I believe also included *reincarnation*.

A jolt of an experience

As well as taking an ongoing interest in fringe matters and spirituality, since back then, I should mention I've had a number of experiences that have forced me to think on the matter of life and death. These are experiences that have helped me to formalise and round-out my beliefs. I mention some of these in the *Fringe Benefits* chapter and won't labour them here. But there is one I'm thinking of right now that I haven't included there. Let me start by asking if you believe in such a being as a *guardian angel*? I know a lot of people do and certainly stories about guardian angels have been around since biblical times at least. I keep an open mind on the whole topic of angels, but I'll admit I'm less inclined to believe in guardian angels as such. Let me give you an alternative viewpoint on this matter. I firmly believe we do, each one of us, have a companion, a guardian, but this is not so much an angel as our own *soul*, or higher self if you prefer. From this higher vantage point, I suggest, we have the capacity to guide and intervene, on our worldly human selves, almost as an external agent, should we get into circumstances where such help or intervention is needed. This may happen most noticeably when our lives are in danger and intervention is required, necessary, and also possible – it won't be in every situation.

You need to make up your own mind regarding the matter but, given this scenario, in the following encounter I choose to believe I was helped out of a dangerous situation by my soul. In any case certainly the experience was that something or someone did help me, that part I'm now sure of. This happened before I read anything by Jung and I was still very much steeped in my non-spiritual beliefs – which made the event all the more unsettling.

This is about my driving home alone, in the early hours of a morning, along a road I knew well. I'd been over to see a girlfriend, the other side of Grantham, and some thirty plus miles from my home in Leicestershire. It was the late Sixties. At that time I was involved in motorcycle racing (which, by then, was the only Sunday service I attended) and fond of speed – I confess I still am fond of the exhilaration one gets from travelling fast but am much less the *boy-racer* these days. When quiet, like it normally was at that time of morning, along that stretch of road, I could really get up some momentum and regularly reached speeds in excess of 90 mph between villages, after leaving Grantham. On this occasion, after a mile or two from Grantham, I caught up with the only other car on the road. This person was driving a Jaguar as I well recall. Their car was very much faster on acceleration than mine – a *souped-up* Mini – particularly on straight stretches of road. By comparison though, they drove very slowly through bends and curves. So slow in fact that the driver was actually, and frustratingly, holding me up on my journey. This situation went on for some miles.

To cut to the chase, I decided there was nothing for it but to overtake this car... I took my opportunity to do so just prior to a particular stretch of road that is winding and runs gently downhill for about three or four miles towards the town of Melton Mowbray. I had caught up with the car once again as we came towards this stretch of road, and, as they braked for the first in the series of bends;

I pulled out and drove past them. It was dry and my car hugged the road well. I pulled away rapidly. The lights of the other car were now disappearing into the distance behind me as I drove through the fast bends that followed. And so I continued on apace towards a final bend that led down towards the town – about a mile away from it.

The bend I'm thinking of was back then, and might still be, a sharpish right hander that led one down a steepish bit of hill. The camber ran away from the direction of the bend too, to add to the potential hazard. With the wind in my sails, and alive with the excitement of finally getting past the other car, I approached this bend at a much higher speed than I should. I braked, and then it happened… One of my rear brakes (on the driver side) suddenly locked with the effect that it threw the car into a dramatic spin and I lost control. Now, merely a passenger, the car spun down the hill for what must have been a full turn and then some. The next clear impression I had was that it was now coming out of the spin and heading across the comparatively narrow two-lane road towards the stone wall of a field. I was still doing a fair rate of knots. My recollection of speed is relative but things were happening quickly. I recall thinking this was it, there was no way I could stop this; the car and I were soon to be going into the wall at speed. I remember vividly bracing myself for the impact. This was also before seatbelts were compulsory in cars too, and I didn't have one.

Suddenly, just as shocking, the car now veered away from heading towards the wall, and now – while facing in the opposite direction to which I had come from, for the second time at least – it slowed rapidly, and next it gently slid and stopped by the grass verge on the side of the road. It looked like, for all of the world, that I was on my way up the hill, and had just parked at the spot. The next moment everything switched off – the lights and engine – and there was silence in the night's darkness that now enveloped me. But only briefly: the other car now arrived and passed by my parked vehicle at speed. Everything had happened so fast that I suspect the other driver wasn't even aware that it was the same car that had passed them, or that anything untoward had happened.

I collected my senses. Hey I was alive and in one piece. I took stock of what had just happened. After a short while I got out and checked the car. It too was in one piece – no obvious damage at all. It all looked fine. I tried the engine and it started without a problem. I soon discovered the brakes were fine, having cooled down. I turned the car around and was on my way again – homeward bound – and giving thanks that, in my mindset, I had gotten away with it. That had been a close call, but *luck* was on my side.[6]

So was it luck or a fluke? At the time I thought it must have been some kind of chance happening. In reality I couldn't really make sense of it. It was outside my understanding. Certainly it was shocking for a number of obvious reasons and it did rattle me that I couldn't quite explain what had happened. I understood why it went into a spin, with the brake locking, but how it was all calmed down and parked safely was something else. It was like someone else had taken over and parked the car. It occurred to me afterwards that had I instead avoided the wall but come to halt in the middle of the road, the chances are, in the circumstances, the other car would probably have run into me. Later, as I experienced other events and began to see things differently, I became convinced that a helping hand did intervene to save me from serious damage that night. The incident gave me much cause for thought back then and still brings back vivid memories and goose-bumps as I write about it.

A guide for beginners and seasoned travellers

I trust this book will provide you with a good down-to-earth, easy to grasp presentation of, what I call, a *thought-provoking, if challenging, spiritual perspective on life and death.* Many of the subjects and ideas presented here can be found in other books, but not necessarily assembled with one overriding intention or vision. You'll find books that tend to focus on one aspect of the prism, be it near-death experience, ghosts, previous lives, mediumship etc. What this book does is draw together a number of these various strands of experience, and associated disciplines, with the intention to provide a more integrated philosophical perspective. It also draws upon ideas that have been around for what seems like an eternity – certainly a few thousand years – and throws in a number of new ideas too. It draws on traditional and esoteric knowledge, on paranormal matters, and a touch more of personal experience.

It needs also to be pointed out that what I have to say here is drawn from traditions, accounts and experiences that are largely still very ignored or overlooked in our world. This is for the most part considered unorthodox, controversial and fringe – and I use the word *fringe* in the book to make this point. It is not to undermine the value of such knowledge. The advice meanwhile is to not let your children read this unless you want them to grow up asking awkward questions about life, and especially that bit we normally avoid discussing – death. Ah, but on the contrary, that is precisely what I would want them to do. Indeed I argue the content I put forward here should be more readily addressed in our educational systems, for young and old alike – that is, if we are ever to become fully functioning and fully rounded spiritual beings.

Throughout I'm asking you, the reader, to consider that the world isn't quite as we see it through the lenses of our *everyday normality* where it is easy to lose ourselves, and lose our awe for life, in the hustle and bustle of *nine to five* – in the constructs we have erected that keep us from considering a fuller extent of reality. We have yet to grasp the whole picture of what we are involved with, and, although it is not beyond us, many of us indeed are afraid to look over the parapet to get a better view, fearing what we might find.

Well, I'm hoping this book will provide you with an alternative vantage point for safe and inspiring viewing. But better than that, join me on this journey and adventure. All you'll need to bring with you is an open mind – and to consider exploring further from the information and resources that are a part of what follows. Are you ready to go? Great, let's saddle up and get started.

See you on the other side… Of course I mean the other side of this introduction – for now. Enjoy your journey.

Notes & references

[1] Franklin, B. (1789) In a letter to Jean-Baptiste Leroy.
http://en.wikipedia.org/wiki/Death_%26_Taxes [Accessed 16/02/2015]

[2] Speaking up. I learnt that lesson many years ago when in odd circumstances I found myself involved in an American radio interview of MP Shirley Williams. This was at Radcliffe College, a ladies college in Cambridge, Massachusetts, US, and Ms Williams was being interviewed about her then latest book, *Politics is for People*. I had turned up on spec, expecting to be part of an audience of about 100 people. As it transpired I was one of a two-people audience in a room just large enough for the small group. During the interview the *audience* were invited to comment on what had been said. I held back but then Shirley put me on the spot saying, "I think Francis has something to say." And sure I did. It poured out. Probably not very coherently but to Shirley it made sense and she answered my comments constructively, in the manner we are accustomed to, from her. Either way, she made me feel I had made some valuable contribution to the discussion. I've always endeavoured to speak my mind since – when I have something to say that is.

[3] I was brought up to believe that not attending mass on a Sunday was a black mark on one's soul.

[4] Jung, C. G. (1972) *Memories, Dreams and Reflections*. Collins Fontana Library.

[5] Watson, L. (1973) *Supernature*. Hodder & Stoughton.

[6] If you want to read about a more dramatic escape, take a look at *Lucky escapes or intervention* - http://lifeanddeaththebook.com/fringe-benefits/lucky-escapes-or-intervention/

CHAPTER 1

THE GOOD LIFE

What is the good life? If we are secure with all, or most, of our sociocultural, material needs and ambitions being met, are we living the good life?

> You are educated. Your certification is in your degree. You may think of it as the ticket to the good life. Let me ask you to think of an alternative. Think of it as your ticket to change the world.
>
> Tom Brokaw, American TV journalist and author[1]

To begin this journey into making sense of life and death, I believe it will be very helpful if we start by reminding ourselves of what it is that a great many of us desire, want, or indeed expect from life.

What we want of course is largely going to be driven by what's available to us, and where and how we have been raised. If you think about it; within the increasingly secular and sophisticated cultural situation in which a lot of us now live, or are beginning to live (and here I'm thinking of countries that are essentially industrialised, driven by modern economies, involving communication technologies, and democracies; with less interference by orthodox religions), we have developed a broad vision of this lifestyle, complete with its stereotypes that we subscribe to, or at least pay homage to. Because of this vision one could argue that this ideal also has a series of identifiable steps or milestones that pivot around where we will want to be, and what we will want to have, by certain points in our lifetime. Of course, while some of us actually live this dream, for a lot of us the ideal remains just that, a dream; a case of wishful thinking for how things might be, or might have been. And yet, no surprise, for others it is something that we consciously rebel against or reject, at least in part, as we seek to find an alternative good life.

The Good Life Milestones

> If you want to have a good life, you should focus on your family, on your business, on your dog, on your fun, and you'll have a good life.
>
> Adam Carolla, American comedian and radio celebrity[2]

To put some flesh on the bones of this, let us look at how our cradle-to-grave scenario might pan out. I'll keep this brief but, give or take a missing milestone or two; it runs something along these lines:

Get a good start in life

We want a good start in life. Ideally we are born healthy and strong, into wealthy family circumstances, with two parents who love us. The area where we would want grow up in will be upmarket and *well-to-do*. These factors together provide the kind of start that has *going places* written all over it.

Get good schooling

There is no doubt that education is a prime consideration at any point in life. We are forever learning and updating our knowledge and skills whether or not we are always aware of it. We do however package the bigger part of our education between the years of four and twenty four in preparation for life – in some cultures even earlier. In our ideal scenario, given the choice we'd probably plump for a private education that sets us up for success in the world. We'd go on to study at a top university and get a good degree – probably going even further and taking a Masters or PhD, or the equivalent.

Make a splash in the world

Our road to success means that we are confident and ambitious. We know what we want from life and we drive forward in whatever career, business or vocation that suits us to achieve our goals. In the ideal this will enable us to make a lot of money, in order to afford a really good lifestyle. Our social world will be brimming with friends, contacts, opportunities and experiences that take us on wonderful adventures – both physically and online. We'll easily meet all our material wants and needs. We'll already own our own home or flat, or be well on the way to it. We may even have a second home possibly abroad by now. We'll have a nice car or two. We're seeking to get a real sense of having arrived, being on top of our game, on top of the world.

The marriage or partnership milestone

Given that we have explored the world, and road-tested relationships, we eventually come to a milestone where we settle down with a partner and tie the knot. This is a big turning point in our lives – and can also be a costly one too if we give it the full works. We are making a lifelong commitment (we trust) and we want the world to know it. In our ideal we would, of course, want to move into a new home around this point. This is going to be a beautiful detached building. It is the first of many such properties we may own during our lives – catering for all our current needs, and is set in beautiful grounds with great vistas. It will also take into account our future children and their schooling.

The family milestone

Doing things in the right order, our next milestone, coming fairly soon after marriage, is raising our children, and this brings with it the need for structure and security. This is the time for settling into reliable and steady work, and becoming family-orientated. This is a time when we can become more aware of our responsibilities to our immediate family, but equally to close friends and work colleagues, and all that this might entail with regard to challenges, companionship and competition. This milestone will inevitably want to include progress up the ladder of success in our chosen career or profession.

Children leave home

For a great many of us the next important milestone is that our children leave home and move on to becoming the successful people we always wanted them to be. This leaves us in the position of reconsidering our own futures and revisiting what we want from life. There's plenty left in the tank at this point. This could be a time to rekindle the relationship we have with our partner. It could be a time to travel more, and move on to new pastures. We'll maybe downsize a bit at this time – rather than be rattling around in our current home. Maybe we'll move to stay in our second home more permanently, or to a new location in the countryside or by the sea. We could be looking for what some people call their *forever home*. We'll probably still want to be within commuting distance to our work at this point, or better still, be considering working from home.

We retire

And so seemingly after a long haul, we come to the next obvious milestone: *retirement*. Although having arrived at this step, and looking back, it may not seem such a *long haul*, as it has come around so soon. This milestone means different things to different people. It doesn't have to mean that everything stops but on the contrary it can be a welcome life change. Ideally many of us would like to choose the timing of this milestone for ourselves, perhaps in our fifties, or earlier if we can, once we have gotten the wealth and security we need to carry us through. If we get it right, retirement can mean the end of work and onto a more active life of *play* – and one might ask as to who, in their right mind, wouldn't want that. Not everyone is probably the answer. Some of us live to work rather than work to live.

If we haven't already done so this could be another opportunity to move away from all the hustle and bustle to a new location. While some of us are off on adventures, probably most of us will be up for taking it easy now, some gardening, trips out and about. Having visits from friends and members of the family, especially our grandchildren, is just what the doctor ordered. Playing golf, fishing, or other outdoor pursuit, might well feature high on our agenda. Being out and about, with some good exercise, is what is important.

Perhaps we will also finally get away by taking that world cruise we always promised ourselves.

We go into a retirement home

This is not such a welcome milestone. Life has drifted on until we're now around our eighties to nineties. We're still ideally with our partner, healthy, and in the sunset of our lives. We are able to say we're having a good innings and are achieving what we always wanted from life. In the best scenario, we skip this milestone and carry on living in our lovely home in the country or by the sea, taking care of each other into infinity. But, given that we know things can change at around this time, we, with our family's blessings and support, begin to entertain moving into a well-respected retirement home for the coming years.

This retirement home is going to be a wonderful place. It is staffed with lovely caring people, and set in beautiful countryside where we won't need to worry about anything. It is where we'll find serenity and peace – and still be able to do many of the things we already enjoy. We decide, *it's going to be wonderful*, and so it may be.

Dying and funeral

If going into a retirement home was an unwelcome milestone then this most certainly is not a wanted component of our good life. If and when death does arrive – for in our ideal it may not be quite so certain that death will arrive for us – we may as well aim to have a good send off, an expensive funeral with all the musical trimmings and speeches that we deserve. In our ideal we'll be buried (or our ashes scattered) in a beautiful and serene spot. Lots of people are going to be there. They will say how much they already miss us. We'll probably be leaving our accumulated wealth to the family, perhaps also a charity or two, and possibly a few friends. And everyone will be able to say, rightly so, what a wonderful person, or people, we were. We had a good life.

What a life...

Well, there it is our good life with its milestones, in a broad sweep, having some or most of the ingredients that I suspect many of us aspire to. But now, let me ask you if it really is what we aspire to? Is achieving these milestones what our modern lives are really about? Is this why we are here? Does it include much of what you expected to be included in this scenario, or did I leave out any important milestone or anything major that you would have wanted to see in the list?

I'm sure that you will get the gist of where I'm coming from with this presentation. I suspect that, if we are being honest, many of us can identify with wanting at least some of this good life even if we take a different route to getting it. We may be single. We may be in a civil partnership rather than a marriage. We may not have children. We may be an entrepreneur, playing the stock market, or an artist or musician, rather than following a more reliable and secure career. Some of us may want it all to take place in a far-flung country – other than here wherever *here* is. The fact that few of us achieve this ideal – there is often something missing in the matrix to stop it happening quite so smoothly or to stop it happening altogether – doesn't stop us from wanting it and possibly envying others who have achieved it. On the face of it, most of it sounds pretty attractive doesn't it?

> The good life is a process, not a state of being. It is a direction not a destination.
>
> Carl Rogers, Humanistic Psychology founder, writer[3]

One of the important points I would make here, picking up on Rogers's words, is that much of our focus is, consciously or subconsciously, set upon destinations, the trappings, that telegraph to ourselves and others that we have it, we have arrived, we are having a good life, *we're living the dream*. Of course we also get the continuous reminders that this is what we need to aim for through television, our online browsing, and other media. All of these aiding and abetting our continuing to seek it. Before I go further let me just state something here so that there are no misunderstandings of where I'm coming from on the matter: from my perspective, *there is nothing wrong with wanting a life of abundance and all the material joy and pleasures that it can bring*. This is not at issue. Rather it is what may be missing from this recipe.

So here's the question again: did I leave anything important out of this scenario that you can think of? Would you say it is balanced? Is there anything I could have added to this list?

What about adding in having *good health* throughout our life as being a primary requirement? Now why I left that out, I've no idea – it's a *given* that we want that. Something else now occurs to me, something easily as significant as health, not stated but assumed – that you might say also links directly to our health – and that is our *happiness*. It is fair to say that we all want to be happy and, as much as possible, stress free as an outcome in all our good life endeavours. It is true, though that one can have all the physical trappings in the world and still not be happy. By the same token, having all one needs needn't be a hindrance to happiness. I'd say fairly, happiness is a desirable ingredient but can also be elusive, hinging on our emotional state, often with disregard to circumstances of abundance. However, let's add it in as an important ingredient.

> The good life is one inspired by love and guided by knowledge.
> Bertrand Russell, English philosopher[4]

So what about Russell's comment here; what about *love*? In tandem with happiness I'd say it is also expected that there is love in our good life. Relationships are in there, of course, so it is implied. Love is something we need as much as want. We can't really live without it, even though it can sometimes be overlooked. But actually, the love I want to talk about here is not just the love we might feel for our partner, our children, our parents and siblings. I think it fair to say that most of us can muster love at this level, almost on autopilot. No, I'm thinking of the love that might require a bit of effort on our part. This is the love and compassion we can feel for ourself, for life, for the natural world around us, for our planet, for our neighbours, for humanity. Bringing this in will no doubt influence our good life expectations and be a likely cause for revision towards what is and isn't of value at each step.

A big missing component

This concern with love naturally leads me onto what I see as a really big oversight in our good life scenario as we currently have it. If you haven't anticipated it already I will tell you; it gives no account for any spiritual dimension or spiritual ambition in the narrative. I appreciate that our good life can have spiritual consequences but that is surely more of an outcome than a driver, or intention behind it.

Now I'm not talking here about religion per se. I'm not about to suggest the ideal religion to sign up for, nor am I suggesting that we should be necessarily introducing our children to religious practices and culture. I'm not really talking about how much time or money should be set aside for one's religion or for good and charitable causes – although *giving* is surely an essential part of any good life plan. No, what I am talking about here is essentially about spiritual health – and herein indeed, lies the possibility of love and happiness being combined within an overarching spiritual framework.

If we add desire for spiritual health into the mix, we could begin to have a bit of a dilemma with our good life scenario as we have thus far constructed it. Possibly we now see the milestones listed as incomplete, with something major missing from them. That *something* may mean they are now looking a bit too extraverted or externalised, perhaps painting us as if we are living in a bubble, and being short on depth and *meaning*.

I'd suggest if we buy into our good life scenario, as listed, much of it can be reduced down to being largely driven by money, by our economy. Am I being fair to suggest that a great many of us assume we have sussed life and the real world when we know how to turn a dollar or two? Possibly too simple an interpretation, but possibly not far off either. We would probably claim that what we reach for is governed by the realities of modern living, with it being the standard by which we tend to measure our success or failure in the world. And money, with all it symbolises, plays an essential part in this. But while our lives continue apace, with all the buzz, noise and dust of modern living, if we look under the foundations of our ideal good life, as it stands, we will find that we have built them upon less stable ground than we might have thought. Indeed, arguably, we have built onto a layer of insecurity, on a sub-terrain of foreboding even. This boils down to a core knowing, denial even, that eventually everything is going to change and that all we have built or gained will one day crumble and/or be taken from us.

More broadly, our good life narrative, as it stands, tends to objectify our world as something we can have, there for the taking, there to be consumed – given that money is no object. And therefore it is also temporary, ever in need of updating, no matter what structure we may have put in place. And we can, if not careful, extend this out to people too, and towards our environment. Everything can become a commodity, having its place and price. We are in danger of becoming disconnected not only from each other and from a huge chunk of humanity, often living in poverty, but also from the world itself, from the rhythm of nature. And indeed from the awesomeness of what we are actually involved in – what is under our feet.

> Can we really believe that we are living a good life, an ethically decent life if we don't do anything serious to help reduce poverty around the world and help save the lives of children or adults who are likely to die if we don't increase the amount of aid we are giving?
>
> Peter Singer, Australian moral philosopher[5]

My contention is that without love, compassion, spiritual health and balance, life, by whatever ideal we try to live it, will fail us. It will be little more than an empty expression, a comfort blanket, an attempt to distance ourselves from the deeper questions and concerns regarding our existence, and that of our planet. I believe these are concerns that we all share in common. It almost goes without saying, too, that our good life needs to include a component of *service to others* – in whatever and wherever we are best suited. This is part of our human and spiritual remit.

Getting a handle on things

If we are versed in a non-spiritual take on life – perhaps an atheist, existentialist, humanist, coming from an orthodox science perspective and/or are *secular* in our beliefs – we are probably going to have a different take on our good life scenario that suggests everything is pretty much okay as it is, on proviso that you can get it. There is no need for any spiritual dimension, just enjoy the years we have and get out of life what we can. Let me tell you, from experience, this viewpoint on one level can be very healthy as it helps one to become discerning, sceptical and less *willy-nilly* regarding what one accepts and believes.

The non-spiritual take is still a belief in itself however. This belief can help to confront and strip away what I consider unhealthy religious indoctrination, as it did for me. On another level though it is ever in danger of replacing spiritual need with belief that I'd contend ultimately offers nothing of great nourishment other than for, what I see as, transitory intellectual benefit. I'll wager too, one thing we can be pretty sure of – regardless of our disbelief in the afterlife – and this is that, if, at the end of our lives, we are given the opportunity to survive on the other side of death, then we will take that opportunity to survive – with, I would suggest, no questions asked. Well okay, there may be a few questions. Which leads me on to a point I will be making throughout the book, and that is, it is better we prepare for the possibility (nay *eventuality* as I see it) of survival than leave it all to happenstance.

Right now I'm wondering... Are we, whilst pursuing our interpretation of the good life, giving ourselves the opportunity to grasp what life might really be all about? Now that we have mapped the genetic code (since 2009), for example, does this mean we have the complete picture of what life is – or that we are in the process of getting to that complete picture if we add *nurture* into the mixing pot with *nature*? Could it be that everything about ourselves, and the rest of the flora and fauna, is now being understood, mystery solved or shortly to be so? If we answer *yes* to these questions then likely as not we will be going ahead pursuing our good life without much, if any, consideration for a spiritual dimension, or a spiritual reason and purpose behind our lives.

But let's slow up a moment. If you ever take a look through a modern textbook (or try the Web such as Wikipedia) covering genetics or topics around genetics, you'll find that what we now know about cells and genes is absolutely staggering; we are really getting a handle on things. But I see something else that is even more staggering: It is the fact that all of which we are gaining knowledge on, the remarkable cells and genes etc., were (and are), already there for us to discover. We may get better at aping life and making modifications through genetics but we haven't invented or created these remarkable building blocks of life, they were already there. Their simplicity, their complexity, their intelligence, already there – and our physical bodies are built with them. For that matter, how remarkable has been the journey of our coming to discover this information – to becoming awake, actually conscious enough to explore it, to actually research, talk and write about it. That's some journey and some miracle don't you think?

Indeed, how remarkable this whole situation actually is. What an enormous move forward we have made from what we knew even just a century ago. I'd suggest we are just scratching the surface, with more of life's magic to be uncovered. Some of this magic, which we will look at together in the following pages, is already made available to us but is, unfortunately, either ignored or sadly denied by the greater majority – and because of this it is not included in our good life scenario as yet. How many of us, for example, seek, as an ambition, to know who we are as a soul? How many of us are seeking to discover (or have already found) our spiritual purpose on the earth? I'm hoping quite a lot but I anticipate that not many of us are doing so, nor are even encouraged to explore at this time.

Where to next

In context with this overview, let us return to reconsider the ending to our good life. As a teacher one of the considerations I usually add in, towards the end of delivering a given course or workshop, is the *Where to next* discussion point. This covers where one might go next to continue and advance one's learning. With *death* in our good life scenario the *where to next* is left hanging somewhat as an unknown, with a number of *ifs* and *buts*. If we take our more sceptical view on the matter we'll probably say there is no *next*, and therefore little point in discussing it.

There are however two commonly held theoretical endings to life that we know of and need to consider here. We either die, end of story, or, something of us continues to live on after death. We can say that whatever we believe we have arrived at after being influenced by – and I would say to a large degree misdirected by – two big and opposing beliefs or ideas. These are: firstly the notion that God, in whatever form, created us and put us here. In this ending we will be judged by him (normally seen as a *he* rather than a *she*) as to where we go next. This is the view of course held by a number of our orthodox religions. Or secondly, with being viewed as essentially mammals, we will go the way of all animals that have evolved on the planet over millions of years – we simply terminate. Our learning ends at death with the *where to next* being, you might say, one of physical dissolution. The latter view of course ties into evolutionary theory as it currently stands.

Well that's about the extent of it, but let me ask you; are these two endings necessarily as mutually exclusive and irreconcilable as portrayed? One offers a spiritual outcome of sorts and the other; well we hopefully can say we had a good innings. On the face of it they do sit uncomfortably with each other. Indeed they are often treated as myth, on one hand, and reality on the other – one based upon faith (some would say *blind faith*) and the other on *a priori* reasoning. But, before closing the door on the matter let me ask you to consider that the spiritual view as presented by a number of orthodox religions is inaccurate, distorted, whilst the biological view is incomplete and misses the equally obvious by a country mile.

I'm going to suggest there is another way to look at this matter. I'm going to propose a perspective on life that can accommodate both the spiritual directive and the process of evolution as being compatible, working together. I present this as an agenda of awakening, of intention, in the coming pages. And let me say here that this synthesis considers we are on the earth for a purpose that is far beyond the good life scenario that I've entertained here.

Teasing out and developing this spiritual perspective, and its soul implications, is the main thrust behind this book. I would like, at very least, to place these thoughts before you to consider in context with your own life and your own journey...

Notes & references

[1] Tom Brokaw on Brainy Quote.
http://www.brainyquote.com/quotes/quotes/t/tombrokaw108699.html [Accessed 23/02/2013]
[2] Adam Caroll on Brainy Quote.
http://www.brainyquote.com/quotes/quotes/a/adamcaroll485689.html [Accessed 23/02/2013]
[3] Carl Rogers quote from Goodreads.
http://www.goodreads.com/author/quotes/102062.Carl_R_Rogers [Accessed 14/01/2013]
[4] From Wikipedia. http://en.wikipedia.org/wiki/What_I_Believe [Accessed 14/01/2013]
[5] Peter Singer on Brainy Quote.
http://www.brainyquote.com/quotes/quotes/p/petersinge471299.html [Accessed 14/01/2013]

CHAPTER 2

ARE YOU READY FOR THIS?

Have you considered what is coming, just over that horizon, just around that corner; and are you prepared for it? I suggest you really ought to be.

If you have yet to give serious thought to what your life is about, whether there is *meaning* behind it or not, now is the time to find out – don't leave it too long.

> Dream as if you'll live forever. Live as if you'll die today.
>
> James Dean, American actor[1]

In this chapter I'm setting out the scene for the rest of this book, by checking in on some important life questions. You will probably need to get your thinking cap on to deal with them. Before getting to that point though we have another little matter to occupy us – and this won't go away.

It's coming... the elephant in our lives

> If it be now, 'tis not to come. If it be not to come, it will be now. If it be not now, yet it will come – the readiness is all.
>
> William Shakespeare[2]

Whether you are having a nice day or not, right now, I encourage you to brace yourself for a very important announcement:

You Are Going To Die...

No doubt about it you are going to die. You will die just like the rest of us – and that does of course mean I'm included. And further, it won't be all that long from now; it is probably closer than you think.

Your work, where you live, your family, friends, and the things you own are not going to save you from this event. Okay they may certainly help speed it up, or delay it for a while. Medical science may help to prolong your life by reversing a terminal illness, or by slowing down your ageing process,[3] but eventually your physical body will break down and terminate. It may not be today or tomorrow but it is coming. It has been on its way from the moment you took your first breath.

It follows that the first big question you might ask yourself to consider, in context with this fact, is:

What are you doing, or going to do, about this coming change?

I'm wondering how you feel right now, having read the announcement. Did it shock or upset you? If it did, well I'm sorry but it was meant to give you a bit of a *wakeup* call. In your reaction you may have been thinking something like, "I knew that already – who doesn't." Or perhaps, "Why remind me, how morbid can one be." Well let's look at this from another viewpoint. Is it really morbid to look at, and give consideration to, what is a natural fact of life? I hope you'll agree with me that it is not morbid. It is as natural as getting up in the morning and going to bed at night. By the way I nearly also added to the announcement, the words, *No one gets out of this alive*, but then I would've had to have also added, *relatively speaking*.

The issue, as I see it, is that we can be so in denial of this aspect of our lives that we know it more as an idea. It is easier to perceive it as something that might happen to us, in the future, than something real that will most certainly happen to us. As children we come to know about the reality of death most probably on the basis of received information, and less so by direct experience – well we certainly hope it is less so by direct experience. We learn about it as a largely unexpected fact of life. Probably no one ever took us to one side, when discussing the facts of life, and said to us, "Just like the birds and bees, you'll also die one day," and then quoted Hamlet regarding, "the readiness is all." This is obviously because no one, particular our parents, would want to be that cruel. We more likely found out about it, in a personal way, through the death of one of our grandparents, or through a pet dying, or we heard through our religious upbringing. It could possibly be through overhearing our parents when talking to other adults about someone who had died, or by means of a kid from school who tragically drowned on a school trip. Certainly, these days, children are more likely to become informed about death quite quickly through our media and online access, and so there is little hope of them escaping the knowledge of death for too long.

Even so, it is probably easier for us as children and young adults to distance ourselves from death. To think of it as something *over there*, that will only happen a long way off, or that happens to others in less wholesome circumstances, to the elderly and infirm, but not to ourselves – not to the young with everything to live for. But of course we come quickly to learn this is not entirely true as young soldiers, even children, caught up in wars may have a very different and painful take on that. If any of us are refugees from war-torn countries, or from natural disasters, we will have a different take on it too. Of course children who have a terminal illness will also have a different take on the matter. But probably for the larger majority of us, we trust, at a young age, we don't have much to do with it; we don't need to contemplate it. We can ignore it.

We know though that at any point death may become an issue, and for some people it may also be a driver for change, a turning point...

> Back in April 2011 Eric Clark was walking out of a church in Chicago (USA) when he was attacked and stabbed thirteen times – and left for dead. He very nearly did die. He was then twenty five. His life at that point was held in the balance. The fact that he survived death is greatly down to his mother's care and healing. This life-changing event, which no sane human being would wish on another, brought him to a crossroads, a major turning point, in terms of his intention, his life's work and spiritual direction. He

now spreads a Christian message to help inspire others – and has written a book about his experience, aptly called The Experience[4].

What Eric's story should remind us is how close death can be at any age and how quickly the possibility of it can arrive.

As we grow older our view of death is also inclined to alter. Probably most of us, by the time we reach fifty years, will have had some direct experience of losing a close friend, a loved one, mother or father, or other family member. Or we will know of someone we saw on a regular basis who has since died and has left a bit of a hole in our lives. We are probably attending more funerals and the increasing likelihood emerges that it is going to happen to us one day. By this age too we are also more aware of our bodies beginning to lose their youth and of our having to work that little bit harder to maintain the impression that we look to be in our prime, and will be around forever.

No one can confidently say that he will still be living tomorrow.
Euripides, Greek playwright

Death actually needs be a healthy concern for all of us – for reasons that I hope will become clearer as this book unfolds. Even so, at fifty or even older, probably still few of us are contemplating what *life and death*, even less our own life and death, is all about. Indeed such contemplation is often considered a taboo and, for many of us, only possible under certain conditions; like obviously when someone else dies you can talk about it, or following a nasty event that we scraped through, we can talk about it. Or, for that matter, under certain conditions or with certain sections of society that are open to such discussion – such as in the process of counselling or religious dialogue – we can talk about it.

And so imagine it. One may have gone fifty years without even really thinking about, or having a discussion about one's life in this imperative way. We might be very highly educated, holding an important career position. We might have a beautiful family, a beautiful home and all the trappings of modern living. We may be very cosmopolitan, travel the world regularly, and able to speak a number of languages. We may be all these things but have given little or no thought to our death. Well apart, that is, from taking care of some of the practicalities of organising a will, taking out a life insurance, maybe paying into a funeral fund. We, of course, seek to protect our loved ones against any such eventuality. Aside from this it is probably something we prefer to keep under wraps, to one side, and not to dwell on too much.

Another big burning question

I make the assumption that no matter who or what we are, or where we come from, we all want to live for as long as we can. On the face of it this may not appear to be true for, say, a severely disabled person who expresses the wish to die, or a person who, for whatever reason, decides to end their life. It may not be true for a person who is suffering under huge life-threatening duress, or for a person who is tired of life. But, if you think about it, such a person is more concerned with, getting out of, escaping from, or getting away from, what they perceive or experience as a situation they are trapped in; rather than a wish to die for dying's sake. I believe that if the person in dire or unhappy circumstances thought there was a realistic alternative to death; that there was a different kind of freedom, that their issues could be fixed, their paralysis removed, the life-threat or extreme loneliness removed, then they would take it. They would choose life every time.

In context, although a great many of us will deny, underestimate or ignore its importance, the truth is that every one of us, no matter what cultural background or creed we come from, is faced with an overriding question in our lives, which boils down to, "What will happen when I die?" or more succinctly, "Will I survive my death?" Will it all end in nothing, or will I, or a part of me, continue to exist? And, if I do continue, *how* will this pan out, and indeed *where* will this pan out? This concern goes with the territory, so to speak, the self-evident fact of our being human, being conscious to being alive and that we also have a limited lifespan.

It's straight forward enough to pose the question regarding what happens at our death, but no way is it so easy to find an answer that we can all agree on or believe in. So far we have yet to conduct an experiment whereby a volunteer would risk losing their physical life to go through the experience of death, and stay dead for, say, a day or two before being brought back into their body to report on their experience. Well of course that's not going to happen, even if there were volunteers out there crazy enough to try. We do however have evidence from some unwilling volunteers who have gone through the process of dying, who have had a near-death experience (NDE) and obviously survived. These have given various and sometimes remarkable accounts of what they experienced. I'll say more about this further in, but to add here that, at present, people who have gone through the experience of being clinically dead, and brought back to life, have been dead for only a few minutes – it has been up to one or two, even three hours in rarer cases – before being resuscitated. What is very interesting about the way resuscitation technique and technology is heading, is that the time delay between being pronounced clinically dead and being brought back to life safely, with less risk of brain damage, is set to get longer, possibly be up to a day. If that becomes true it may well revolutionise our way of thinking about the experience of death and what *to be dead* actually means.

Shades of Pascal's Wager

Note: It was only after drawing on the logic, I used below, that I realised it was following a similar argument as posited by the French philosopher, Blaise Pascal (1623–1662). This is now known as *Pascal's Wager*. He argued, on logical grounds, why it was better to believe in God than not believe in God.[5]

On this question of death, and survival, it is my understanding that the answer we come to find, come to choose, come to believe in regarding what happens when we die, at whatever time in our lives, will have implications, even profound implications, for the way we will tend to live life, the way we will tend to view the lives of others, and the world around us. Of course it will. It really is that important. To explore this further, let me first put things into a more logical framework. Let me start by saying that although, from my perspective, there is an abundance of evidence supporting our survival of death – some of which this book will deliver – it is the case that without the kind of proof that we can all begin to accept or agree upon, our most logical position is to say we *believe* we survive death, or we *believe* in there being an afterlife. In this situation the opposite has also to be true: proof, that we can all agree upon, is also lacking to indicate death is actually final. We can only say we *believe* we do not survive death, or *disbelieve* in there being an afterlife.

To help lay out the logic of what we know, don't know, and/or believe, in this dialogue, I'm going to use two people: Person A is a *disbeliever* in the afterlife. Person B is a *believer* in the afterlife. From what both sides of this debate can anticipate, or agree on, the following arguments can be made:

1. **Physical death**: Both Person A and Person B will go through physical death regardless of what they believe.
2. **What they believe going into death**: Person A will go to their death believing there is nothing on the other side. Life ends at that point. Person B, on the other hand, will go to their death believing that there is an afterlife; that something transformative will happen to them. Person A believes death is the end of everything and that by deduction life ultimately has no meaning, other than what meaning they give to it, through being alive. Person B meanwhile believes in something that is ongoing. Person B sees life as meaningful and spiritual in essence.
3. **Consequences of their beliefs:** No matter who is right, one outcome of this scenario is that Person B's belief gives cause for them to be less fearful and less stressed over their eventual death than Person A. Person A can only view his/her life as finite – what's left in physical years from where they are now – whereas Person B

is less restricted and can choose to view their life as ongoing and indeed infinite.

4. **In actuality**: In the actuality of the event, if there is nothing on the other side of death then the beliefs of either party are of little consequence, as neither Person A or Person B will be in a position to comment or care about it. If, on the other hand, there is an afterlife, Person B is likely to be better prepared to accept they have passed out of their physical body and are now in new circumstances – the circumstances they believed would happen. By comparison, Person A is now experiencing something they didn't expect. It could be a nice surprise but given they have carried their disbeliefs with them they will probably be in denial that they have actually died, and therefore are now in danger of becoming stuck in a confusing limbo situation with no immediate resolve.

Given this scenario, one is now asked to consider which of the two options it is better to believe in. Which subscribes to the more optimistic or favourable belief about life and death, and which the more pessimistic? Indeed, placing the eventuality of death in context, which belief best supports one having a joyful and a happier life in the here and now? Is it Person A or Person B? To my mind this is a no-brainer.

What we believe about life and death will have impact on our lives, our values, our attitude, and our expectations. There will be important differences between holding the view that one is a spiritual being, a soul who continues on past death, and the position of believing one is essentially an animal, a physical being who is only around for the next few years. It is not so much that this would necessarily be noticed in our everyday behaviour. Whether we have a spiritual belief or not, doesn't stop us from living by a healthy moral code. Can we love our family, our children and others around us just the same? Of course we can. Can we be as loving as the next person towards humanity and the world? Of course we can. Where it will most likely be different is the context by which we place all of our experiencing into: how we interpret what we experience, what helps to drive us forward and becomes our reason for existence. Importantly it will be what gives our life meaning.

If I live my life believing that I will eventually die and that will be that, I will tend to drive my life forward from that imperative. While my family, friends, my interests, my work and my things give meaning to my life, indeed my passion, I will be less inclined to see my world as having any meaning in a bigger and symbolically sense, or containing anything invisible and – notwithstanding natural forces and human powers that be – bigger than myself, in terms of influence. I'll be rather more inclined towards a pragmatic, *life just is,* philosophy and buy into natural causes and coincidence for my explanation to events. Perhaps there'll be a bit of *sods law* thrown in too as I'll probably be much less inclined to see my *responsibility* in everything that happens to me. Taking responsibility for everything that I draw towards me, or happens to me, can be a tough deal for anyone to accept. I will be inclined to be less attentive to important cues and signs around me such as might be flagged up by elements of synchronicity, my intuition, by my dreams, by communications with such other worldly beings as guides or angels – I'll probably give a wry smile at even the mention of the latter two beings. I'll probably deny the power of my dreams to foretell events, and deny the power of my subconscious to influence my external reality.

I probably won't hold to any belief that life is a journey, or series of journeys, towards enlightenment or consciousness. Further I probably won't believe in there being such a thing as the law of karma (or its modern equivalent, the *law of attraction*) and by that I will choose to miss out on grasping such a fundamental as to how life works from a spiritual perspective. In summing up I will tend towards having, what could be described as, a *brain-centric* – our brain and physical body is the extent of who and what we are – view on life, that explains how we are thereby conscious, and I'll be inclined to be sceptical regarding anything that falls outside this view of things. Probably this will include an intolerance, or suspicion, of alternative, holistic ideas, and anything deemed as spiritual.

And how can I say all of this is possible? Well much of it follows once one takes up what is essentially a non-religious or non-spiritual worldview, which is where I once lived. My worldview was once based entirely on what I could see or sense with my physical capabilities and I certainly was inclined to rubbish anything not fitting in with this *intellectual* take on things – which was also, I have to say, ultimately pessimistic in outlook.

To be fair, this view wouldn't necessarily be true of the person who retains a more agnostic approach to life – of which many of us do of course. I'm talking of those of us who, although not holding any strong spiritual beliefs, nevertheless endeavour to keep an open mind on such matters – but which can also be a bit wishy-washy, and a less than desirable position in the scheme of things. Even so the above should give you a flavour of what I am angling at. There is a difference, and in many respects it really does boil down to starting from whether we see *meaning*, symbolical, connective, synchronistic meaning in our world of experience, or not as the case may be. And let me add that for those of us who aren't able to get even a glimmer of this, what I'd call *reality*, really are missing out and are the poorer for it.

Father Christmas – a rite of passage

Much of what we come to believe about our world, and our place within it, has its beginnings in childhood. I mean that what was presented to us by our parents, our teachers, religious upbringing, culture, traditions, our peers, and our environment, will have impacted upon how we handle our lives. As we get older and wiser, we may hopefully come to see and acknowledge the contribution our childhood experience has made to our adult perception of things. If we can begin to see that, then, with some effort, we can place ourselves in a better position to make a choice regarding whether we accept the worldview as provided for us, in part, or in its entirety, or whether our view of the world needs to be somewhat adjusted, perhaps radically so, and maybe given a new interpretation – our own interpretation.

If our early experience was emancipating, encouraging our freedom to play, to explore and find our own path in life, then great; "The lines are fallen to me in pleasant places; indeed, my heritage is beautiful to me." (Psalm 16:6). We know of course, from experience, that not all of us have fared so well in our upbringing, and a lot of us carry leftover, often unhealthy, baggage as a result of our childhood. Given that, it needs also to be said that in a broad sweep our parents, and other figures influencing our young life, were who they were (with their own baggage) and no doubt did the best they could for us. For the most part, of our upbringing, no harm was done to us – at least not intentionally.

On the other side of the coin; from a parental viewpoint, some traditions, and external influences, place pressures upon us so as to behave in a certain way in how we raise our children. There are of course all kinds of initiations, expectations, laws and social codes regarding how we live with each other, and how we behave in public. These in turn can have a profound, if sometimes subtle, effect upon our children. Again it is done with good intention behind it. One of these influences concerns how we learn from an early age not to be *taken-in*, or taken for a ride: when and how we trust others, and how much trust to put into anything that we can't necessarily see or experience directly for ourselves. We learn early on how not to be conned out of something we own for example, or to have, the wool pulled over our eyes into believing some obviously untrue story.

Knowingly, or unknowingly, one device we adults use to get such a powerful message home to our children is our modern-day Christmas story. Father Christmas or, if you prefer, Santa Claus (St Nicholas) is a magical being who knows all the children in the world personally – and, as we know, brings them presents at Christmas. What a thing to be a child and yet know that someone so magical knows your name, and will visit you on that special night. That makes you special, right? Yes of course it does.

For the child our story runs along the lines of a mother or father saying; "Go to bed now Tommy or Father Christmas won't visit and bring your presents this Christmas." Tommy, all excited, goes to bed quick sharp, and of course stays awake for ages hoping to spot Santa. He comes to a point where he can't keep his eyes open any longer and drifts off to sleep. He misses seeing Father Christmas, but next morning all the presents he wanted have miraculously arrived. He checks with his mum that Father Christmas had the mulled wine and biscuits left out for him, to help him on his journey. She tells him that he did. How magical that Father Christmas didn't forget him – he was actually here in his very home during the night. That's a wow. Tommy thinks to himself, "Santa must have come just after I fell asleep – oh I wish I had seen him."

Let's say Tommy is only four. We know a year or two down the line he's going to find out the truth. Maybe another kid will spill the beans, or he'll pick up on something and end up asking his parents about the matter. I recall so well challenging my mum regarding Father Christmas not being real. This was after receiving a Rupert Bear book for Christmas. I was able to say that I had read most of it before Christmas Day. The reason being I had discovered its whereabouts a week or so previously. I recall being somewhat afraid to let her know that I knew. I think it was because I was aware that I was spoiling it for her, and my younger sister, Pat, at the time. But anyhow I couldn't hold it in and I told her I'd been reading it. My mother adamantly stuck to her guns: the book was especially delivered early for Christmas, and she was told to hide it. But for myself I could no longer buy the Father Christmas explanation – and I have to say, I recall so well that the magic of Christmas was never quite the same afterwards.

For Tommy, likewise, the truth will out, that Father Christmas isn't real after all. But now let's look at what has actually happened here: It transpires that Tommy was taken in, by of all people, his parents, the people he loves and trusts to guide him into the world. He was duped into believing in a magical being who visited him once a year with presents – and he bought into this myth year on year. He then found out later – probably through someone other than his parents – that this being didn't after all exist. If it was through one of his peers the message could also have been reinforced with Tommy being made to feel pretty stupid for not knowing – kids can be cruel to each other at times. And this was all happening at such a young age.

We adults tend to treat this event as an innocent act, a *no harm done* matter, as we want to let our children have their moment believing in the magic of Christmas, before they grow up and discover a very different story. It is done with all such good intention, but it doubly serves as a rite of passage, a salutary lesson to the innocent child to never again be quite so trusting or gullible – particularly where other worldly beings are concerned. *Father Christmas doesn't exist.*

Do you see where I'm going here? It goes into the young mind, the seed is sown and it will take some undoing. It's a kick-start to our, "Yes pull the other leg," response to life. It is experience such as this that can compromise our awe for life too. Our spirit dampened, we can come to miss seeing the obvious magic that is actually all around us. We come to sublimate our inner child needs, for the magical, into more mundane avenues: into the world of fantasy movies, television, novels, sci-fi and such as online games where we can interact and our imagination and fantasy life can run riot. I suspect some of us, as near as damn it, live in this other *online* world, and would move there, lock, stock and barrel if we could. In effect, through such alternatives we can find safe expression for our needs and dreams of the magical neatly compartmentalised in a boxset or piece of online software. It is not all bad either as it provides us with possibilities, a different kind of reality that we may be able to somehow bring back into our physical world through our creativity. But probably none of this interactivity may challenge or shift what we have grown up believing about ourself and our physical reality.

In the film, and book, *The Secret*[6] (one of many sources for the law of attraction concept), we are given guidance regarding use of the law of attraction; and how magically we can bring into our lives what we might otherwise describe as the magic of Christmas. We ask for something, from something bigger than us, the *Universe*, for what we want. The Universe then responds by providing it for us. It is that simple. Well it's not quite that simple as it is also an art-form involving practice at using visualisation and invoking good vibrations or feelings in oneself. It also involves taking action, to pull what we want towards us. But hang on, it is not that simple anyhow as we've been taught a hard lesson as children, not to believe in Father Christmas. Replace *Universe* with *Father Christmas* and there's our dilemma. Could we but regain that wonderment, that trust that life and our world is, after all, a magical place that will provide for us. Ah, if we could who knows what might be possible. That takes some believing however. It can be done of course.

We will need to work at it, to undo that childhood double-whammy. Remember it wasn't just that we found out Father Christmas doesn't exist but that it was those who love us the most who set us up for the con. This *undoing* may become important for you to consider as we move through this, and the following, chapters. It can be so tempting to place a lot of what I'm discussing here into the, been there, done it, *Father Christmas* pigeonhole, and leave it there – I hope and trust you'll stay with it for the duration; and the magic yet to be explored.

Soul Journey Start

One of the first milestones we need to come to accept on what is part of this undoing, and an opening ourselves up towards the journey of our soul, is linked to the very beginning of the journey. What this is, is that we need to understand we attract towards us the circumstances that we are to start out with. Our parents and siblings, the upbringing we are likely to have, and our physical and mental capabilities are all symbolically tied into this attraction. This is part of our path, our learning. It is all potential at the start with no certainty regarding outcomes. I happen to believe that always there is a great deal of love around at the start. Never is our situation intended to scar, even though from that starting moment the road ahead has every chance of providing challenges, difficulties and woundings through our interaction with our environment and people. The future, our future, is not so written in stone as those who believe in fate, or everything fixed, would have it.

To accept this state with all its ramifications, we have to also consider we are not quite the tabula-rasa we may think we are at the beginning. We arrive ready-wired with our propensities and proclivities yet to be given external form. We seek the time and place of our birth and, as the central character, we take centre stage in our own developing drama. There is direction from the outset albeit at a subconscious, part open-book, level.

As adults we may come to learn too that this power of *attraction* is dynamic and continues throughout our lives. The better we are able to know ourselves, then the better we are able to improve on what we attract towards us. We are also likely to be in a better position to curtail passing the emotional knots, and baggage, that we have acquired from our travels, onto the children now in our care. Instead we enhance the start they need from a more open perspective. Hopefully there is progress towards encouraging a more open-minded approach with each generation. But the reality is that this process can so easily become a comparatively closed circuit of reseeding old dark beliefs, habits and traditions, family or otherwise, that allow for only a small chink of light to come in – or only to very gradually open up our children to other perspectives, wider viewpoints, other opinions, other valid beliefs.

It is still a few weeks too early in our human development to present a more fact-packed approach to unravelling what our lives are about from a spiritual perspective. Surprisingly few of us endeavour to see the larger picture of life, or place our own lives in context with the absolute wonders around us. And yet time passes, a given life is finite, and really none of us can afford to get too comfortable. Ah but that does indeed conjure up the old truism, *Ignorance is bliss*, and for many of us the earth show goes on without our willing participation – for now at least. I think sometimes it is better to remain in blissful ignorance than to dip our toe in the water and only take a peep at what might be going on. I'm thinking of another old truism here; *A little knowledge is a dangerous thing*. The suggestion is therefore that if you are going to take the plunge, to look into such spiritual matters, then do it with intention, determination, passion and commitment.

It is my concern and desire that at the very least we should, from childhood, be given every encouragement and opportunity to explore, discuss and consider our life (and death) adventure. One way to encourage this process is by giving ourselves the opportunity of asking, and being asked, some leading and open questions that we as children and adults can explore and seek to answer. And so here they are... I'm sure once you have the gist of this, more questions will occur to you too.

Life and Death Questions

> Isn't it sad to go to your grave without ever wondering why you were born? Who, with such a thought, would not spring from their bed, eager to resume discovering the world and rejoicing to be part of it?
>
> Richard Dawkins, biologist, ethologist[7]

The above discussion has largely been by way of a preamble to our taking time to look at, and to seriously consider, the following questions – which I've narrowed down to ten areas. I suggest these are amongst the most important questions any of us can ever ask of ourselves and seek to answer at the level of human consciousness and spirituality. They are not that original; on the contrary they have no doubt been pondered by countless lives – although I'll bet by not as many lives as there might have been or needs to be. That said, it is possibly new my lumping them together like this. They are ancient, so ancient indeed that it would be fair to surmise that some have been around since the dawn of consciousness in mankind. Yet they are ever new and ever the property of each person. Given the opportunity you may have phrased them a little differently, but putting aside all our other daily life concerns and getting down to what really matters, these questions are, or I believe need to be, fundamental to understanding our human condition. They need to be the base, the foundation, upon which all our other concerns rest, and whether they rest peacefully or not will depend upon how we answer them.

Do give them serious thought. Try to avoid snappy glib answers where possible – well okay get your glib answers out of the way and then think about the questions more seriously, more deeply. In any case I would argue that glib answers to these questions only reflect a learnt cultural response rather than a response coming from who we truly are, or feel inside. Give yourself the opportunity to answer them with the seriousness they deserve. If they disturb you – and one or two really ought to, at very least, make you think – or fill you with concern to understand and answer them thoroughly, you are probably already embarked upon the adventure of finding and regaining your soul – whether you fully realise it yet or not.

I might suggest jotting your answers down somewhere, even dating them, should you want to revisit them at a later time – but I'll leave that with you. Along with your answers try to give reasons for your answers. I suggest it is really important that you stop to consider these before moving on through the book.

Ten big questions

Q1. Who and what are you?

This first question is perhaps not as simple as it may sound. Are you your name, your nationality, or perhaps your profession or job? Are you what your friends, family, colleagues or the State says you are? Or are you a combination of all the above that defines you? Could it be your gender, colour, culture or language that you strongly identify with? Do you consider yourself to be a genetically driven bundle of molecules, in every sense an animal? Do you perhaps consider yourself to be a spirit in an animal body, or something else? If something else what would that be?

If you believe you are no more than a physical being, a product of evolution, what makes you so certain this is true – and importantly how did you go about finding this out for yourself? If you believe you are more than a product of evolution, what is this *more*, and importantly how did you arrive at this view for yourself?

Q2. Where did you start out from to get here?

Put another way, where were you before you were born? Did you even exist back then?

Was it perhaps as simple as your father providing the starting point, or was it your mother's womb – an obvious starting point? Or was it perhaps the earth itself, or the stars, or the *Other Side*, in whatever that means to you? Would you say you started out from God, or was it somewhere else that you started out from? Perhaps you never started from anywhere? There may be more than one answer to this question. Nail it, if you can. It is important to establish an origin and baseline for your beliefs.

Q3. Why are you here and here now?

So why are you here right now? Do you have a reason or purpose for being here on the earth at this moment in time? Apart from what you might consider obvious day to day reasons, such as your family life or your work, or social life, are there perhaps further reasons, even entirely different reasons – a purpose or destiny perhaps – to your being here during this time? Are you here to possibly find out something or to achieve something, to take something or to give something? Is it possible that you are simply here by accident? Could you feel the reason you're here is actually outside your control or say-so? If so who is responsible for you being here and why now?

Q4. Have you been here before?

This question links to reincarnation or rebirth.

Do you believe you have had a previous existence before this one? Have you perhaps some vivid memories, or recurring dreams that have no obvious connection with your life? Do you possibly suffer with, what one might describe as, an irrational fear or phobia that you cannot easily explain – unless placed in context with something deeper, less personal, a possible previous existence? Such experience (as vivid memories) can be particular powerful during childhood. Just as important; if you do believe you have been here before, then, why have you been here before? And leading back to Q3 – for what purpose might you be here again?

Do you alternatively buy into the, *I'm only here once* belief? If you do believe this then what do you actually mean by it? I ask this question here as it can depend upon what perspective this comment is being viewed from. For example I believe in reincarnation but also believe that I'm only here once – I'll explain my take on this, further in.

Q5. We are conscious beings. Why do you think this is so?

This question can open a Pandora's box of questions too. Evidently we are more conscious, or let's say more self-aware, than other creatures or plants around us. But hang on is that really true? If true, do you think the reason for this is simply a quirky outcome of *evolution*, or possibly an outcome by design? If by design to what end or purpose could this be? Could consciousness be perhaps intended to serve some higher purpose not yet clear?

Importantly, do you see consciousness as stemming from our brain, or our brain as an instrument for consciousness to be expressed or applied in the world? Could consciousness, in other words, stem from elsewhere, perhaps the mind or soul, could there even be another, and different, source?

Q6. Have you ever experienced something paranormal, an unexplainable event in your life?

Perhaps on occasion you saw something, heard something, felt something, or experienced something, with any of your five senses, that didn't make sense in terms of what you regard as normal. Perhaps you have experienced something that ran contrary to known forces – such as defying gravity. Could it be you regularly experience what to others would be "paranormal" or unexplainable, and in such a natural way that to you this is completely "normal" – perhaps so much so that you even consider it odd to learn others don't experience the same? If you do have, or have had, such experiences, how has this affected your beliefs about life and death? If you haven't knowingly had such experiences, how has this affected your beliefs about life and death?

Q7. Do you believe life is meaningful?

One can append the issue of whether you believe in fate or freewill, to this question.

Are the events taking place in your life, and the lives of others around you, entirely random, coincidental, or happening for a purpose? Is it really all just the *luck of the draw* or is there *meaning* or *symbolism* operating in life, in your opinion or experience? Could you possibly be living in a dynamic, interconnected situation, where attraction and synchronicity are involved in the events that you create and/or experience? Have you, for example, ever considered, at times, that life may be *trying to tell you something*?

Do you believe in fate and see your life and direction as fixed from birth; there by some higher design or destiny that you may or may not know about? Alternatively do you see your life and direction as determined by who you are, and by the decisions and actions you are taking – whether consciously or subconsciously carried through? If you regard your life as essentially an existential or meaningless experience, let me ask you what drove you to pick up this book and start reading it? It's a serious question.

Q8. Do you accept there is the Law of Karma at work in your life?

Here's a question that directly ties in with the last question, as well as most other questions listed. Bear in mind, when answering here, that if karma truly is a law it will make little difference whether we believe in it or not; it will simply operate in our lives. In context then, have you looked into what karma is and how it works, or is supposed to work? If you do believe in karma, how are you working with it in your daily life? If you do not believe there is such a law operating in your life then why not, what alternative view do you hold with? Try not to glibly endorse or deny this law, give yourself reasons either way.

Q9. Do you believe you are a soul?

When we talk of psyche, mind, spirit, higher self, atman or soul do you think we essentially mean the same thing or are there differences in your view?

Not every spiritual discipline, or religion, believes in the soul – Buddhism being a prime example. If you believe you are a soul have you ever considered what form your soul takes, and for that matter where it resides – somewhere in the body, outside the body, all through it?

Bridging back to *Q5*, is it the brain perhaps that you see as really being the soul that people talk about? Alternatively, if you believe you are a soul, how does your belief fit in with *consciousness* in the scheme of things?

If you believe you are a soul, do you/your soul have a purpose or plan of action? If you do, then what is it? If you believe you are a soul, is it the same you, as you know yourself, or something else? Could you exist without being a soul? Also, if you believe you are a soul, what about other lifeforms; do they also each have a soul or something else?

Q10. What do you believe will happen to you when you die?

Okay, a final but critical question. Will death be it, an end to you, or will you, or a part of you, survive death? If you believe you will survive then in what form will you survive? Also what do you think is going to happen to this form of you, once on the other side of death? Do you believe you will be going to heaven, hell or perhaps purgatory for a long stay – or perhaps some other place, what we broadly call the Other Side? If you believe it's the Other Side, what do you consider this to be like, and how will you live there? If you do believe you will survive death, are you likely ever to return here, back to the physical world?

Finally, in the event of your death, will it make an iota of difference whether you are buried or cremated? Will it matter whether you are buried in or outside of a churchyard – or possibly even in a remote location such as a desert or at sea? In the event of your death, under what circumstances would you be most at peace, and why?

Commentary

Fairly this list, of ten broad question areas, does not exhaust all conceivable and related questions on the matter being looked at here, but, nevertheless, it does aim to get to the nub of the situation. Certainly the nub of the situation I intend to address, which is making sense of our life and death, our spiritual situation on the earth and beyond.

On a personal level, looking back, I would like to have been encouraged to explore these questions, possibly as a child but certainly as a young adult, as part of my development. I was never asked them, or anything like them, not in my learning at school, not by my parents, or indeed by anyone charged with my education. You might be forgiven for thinking these questions are for adults only, but an exploration of any mainstream religion will show it is not the case. My Roman Catholic upbringing, for example, endeavoured to deal with similar. Actually it not only posed big spiritual questions but also supplied ready-made answers. I didn't have to think in other words. Yes I learnt the basic catechism by rote as a child. Although I don't buy into this narrative now, in the same way as I did as a child, the message has certainly been lodged in my mind – I can still repeat a part of it, that, "I'm here to know God, love Him and serve Him in this world and be happy with Him forever in the next." It is in there and so easily rolls off the tongue – requiring little or no thinking.

I reckon more so as an adult, there can be the assumption that we don't need to ask or answer such questions. They are either not seen to relate, or are not that important in our daily lives. They can, and often do, sit uncomfortably with us. Probably most of us rest in the knowledge that they have been, or can be, answered for us by others of more expert opinion – if we need them answering that is. And there is a lesson in that too: *No one, but no one, can answer these questions better than you can for yourself.* Let me tell you, as if you didn't already know, we live in a world of reason, opinion and belief where these matters are concerned. Let it not be those who speak the loudest, or appear dressed for the part, who necessarily have the greatest influence over what we believe. Okay so let us call on authoritative opinions, check out the views of neighbours, views on the Web, weight up the pros and cons, but in the end let us seek to discover our own answers that we choose to live by – and, for that matter, die by.

Remembering where we are

Working through this book and answering these questions with an open mind, and open heart, can, I believe, help you to bring about positive changes in your life. It can help you to better understand who you are, help you to find your place, and with it peace and happiness. The process will encourage you to travel to places in your inner and outer worlds that you perhaps never knew existed, and also help you give yourself permission to live by your answers.

The best way to begin this process is by remembering where we are. I believe it helps to occasionally look up at the sky and remind ourselves of what a weird and wonderful place we exist in, or more accurately, live on. I'm talking about our planet Earth of course. We are brought into the world and may, if encouraged as children, grow up with wonderment in our hearts at what we see around us. I recall as a child, that one of our infant school lessons was to go out on a nature walk, through a nearby lane and local fields, and identify plants, trees, birds, other animals and insects. I loved those trips and maybe it has had more influence on my view on matters than I can imagine. It is the case though that, more likely, we grow up rapidly adjusting to the world of our parents and our peers, and pretty soon forget where we really are. We replace *remembering* with the agenda of our human needs and culture – seeking indeed to create the good life I discussed in the last chapter. We forget we are in space, on our good ship Earth. Think about it. We are travelling through space on our planet, and by each moment we are a lot deeper in space. Our ship is rotating at around a thousand miles (1.6 thousand km) per hour at the equator and is falling at approximately 67-thousand miles (108 thousand km) per hour around our Sun, some 93-million miles (150 million km) from us. Further our Sun and its solar system are also falling at a colossal speed around the centre of our Milky Way galaxy – the speed is estimated to be as much as 568-thousand miles (914 thousand km) per hour. Something to think about alright... would you agree? This is the backdrop to our physical experience, our lives on this planet.

Let's talk about *awe* for a moment

Awe, I think, is one of those words that you have a better understanding of once you see it. I felt using the word 'awesome' was totally appropriate when it came to describing what the planet looks like [from space].

Nicole Stott - Shuttle/ISS Astronaut[8]

I think it fair to say that few of us give much thought to where we are. We soon enough develop blinkers to the world that is going on beneath our feet, and around us, while living in our towns and cities. We've constructed a seven day week and, in it, we usually work for five days and then have weekends off – I certainly try to and most often fail. We work through our year with our public holidays and all the other calendar structures in place. Okay we may take holidays to exotic places and know with pinpoint accuracy their locality, language and local customs, and also that, of course, these destinations are on the same planet. We know stuff existentially and intellectually but we don't so easily feel this, and, even less likely to the point of it encouraging engaging questions about the nature or purpose of our lives.

I hope you are getting my drift with this; we are ever in danger of losing our awe for life – and taking life, our modern version of it, almost for granted. But can I be blunt here: we are also a bit afraid of engaging in the awe of life. We even have a word for anything having too much awe – we call it *awful* – something we'd sooner not know about or experience. Having a world without awe, it seems, is an easier state to slip into. The world could literally be flat and not moving for all we think about it and experience. On the contrary though we are living on what I accept as a living thing, our collective mothership that is giving out life, endlessly moving and changing its position – in relation to our solar system and Milky Way galaxy.

> To have that experience of awe is ... to let go of yourself, to transcend the sense of separation. So it was not just that they [the astronauts] were experiencing something other than them but they were at some very deep level integrating, realising their interconnectedness with that beautiful blue ball.
>
> David Loy – Zen Buddhist teacher[9]

Let me see if I can put this across differently. Back in 1948 the astronomer Fred Hoyle was quoted as saying that, "Once a photograph of Earth, taken from outside, is available ... a new idea as powerful as any in history will be let loose." Well, twenty years later, in 1968, Apollo 8 went to the Moon, and at one point, as the crew were orbiting the Moon, one of the astronauts casually turned the camera around to show us what planet Earth looked like from space... And yes, this was the moment that Hoyle had spoken of. For anyone watching at that time it could have been quite awesome. Frank White, author of the Overview Effect[10] (the overview effect is the experience that astronauts can have when seeing the earth from space), certainly thought so. He remarked that he was watching and said, "That was the first time I had ever seen the planet hanging in space like that and it was profound."[11] It is this, "hanging in space," that we easily lose touch with in our flatland lives on the planet.

> The universe is a pretty big place. If it's just us, seems like an awful waste of space.
>
> Carl Sagan, astronomer, author[12]

Most of us will have seen images of Earth from space by now. We know from this and our space voyages that if we are able to see it from outer space it has a beautiful blue hue. Because of its atmosphere and life, it actually glows, like strip lighting, on the side facing the Sun. If we look towards our nearest neighbour planets, firstly in the direction of the Sun. Relatively close by is Venus. Venus is similar in size to our Earth but too barren, and hostile, for life as we know it. If we look to the outer side of us, away from the Sun; there lies Mars. Again we find a barren landscape with indications of possible life being there at one time – and possibly, at a micro level, still is there. Although we anticipate life most probably will exist, nay definitely exist, in abundance elsewhere in our Milky Way galaxy – with the likelihood that some of it is already visiting us, and has been for some time – we may have to accept the fact that it does not exist in any great abundance elsewhere in our solar system, not as yet at least. Maybe simple life will be found in the waters on Europa (one of the Moons of Jupiter) but we can accurately anticipate we are not going to find the complexity of lifeforms as we experience here.

This is so easy to say but our solar system itself actually covers a vast area in space. The planetary bodies we are talking about have huge masses. Jupiter for example is nearly eleven times bigger than our Earth. It is not the furthest planet from the Sun in our system but even so its mean distance is 483-and-a-bit-million miles (778.5 million km) from it. It is over five times the distance we are from the Sun. When we talk of Neptune then we are nearly off the scale of imagination – Neptune is 2.8-billion miles (4.5 billion km) from the Sun, and that planet is falling around the Sun, as we are – only taking a bit longer, some 165-earth-years to get around it.

What we are a part of is vast, and we need to remind ourselves of this occasionally at least.

> Exploration is in our nature. We began as wanderers, and we are wanderers still. We have lingered long enough on the shores of the cosmic ocean. We are ready at last to set sail for the stars.
>
> Carl Sagan[13]

Well we are getting close but not quite leaving the shores at this point in time. Taking on-board Sagan's comments, let us take this a step further by conjuring up, or recapturing, something of our wonderment and awe for life – by using our imagination.

Let's suppose for a moment we have boarded a rocket bound for Neptune. After years of preparation, the moment has arrived. We have carried through all our checks, and have blasted off. We have left Earth and are travelling towards the outer planets. We chose a time when they effectively lined up with planets closer to home, so that we could use the gravitational pull of Mars and Jupiter to help slingshot us on our way to getting there. And so we have gone out, past Mars, then onto Jupiter, then Saturn, and beyond to Uranus and finally, getting out to the known extremities, we have arrived at Neptune. It has taken us some time to get here... By our current rocket technology we are contemplating years of travel to get to any of these remote places. For instance, back in August 1977, *Voyager 2* spacecraft was launched and took twelve years to get out to Neptune. So, to keep it simple, let's say it has taken us ten years to reach Neptune. Also, due to the negative effects of being away from Earth's gravity, we should note that astronauts rarely spend much longer than six months, at a time, in space. In our scenario then we are really stretching our imagination. Let us assume that we'll remain healthy throughout this journey, and be able to adjust to gravity when back home. Now, as if we didn't know, we've taken this journey to get a closer look at Neptune's fourteen moons, with particular interest in getting close-up images and measures of Triton – for the possibility of life. Speaking of life, we certainly didn't expect the objects, we observed, once outside the Earth's atmosphere, to have followed us for, at least, part of our journey, which they did. But, for all that, we remained safe.

Moving on, let's say we spent, what would be, seven earth days orbiting Neptune, while keeping a close eye on Triton, and we have now turned our ship around and are heading back home. We are fortunate indeed to have the rocket capacity to be able to do this. At this stage, using our current technology, we wouldn't get back.

Now a further ten years on, and therefore twenty or so years older, we are nearing home. So now imagine the sight, how pleased we are to be returning to our blue planet, our home, and its moon that has shone in the half-light for well over a year. Now we are close enough to make out the shape of our continents and oceans – what a sight! The anticipation of getting home is overwhelming. Let's say we are now re-entering our atmosphere and more closely we are able to view the land, the seas; now even the mountains, forests and some of our remarkable buildings are visible. We land safely, and soon enough we are back on home soil, back with our people, our friends and importantly our families.

We are going to need a lot of time to adjust. Not just to being back on terra firma, and gravity again, and not just to adjust to all that has happened in our lives, during the last twenty years, but to all that has happened in the lives of our families, and in world events that have taken place on the Earth, over the time we have been away. Children have grown up, people have aged, moved house, had their own children, and people have died. But let's consider for now the lasting effect of how beautiful, unusual and fragile, so alone, and homely the Earth seemed to us as we were returning – especially after all the uncertainty and dangers we encountered being away. The impact has been enormous and that experience is ever now vividly with us – yes, what a beautiful blue gem our home planet really is to us.

> We are all in the gutter, but some of us are looking at the stars
> Oscar Wilde, author, playwright, poet[14]

It might also be something of a sad return and experience too. Our journey has given us a wide, solar system wide, perspective on life, and we can see more vividly now, than those years before, the way a lot of us live on our finite and precious world. How primitive, sometimes dangerous, petty and even mad so much of what we collectively believe, value, do and say, now appears to us. If only more of us could raise ourselves and be looking at the stars, at the bigger picture. If only all of us could take such a journey, even in our imagination, we might have a more loving and wakeful approach to life... and be leaving Oscar Wilde's, "in the gutter" behind.

Notes & references

[1] Quote from Goodreads.
http://www.goodreads.com/author/quotes/1505445.James_Dean [Accessed 14/04/2013]

[2] Shakespeare's Hamlet: Act 5, Scene 2.

[3] There are two main theories regarding how the ageing process works. Our genes are thought to account for much of it – we are pre-programmed to age - then there is damage to our DNA/molecules through the wear and tear of life/environment. If we could change these conditions the idea is we might live for longer. However we would still eventually die or fall to bits (would we not?), as parts are going to continually be knocked, in need of repair or being worn down. The cells in our bodies are continually dying and being renewed. It is believed we have a complete change by the end of every 7 years but nevertheless it is an ongoing process. With each 7 year cycle there is a generation being built on the last generation. In context it helps to liken the ageing process to making photocopies of photocopies. Each time a photocopy is made of the last photocopy some definition, some information is lost which can't be regained.

[4] Clark, E. M. (2012) *The Experience (Near to Death)*, Friesen Press.

[5] Pascal's Wager. Pascal proposed that it is better to believe in God - and live morally by the constraints of that belief - than not to believe in God. The argument being that if God does not actually exist, such a person, at most, will only suffer finite losses in some pleasures and luxuries, whereas, if God does exist, they stand to receive infinite gains in Heaven and avoid infinite losses in Hell. Read more https://en.wikipedia.org/wiki/Pascal's_Wager

[6] Byrne, R. (2006) *The Secret* (film), TS Production LLC. Also Byrne R (2006) *The Secret* (book), Atria Books.

[7] Dawkins, R. (2000) Unweaving the Rainbow: Science, Delusion and the Appetite for Wonder. Mariner Books

[8] Quote from the film *Overview*, from Planetary Collective – visit overviewthemovie.com [Accessed 14/04/2013].

[9] Ibid., from the film *Overview*.

[10] White, F. (1998) *The Overview Effect: Space Exploration and Human Evolution*. American Institute of Aeronautics & Astronautics.

[11] Film *Overview*, op. cit.

[12] Sagan, C. (1997) *Contact*. Mass Market Paperback. First published 1985.

[13] Sagan, C. (2002) *Cosmos*. Random House. First published 1980.

[14] Wilde, O. (1892) Lady Windermere's Fan. Act III Lord Darlington.

CHAPTER 3

FRINGE BENEFITS

Could we, in our wildest dreams, learn anything about ourselves from reports of paranormal events and experiences? Could people who have had a near-death experience, or those who have discovered they had a previous life, through past-life-recall, possibly provide us with valuable insight into the true nature of our existence? More broadly, could there be any benefit to our understanding of life and death by exploring what are often described as *fringe* matters and beliefs?

Well, from my perspective, it is a resounding *yes* in answer to all of these questions. In this chapter I'm going to explore some of the more prominent areas of fringe interests and provide evidence that should give us grounds for looking into life, death and spiritual matters more closely, and indeed more seriously.

Let me add to this that while it is quite usual for us to ignore or side-line much of what I will be discussing here – hence why it is deemed as fringe – it is, I'd argue, only by exploring these areas, in the round, that we can readily see a more holistic, meaningful and spiritual picture begin to emerge. I further believe this will give us cause enough to take heart and consider our survival of death is better than likely. Indeed some of the evidence for this being the case is mounting up and already at a point for serious enquiry and debate.

> Death is simply a shedding of the physical body like the butterfly shedding its cocoon. It is a transition to a higher state of consciousness where you continue to perceive, to understand, to laugh, and to be able to grow.
>
> Elizabeth Kubler-Ross, psychiatrist, pioneer near-death studies[1]

Ten reasons why I believe in the afterlife

Before going any further I'm going to list what amounts to ten pointers that convince me there is more to life than we currently know or accept. These ten pointers also provide reasons why I believe, nay *know*, I will survive the termination of my physical body. Placing these here serves two purposes: the first is to lay before you the foundations for my own beliefs – some of which I have wrestled in order to come to terms with – and the second; to flag up that some of these pointers also influence the direction of this and subsequent chapters. The ten are:

1. *Personal experience*: A series of experiences, such as learning about past lives that make sense in context with my current life. I have seen ghosts. I've had other paranormal and, for that matter, synchronistic experiences, that have caused me to be less dismissive of such otherwise, *off-the-wall* interests. Indeed I would say I have become more questioning of life and existence as a direct result. I draw on some of these experiences below – there is also one discussed in the book's *Introduction*.

2. *Nature – change and transformation*: We probably need look no further, than what we call *Nature*, to see clues to change and transformation. For example trees and plants appear to die off in the winter only to return to life in the spring. Caterpillars transform into butterflies or moths, tadpoles turn into frogs. Is our body us, in our entirety, or a vehicle leading to something else? You probably won't be surprised if I say I believe it is the latter. And do we also return in our season? I believe we do, if that is so required of us.

3. *Paranormal events*: There are accounts throughout history that offer rich evidence of forces at play that we don't yet fully understand, or rarely seek to understand. I'd say we rarely treat these with the importance they deserve. We are more likely to ignore such events, but, as I want to explore in

this chapter, they can, and I believe do, help to throw light onto our spiritual situation.

4. *Near-Death Experiences (NDEs)*: A large number of people who have clinically died, and who have been resuscitated, have reported experiences that describe what could be awaiting us on the Other Side of life. I find this convincing evidence. I will be drawing on NDEs in this and subsequent chapters.

5. *Past life recall of children*: Children who remember a past life with enormous clarity and detail provide reliable witness to help endorse a belief in reincarnation. It stands to reason that they are less likely to know about such belief, or have any kind of hidden agenda for doing so. A verifiable number of cases have been reported and we will visit a few of these amazing cases below.

6. *Past Life Regression*: Regressing back to one's early life, or possibly past lives, under hypnosis, that can impact favourably on one's present life. The process of PLR, done professionally, is intended to be a healing therapy. What I find interesting here is less the healing aspect and more the evidence it may provide for possibly tapping into previous lives. PLR has, in a number of cases, been found to provide very accurate information and be equally enigmatic.

7. *The evidence of mediums*: As I see it, it is a completely reasonable explanation that mediums receive impressions or communications from those who have passed over to the Other Side. The claim that they use some other means of acquiring their information, such as *cold reading*, simply doesn't hold up when one actually attends a one-to-one session or public demonstration – I have experience of both, and the latter I have attended on many occasions. I'll be saying more on this below.

8. *Astrology*: Back in the Seventies I began what has transpired to be a lifelong study of astrology. If one looks at this topic, in depth, one can hardly do so without considering its

philosophical implications. These implications are with regard to there being *meaning* or *purpose* to life. It is hard to escape noticing it. It is interwoven within the very fabric of this art. Astrology, in my opinion, provides the most useful handle for an individual to understand their current life journey.

9. *World religions and ancient burial practices*: Although offering differing perspectives, most world religions believe in life after death – and also that the outcome/s one faces at death is linked to how one has lived. Ancient burial practices, some of which I have been fortunate enough to explore first-hand, give evidence for this belief being very much older than many of the religions we know of today. Leaving aside whether our orthodox religions have gotten how it all works right or wrong, clearly they do show the idea, of there being another existence beyond the grave, isn't new, and, if nothing else, this should cause us to think – there is *no smoke without fire* in other words.

10. *Consciousness*: The fact we are here and conscious is, in my humble opinion, absolutely remarkable and further convinces me that there is a bigger purpose operating behind our lives. I firmly believe consciousness (as I see it, the awaking soul), to be the driving force on our planet and beyond. Links between the findings of quantum mechanics and consciousness is a growing and exciting area of science that will, I believe, eventually prove and clarify the existence of an overarching spiritual dimension to physical life.

Okay, let us now get underway and begin by taking a look at the paranormal...

The Paranormal

Normal reception will be resumed as soon as possible.

Mostly we live in a land of *normality* that we humans have constructed. When we talk about normality we can mean many things of course. For the purpose of this book I'm thinking normality means our physical world behaving as we predict it to behave, according to our current understanding. I'm thinking of normality as being linked to our beliefs, our attitude, our culture, our traditions, also our expectations of each other, our behaviour, whether in groups, in family, work or social life, and, in context, our predictions of outcomes.

What I believe we are looking for when we talk of things being normal, is regularity, reliability, predictability, identity and security. It's a case of knowing that although things change, what we can trust today will be, more or less, the same tomorrow, and the day after. In truth, of course, one country's normality or one person's normality may be very different to another. Even so there is usually a spoken or a tacit agreement of what is acceptable and therefore normal. And indeed it can be striking when people step out of the expected norm either for effect, as a fashion statement, or out of strength of belief or conviction. In my own culture I'm thinking of obvious examples like the *hippies*, the *skinheads*, *rockers* and *punks*. These were, presumably still are for some people, obvious groupings that sought to stand outside the bigger conventional norm, and in doing so created their own normality with their own identity, music, rules and expectations – and probably with the passage of time most of them now looking as normal, in the conventional sense, as anyone else.

From a physical perspective we come to trust that what we experience with our five senses serves us with all, or most, of what we need to know about our world in order to negotiate it. We trust the Earth will do its daily rotation. We trust the forces of nature to remain as we know them – well we hope they do. We trust physical things to remain held in place by gravity, unless another physical thing (or things), that we can see or measure, moves them. And should anything seemingly odd happen in our world we look for, and indeed need, an explanation that best ties in with our perception of normality, to accept it and move on with it, or from it.

For example we all know an earthquake can radically change the world around us and place us in very abnormal, distressing and dangerous circumstances. However, as terrifying as it can be, we know now (we didn't always know) an earthquake is due to natural causes – the result of huge pressures such as produced by tectonic plate shift (or possibly triggered by human intervention). We understand how and why it happens and we know earthquakes tend to happen in certain parts of our world more frequently than others. In the event of an earthquake, eventually we clear up the devastation, it has caused, and move on with our lives. Okay I've made that sound pretty straight forward and easy. I'm well aware it is not, that it can, and usually does, have tragic consequences. It is though a situation we can explain and thereby even factor in on policy decisions to help negate the loss of life and structure – good building design, under strict building codes, as obvious examples.

But now think about this: **What is our *paranormal* of today will become our *normal* of tomorrow.** We've gone through a huge amount of learning, in the last two-to-three hundred years, that has largely been pushed along by our industrial revolution and technology. This has brought on developments in architecture, in farming, in weaponry, in the development of health care and surgery, in a better understanding of the human body, a better understanding of diseases, of genetics, in a better understanding of ecosystems, in the development of the car, the aeroplane, the radio, television, the microchip, in exploring the sub-atomic world of particle physics, and let's not forget the Internet, just to name a few. In context our understanding of what is *normal* has had to change and broaden apace. Oddly enough though in our efforts to keep up with the changes taking place around us, we don't necessarily notice our perception of normality is continually being put under review. It is like we quickly take on such developments as becoming part of our normality; but we can so easily miss the implications in these developments. The implications being, they could, probably should, lead us to being more open-minded to other possibilities besides.

> It is possible that there exist emotions that are still unknown to us. Do you remember how electrical currents and unseen waves were laughed at? The knowledge about man is still in its infancy.
>
> Albert Einstein, physicist, philosopher[2]

Of course the human invention or human cause, behind these wonders, allows us to more easily absorb and accept them onto our framework of normality, even though we may know little or nothing of the magic operating behind them. For example we may not know how a computer or tablet actually works yet it is enough to know someone amongst us does, and that we do know how to operate it. Probably the same for our car too – as long as we know where to top up the petrol, oil and water, or whatever resource it runs on. But now imagine a person being resurrected from the mediaeval period, or even later, it could just as easily be the 19th-century, into our modern world, into a city such as London, with all its vehicles, huge building structures, buzz and gadgets. Wouldn't they think a lot of it quite weird, indeed quite scary, and the very opposite of their perception of normality? If they already knew of the word, they'd probably call it *paranormal* – nothing like they ever knew as normal. They would be seeing carriages moving without horses, machines that fly, buildings stretching into the clouds, people using gadgets, with no wires, and able to communicate with each other, even across to the other side of the world – while at the same time strolling down a street. You get the idea…

You can't be serious

> Poltergeist activity is so inherently improbable that most rational people simply cannot believe it. And when they see it and have to believe it, they find it very hard to convince anybody else that it really happens.
>
> Guy Lyon Playfair, parapsychologist[3]

And so on to the fringes… Within the comfort zone of our normality, we can talk about anything we like, such as each other, our jobs, our ambitions, sport interests, our cars, our lovers, our friends, family, the weather and so on. And in the main, this is on the proviso that we steer clear of certain taboo areas such as politics, sex and religion. Certainly one has to be cautious in public anyhow if one wants to avoid getting into heated exchanges. We can talk about the birth end of life but we know it's not so okay to talk about death – unless associated with some event making it okay to talk about it. However, if you really want to keep your *street-cred* up there then avoid at all costs raising anything to do with fringe matters. Into which can-of-worms we can throw the paranormal as a general topic, the tarot, astrology, palmistry, UFOs, the occult, crop circles, angels, fairies at the bottom of the garden, the list goes on… It's all the stuff that we are not meant to talk about, or take seriously, that borders on the wacky and the superstitions of the uneducated.

> In all affairs it's a healthy thing now and then to hang a question mark on the things you have long taken for granted.
>
> Bertrand Russell, philosopher[4]

It is interesting to observe that whenever fringe subject matters are raised – and it is fair to assume they rarely are in most social circles – it is usually done in an atmosphere of levity, derision, embarrassment or denial. It is probably worse than admitting which television *soap* we regularly watch – and that's pretty bad. In general, unless you happen to live in one of a number of the more bohemian small towns in the UK (I'm thinking of say Glastonbury or Totnes) or in say southern California, or perhaps Sedona in Arizona, and other such locations around the world, or just happen to have friends around you of a like mind, it is a *no-no* area to enter into.

Take ghost or poltergeist stories for example – you've got to laugh. Nothing in it, right? Well it certainly made me smile when I was watching a UK television programme in which, Deborah Hyde, the editor of *The Skeptic Magazine*, was giving reasons for denying certain poltergeist activity being real. This was in relation to the

Enfield Poltergeist story, which I will discuss in a bit more detail below. It was the part where she added to her commentary:

> Human beings are remarkably bad at remembering things accurately and seeing things accurately. We see things that aren't there, we don't see things that are there, and we misinterpret things that are there... It's very easy to impose what's called, *top down processing* – the ideas you already have about the world get imposed onto the world and the things you are seeing.[5]

Without doubt there is obvious truth in her comments. If I witness seeing something odd, a ghost for example, and I believe such events can happen, I may be prone to exaggerating or embellishing the experience, to fit in with my worldview that this, or odd things, can happen. Or equally, I may embellish it in order so as to tell it as an exciting story to others. Even so, unless I am making it up completely, all the spin doesn't change the fact that I witnessed something out of the ordinary. If what I saw could be argued to have been a trick of light, or other natural phenomenon, then I could have got it wrong and misinterpreted. This might be the case on occasion, but let's keep in mind here too that most of us negotiate our world successfully from one day to the next and we get streetwise regarding what is real and isn't real – well don't we? The fact I believe *Emmerdale* is a real village in Yorkshire where my partner and I will one day buy our *forever home* and make the Woolpack our *regular*, is beside the point. Of course the other worrying fact about Emmerdale is that it is not really a UK TV soap drama, that everyone has been duped into believing, but rather an actual community that has been hijacked by TV crews, and scriptwriters, trying to cause mayhem and unwelcome relations for the inhabitants. And thinking on, this activity needs to be stopped, especially before we move there. Seriously, if we should be entertaining doubt about what we are witnessing when it is out of the ordinary, then, should we not equally apply doubt to what we witness of the ordinary? Let's for example consider Eve's story. She and Adam are having a conversation:

Eve: "I saw, what I thought, was a Labrador dog go across the road in front of me this evening, as I was driving down for our groceries. Admittedly it was just getting dark... but I definitely saw it."

Adam: "Now hang on Eve that sounds a bit bizarre. Are you sure? You know you've been under a lot of stress recently. I'd suggest you only thought you saw a Labrador cross in front of you. As you say it was getting dark and we know how the lighting at that time of twilight can play tricks on us. I don't think you saw a Labrador or any dog at all."

Eve: "Oh come on Adam, of course it was a dog. I mean what else could it have been?"

Adam: "Well, let me ask you, was it black?"

Eve: "Yes."

Adam: "Was it by itself?"

Eve: "Yes."

Adam: "Well then the chances are what you actually saw was a panther."

Eve: "A what!?"

Adam: "A panther. Don't be surprised. Look at the facts Eve; try reasoning it. Firstly dogs are not allowed out on the road unless they are on a leash these days – so it couldn't have been a dog, let alone a Labrador, unless you also saw the owner – and you didn't, right?"

Eve: "Well no that's true, there was no one around."

Adam: "Secondly, a big black cat, often described as a panther, has been seen in these parts and, as believed, is thought to come into this neighbourhood looking for food. So it's obvious; the chances are it was a panther that you saw and not a Labrador. You're not going mad; it's an easy mistake to make."

Eve: "Well now come to think of it, I suppose it did look a bit cat-like."

Adam: "You see. If you reason things out there is usually a simple explanation. Anyhow, you shouldn't let things like this bother you, and particularly this creature, for as you know, providing you stay in your car, and keep your doors and windows closed, and the engine running, there's really nothing to worry about."

Eve: "Oh gosh, thanks Adam. That really helps to explain what I saw. I'm so glad I talked to you about it. A problem shared... I was starting to get a little worried that I was seeing things. I'll sleep better tonight knowing my mind is at rest again. What say we have some cocoa to help us relax? I need to wind down a bit. It was still a shock to the system regardless of your explanation."

And with that Eve goes off to the kitchen to get the cocoa – her normality restored, well as good as.

But back to my *witnessing a ghost...* issue. If others were with me at the time and also saw strange goings-on, or what they believed was a ghost, then my story has corroboration and carries some clout, does it not – yes, no? Okay, admittedly, it could be some form of *collective hallucination* we're all under. Anyhow, so what made me smile about *The Skeptic Magazine* editor's comment, above, was this: She made her observation during an interview that included Janet Hodgson (who, as a child, was at the centre of the Enfield poltergeist affair), and Guy Lyon Playfair (one of the two, Society for Psychical Research, researchers[6] looking into the matter, and who wrote the book, *This House is Haunted*,[7] about the affair). While she was expressing her doubts as to there being anything paranormal in the series of events witnessed at the house – which was claimed, and corroborated, by a number of people over a period of many months – it transpired that she had not been a witness to any of it. The reason this was so is because, as both Hodgson and Playfair pointed out in the interview, she hadn't actually been there. I wonder, did she miss the obvious irony of her point regarding, "top down processing?" Could this top down processing just as easily apply to the sceptic as anyone else; and was she imposing her, "ideas you already have about the world ... onto the world and the things you are seeing," or *not seeing*, as in her case? I'll leave you to decide on that.

> In the spiritual search doubt is beneficial, a closed mind is not. Doubt used wisely assists enlightenment; a closed mind assists ignorance.
>
> Ian Gardner, author[8]

Like most of us, the sceptic is looking to explain events happening around us in terms of a normality that they, or we, can accept – and often they may be spot-on with their assessment. Let's not forget however, as I indicated above, that our normality is subject to change and develop as we learn more about ourselves and our world, and absorb those changes.

Let's just approach this concern from another angle for a moment. Let's say you live by what most of us would describe as a normal existence. You are educated, have a demanding job and are married with children. You have a sound and healthy interest in your career, in your family and everyday matters that grab your attention. For all intents and purposes other people consider you a regular and reliable person. You negotiate your world with sobriety, you look after your interests, and you are no one's fool.

One day you happen to be looking out of an upstairs window, at the front of your home, and you get a glimpse of someone passing by who looks very much like an old friend, that you still keep in touch with, if infrequently these days. Now by itself you consider this event odd and unlikely for, if it was your friend, they are a long way from home – normally some fifty miles or so away from you. Being inquisitive to establish it can't be them, you come downstairs and dash out the front door to check. At this point though whoever it was has now moved on. You wait on the pavement for a short while, in case they were looking for you and have called at the wrong house. There is still no sign and so you return indoors. This brief event however has left you strangely uneasy. This is partly because you had only been thinking of this person earlier in the morning, and ever since you have had an odd feeling. You can't really describe what this feeling is, a little tightness in the stomach perhaps, but somehow you just know something is not quite right and somehow it seems to link to your friend. A while later in the day however and the feeling goes. You reason the episode is just the surprise of seeing someone reminding you of your friend. And, as likely, the tightness in your stomach may have been totally unrelated – probably linked to the burnt toast you had for breakfast.

But this little episode has in any case left you curious to catch up with your friend and know they are okay. You decide to leave the matter for now. The next day, curiosity gets the better of you, and you take the trouble to call this person, just to say hello. It's been a while so you have good reason to call and catch-up. You ring and the phone is answered, not by your friend but by what turns out to be a family member. They sound distraught, and not up for much conversation. You then learn the dreadful news that your friend suffered a road accident on the motorway and actually died in the crash – and shockingly this happened yesterday. Now this news has thrown you, and obviously for more reasons than just the event and the loss itself...

Let me say, as an aside, such an experience – of sensing something has happened to someone you know, or is close to you – might seem very odd but it is not entirely uncommon, nor for it to happen in conjunction with seeing the person, or someone who reminds you of them, as you were thinking of them. In happier circumstances the other person may also have been thinking of you and may suddenly decide to get in touch – seemingly out of the blue.

Back with our scenario, and the question arises as to how you deal with this. This news is tragic; you haven't just lost a friend but have lost them within, what could be described as, bizarre circumstances – certainly from your viewpoint. If you are like the majority of us, who depend upon the safe and regular world around us, then in all probability you will find some simple way to explain what has happened and maybe put it all down to coincidence. The experience might have generated a little crack in your beliefs however, a little doubt in your mind that what you think you know about the world is not quite the full picture. One thing is for certain, it will need to be dealt with, to get it into context. It's not so much the oddness of the event but the loss of a friend that will keep it in the frame, and not allow you to so easily drop it or forget about it.

> There are no mistakes, no coincidences. All events are blessings given to us to learn from.
> Elizabeth Kubler-Ross, psychiatrist, pioneer near-death studies[9]

For the time being it would probably be best not to talk too much about what has happened, or alternatively to be very selective with regard to whom you do speak to. This is obviously because it's a sensitive matter and you'll need time to process and work through it. There is a chance that you are going to be judged, as not yet dealing with things clearly, if you attempt to make something of an issue of it. This may be a fair judgement in context with the setback you have now suffered. Let's say you decide to confide in a colleague at work about your experience. Unless this person has an open mind to such matters then in all likelihood you will be told that the events, what you saw and felt before learning about the accident, were the result of simple coincidence, and just because your friend did actually die doesn't make it any less of a coincidence.

And so wanting to get back to that sense of security and normality, you eventually get over the loss of your friend and pass off the whole caboodle as a bit strange but no more than an oddity, without needing anything *meaningful* being written into it. The notion that you may have had a little spiritual nudge or that you have latent psychic abilities, attempting to break out, didn't really get entertained this time, and so gets shelved. The thought that you may have been tapping into something that you've been taught is impossible was all too scary to face and deal with differently. The implications from that one experience can therefore be big.

Ghosts and Poltergeists

> There is no mystery greater than that posed by the poltergeist. The noisy ghosts of folklore and legend represent some of the most complex phenomena known to science.
>
> D. Scott Rogo, writer, journalist, parapsychologist[10]

Probably we all show some interest in ghost, poltergeist and other *bump in the night* stories by their very other-worldly and scary nature. I'm sure that quite a lot of us enjoy movies on such topics and, for some, the more horrific and scary they are the better. It can actually help endorse our sense of normality and make our lives a little more interesting, even nourished, to be reading about such things on the *morning-break* page of a magazine, or newspaper, while at the same time knowing we are safe. Bottom line though we mostly doubt there is really any truth in them. Don't they belong in the realms of vivid imagination and Harry Potter...? Besides these reported events are happening *over there*, in that house or to that person, to that family. They are experiencing the *para-normality* not us.

> I think everything I do is normal, not paranormal but normal. It's using the power of the mind to achieve whatever we can endure.
>
> David Blaine, magician, illusionist[11]

We may say to ourselves that it hasn't happened to us in all the years we've been kicking around. Okay, so we've seen some disturbing movies. *The Exorcist* for example was particularly shocking and real, but that was before we became more familiar with special effects and how it was being done to look real. We can leave aside the blurb, that the film was actually based upon a true story, as just hype at the time to get us to watch it. We've seen illusionists and we know it's all tricks, smoke and mirrors stuff. As Richard Wilson would say (from the UK, *One Foot in the Grave* comedy programme), "I don't believe it." But then on that note, can we really explain away someone like David Blaine as just another illusionist? Maybe we can, but isn't he (and others like him, such as Steven Frayne), in the way he uses his mind, stretching the boundaries of illusion a bit more than he should? Maybe not; no doubt we'll find mirrors up his sleeves. But what someone like Blaine does might make us think on the matter, and we may, for example, be next giving in to pressure from friends to going on a paranormal adventure, a ghost hunt, just for the adventure and fun of it. If we do go we know we'll experience nothing really paranormal – we're not fools – but, at the same time, we hope that something might just give us a bit of a jolt. It's all a shame really as we would like to be living in a more magical world of greater possibilities. Well perhaps we are, more so than we yet realise...

The word *poltergeist* comes from the German word *poltern* and literally means *noisy ghost*. Right now I'm thinking of two well-known cases of poltergeist activity that took place in the UK – one to my knowledge is still ongoing. Admittedly I haven't experienced either at first hand. I have read about them from different sources and viewpoints. I accept the accounts as given, by people who have witnessed the events. Let's say I'm embracing wider boundaries to my level of normality. These are the *Enfield Poltergeist* and the *Mackenzie Poltergeist*. You may well be familiar with both cases but bear with me and let's take a look at them…

The Enfield Poltergeist

This episode took place in 1977 – better to say things *began* to happen back then – in a North London council house (in Green Street, Enfield). In the semi-detached house lived Peggy Hodgson and her four children – Margaret (twelve), Janet (eleven), Johnny (ten), and Billy (seven), so we're considering a young family here. Peggy was a single parent (after being divorced), which couldn't have been easy for her. Her situation most probably didn't help redress the needed energy balance that two parents can bring, to provide boundaries and security for four children. Leaving aside any paranormal activity, I imagine there was quite an amount of angst, fear and vulnerability in the situation.

What they witnessed and went through was by all accounts horrendous. Active phenomena included furniture moving by itself, knockings from inside the walls and ceilings, spontaneous fires, pools of water appearing on the floor, cold breezes, physical assaults, the appearance of graffiti, equipment malfunction and failure, and various items, toys, plates, cutlery, books and pictures being thrown around the house, and/or circling around rooms.

The case is well documented (visit Wikipedia for example to find out more)[12] and certain events were witnessed by up to thirty people. This included a neighbour, Vic Nottingham. He is described as a "burly builder" who, so the account goes, went in to help on one occasion but couldn't make out where the noises were coming from. He experienced knockings, got scared off, and got out of the house as quick as he could – and who could blame him. There was a policewoman, WPC Carolyn Heaps, who saw a chair move across a room by itself. Heaps bravely checked out the floor, the cushions for wires, and all possible physical explanations, for what had happened but said she couldn't find any explanation for what she saw.

The Society for Psychical Research got involved with an investigation led by Maurice Grosse and Guy Lyon Playfair. They spent a total of fourteen months on the case and catalogued a number of inexplicable occurrences – boxes that flew across rooms, ornaments that floated in mid-air, books that mysteriously appeared and disappeared, strange knocking sounds.

One morning when Playfair was at the house there was a "sudden violent shaking sound, and it was immediately followed by total panic." He barged into the girls' bedroom where the noise was coming from, and there he found quite a commotion and disturbing scene. What met him was the "entire iron frame of the gas fire had been wrenched out of the wall, and was standing at an angle on the floor, still attached to the half-inch diameter brass pipe that connected it to the mains … This was a major demolition job, for the thing was cemented into the brickwork…" He added that when it was finally dismantled it was a job to move it and, "must have weighed at least fifty pounds."[13] A point being made here, by the way, is that a number of people suspected the children were causing all this mayhem through playing pranks on people. Janet Hodgson, and her sister, did indeed admit to playing tricks on one or two people sent to investigate. From what was said, it appears their antics were due to being fed up with being tested so often. However this only added fuel to the argument that the whole thing was a hoax.

But too much was happening for the children to be the cause of it all – they certainly couldn't consciously make things levitate, and move them around rooms, as things did. The main focal point for the activity, however, was Janet. Janet is quoted as saying more recently that, "It lived off me, off my energy."[14] On more than one occasion she was dragged from her bed by an unseen force. She was seen being levitated in her bedroom. She was also hauled down the stairs on one occasion – witnessed by Grosse.

Most bizarre was the disembodied gruff male voice that began speaking through Janet. It is believed to have been the voice of *Bill Wilkins*, a sad and foul-mouthed grumpy man, who died alone in the house some years previously. His son later confirmed, from the details the Bill entity gave, that it was indeed his father. He had died from a brain haemorrhage while at home and seated in a particular armchair. Grosse said that one hundred and eighty hours of tapes were made of the voice. Wilkins apparently knew he was dead – although it is hard to believe he fully understood what that meant. He knew he was indeed invisible to people, that he was a "ghost," and appeared to be the cause of the problems in the house. Even so he existed in fear. He told Grosse, at one point, that he was scared he could be "killed off," and when Grosse asked how he could be killed, when he was already dead, he said, "by praying to God." Being earthbound, stuck and ignorant of his true spiritual nature, afraid to go towards the light as he was, this latter comment makes sense, and possible grounds for his frightening actions – essentially to scare people, and keep himself alive, in his warped understanding. What remained of his identity, as he perceived it, was with the house and if forced out of the house he could reason he would disappear. Whether he caused all the mayhem, or was a part of it, he certainly helped to create a terrifying atmosphere.

After Peggy Hodgson died, the Hodgeon's left the house. It was then occupied by another family: a Mrs Bennett and her four sons moved into it. She reported feeling uncomfortable in the house from the get-go. She sensed there was some kind of presence. Her sons would wake in the night, hearing people talking downstairs. One of her sons, fifteen at the time, told her how he awoke and saw a man come into the room. Mrs Bennett then found out about the house's history. They moved out. This was only two months after moving there. At the time of writing I understand the house is occupied by another family, who wish to remain anonymous.

The Mackenzie Poltergeist

Another well-known and miserable phenomenon is what is called The Mackenzie Poltergeist – linked with Sir George Mackenzie. It happened, and is believed to still happen, in Greyfriars Kirkyard, a graveyard surrounding Greyfriars Kirk in Edinburgh.

There are differing versions regarding how it all began. One story has it that events were sparked off in 1999, after a homeless man tried to stay the night in the mausoleum belonging to Mackenzie. I'll come onto other versions of how it began shortly, but let's just pause for a moment to put some flesh on the story. This site has been considered haunted throughout recent history and most probably ever since the atrocities that were carried out there back in the 17th-century.

Mackenzie, who died in 1691, was a judge with a nasty history and reputation behind him. He was known during his lifetime for being a hanging judge – and had the nickname of "Bluidy Mackenzie." He is particularly remembered for his persecution of the Covenanters. Keeping this brief, the Covenanters[15] were a powerful Scottish Presbyterian movement who were opposed to Charles I rule of Scotland, as head of the Church. They signed a national covenant proclaiming loyalty to God, as opposed to the King. As an army, of some thousands, they stood their ground against Charles I. Much later though they were defeated by his son, Charles II, with many of them, it is claimed twelve hundred, being taken prisoner, with possibly a third of these imprisoned in the Covenanters Prison. Called a prison but this was an adjoining secure field to Greyfriars Kirkyard. With no shelter, and little food, many of them perished either through the harsh winter, or the horrors of public execution. Others were sentenced to transportation and died on the journey. It is believed that up to eighteen thousand Covenanters, all told, may have died, and mostly at the hand of Mackenzie. Some of those souls, and Mackenzie, are buried in Greyfriars Kirkyard. So you get the picture; what a recipe for gloom, injustice, sadness, hatred, dark rage, a seeking of revenge, unfinished business and tortured souls.

Coming forward to 1999, the homeless man possibly decided to stay the night in Mackenzie's mausoleum, to get out of the weather. It is claimed he either desecrated or caused some damage to Mackenzie's coffin, even disturbing a hidden chamber, below the tomb, that contained further unidentified coffins. So the story goes, he was subsequently witnessed running and screaming in terror from the site – to be found later in a state of delirium by police.

Whether this is an accurate description of what happened or not is unclear. It is certainly believed to be accurate. Another account indicates it was a schoolboy who hid in the vault to escape a beating from a master at the George Heriot's School close by, and effectively went mad after seeing the ghost of Mackenzie. This story however may be a retelling of a story that Robert Louis Stevenson wrote of in his book, *Edinburgh Picturesque Notes* (published in 1897).[16] Of Mackenzie's mausoleum he wrote:

> Here, in the last century, an old Heriot's Hospital boy once harboured from the pursuit of the police. The Hospital is next door to Greyfriars ... the fugitive had managed to conceal himself in the tomb ... and there he lay in safety till a ship was found to smuggle him abroad. But his must have been indeed a heart of brass, to lie all day and night alone with the dead persecutor...

Elsewhere Stevenson recounts how, "foolhardy urchins [considered it] a high piece of prowess to knock at the Lord Advocate's mausoleum and challenge him to appear [with the words] 'Bluidy Mackingie, come oot if ye dar'.'"

Leaving aside the vagaries of how the poltergeist phase began; since the disturbance took place, in 1999, weird phenomena have been experienced in the Kirkyard and the surrounding area. There are accounts of neighbouring houses being plagued by objects flying around the rooms and crockery being smashed. It is reported that there have been more than 450 attacks on visitors to the site. People have experienced feelings of extreme heat or cold, suffered cuts, bites and bruises, had their throats squeezed, coats tugged violently, and were, on occasion, even knocked unconscious by an invisible force.

According to commentaries, there have been two exorcisms carried out to bring a closure to the phenomena but both have failed to halt things.

Not missing a trick, there are regular ghost tours to this Edinburgh site. People do love to be scared and there is money to be made in such events. The tours began in June 1999 – the same year as the "homeless man" was supposed to have started all this mayhem. Visitors (not all) to the site have continued reporting odd things happening to them – notably bruising, people passing out, having one's hand held, one's hair pulled. The person who set up the *City of the Dead Tours*, Jan-Andrew Henderson[17], wrote in 2005 that:

> The period between the first recorded sightings in 1999 and the present, have seen over 450 documented 'attacks' in the Black Mausoleum and Covenanters Prison. Of these attacks, an astonishing 140 have caused the witness to collapse.[18]

On his website (in 2012), he had added that, "I now have 75 pages of eyewitness accounts, and there are probably many more people who encountered the poltergeist but didn't write to me with their stories."

Admittedly the tour also includes what's affectionately called, a *jumper-outer*, the person who has to make sure people get their money's worth by being dressed in costume and who jumps out to scare people – people who are already in a heightened emotional state. Even so it is clear that, if these reports are to be believed, things

---

are happening at times to make the jumper-outer as good as redundant.

We're still in Fortean Times

Just to be clear from my perspective; both the accounts of paranormal activity described above may carry some embellishment – I believe a lot less so in the Enfield story. But whereas I may quibble the detail I have no problem accepting there is more than *something* in both. This is because firstly I can accept that such events happen, and don't necessarily happen in complete isolation. Do a search on the Web and you will find there are parallel reports from elsewhere in the world. With regard to a parallel to the Enfield poltergeist, for example, we could stay in the UK and call around 30 East Drive in Pontefract, Yorkshire, where poltergeist (or poltergeists) activity, malevolent in nature, is reputed to have been taking place since the 1960s. Secondly, similar has been happening over centuries...

Anyone who has read Charles Fort, *The Book of the Damned* (first published in 1919 and which later became the springboard for the *Fortean Times* magazine)[19] will know odd things have been happening for a long time. Fort, back then, drew attention to the ongoing denial by experts and scientists of there being anything in stories of odd things happening. Of course that denial was the driver for his writing the book – the clue is, as they say, in the title.

Fort drew on anecdotal eye witness accounts of all kinds of odd occurrences, particularly aerial phenomena, such as odd rains that dumped small animals and inanimate objects, like blocks of ice, pebbles, even what looked like axe-heads, onto the land. He listed reports of phenomena being seen, sounding very much like what we would now describe as UFOs. These were being reported during the 19th-century and earlier, in such as *Notes & Queries* publications and in newspapers at the time.

One major drawback of *The Book of the Damned*[20] is that it isn't organised into proper chapters – so it has no table of contents or an index at the back. One is therefore obliged to trawl through it to find the nuggets of information one is looking for. On the poltergeist front, I found two reports in the book that fit the bill – there may be others. These were both from the London Times. The first dated September 16th 1841, wherein,

> In the home of Mrs Charton, at Sutton Courthouse, Sutton Lane, Chiswick, windows had been broken 'by some unseen agent' and every attempt to detect the perpetrator failed. The mansion was detached and surrounded by high walls. No other building was near it. The police were called. Two constables, assisted by members of the household, guarded the house, but the windows continued to be broken both in front and behind the house.[21]

The second dated April 27th, 1872:

> From 4 o'clock, Thursday afternoon until half-past eleven, Thursday night, the houses, 56 and 58 Reverdy Road, Bermondsey, were assailed with stones and other missiles coming from an unseen quarter. Two children were injured, every window was broken, and several articles of furniture were destroyed. Although there was a strong body of policemen scattered in the neighbourhood, they could not trace the direction whence the stones were thrown.[22]

Do the above reports sound like poltergeist activity? They do to me.

Ghost and poltergeist stories not new

Note we are going back to 1841 with these records from Fort; not particularly early in history you might say. It does however underline that such events are not a modern attention seeking scam, nor a Hollywood invention. There is an earlier record, called the *Drummer of Tedworth*, as relayed by Joseph Glanvill in 1668, in his, *A Blow at Modern Sadducism*. The story goes that a local landowner, John Mompesson, owner of a house in the town of Tedworth (now Tidworth, Wiltshire), had brought a lawsuit against a local drummer, William Drury, whom he accused of extorting money by false pretences. He won the judgment against the drummer and became the owner of his drum. And this is where his trouble began. Historical researcher, Michael Hunter, who reviewed this case, in 2005, writes of Mompesson's experience:

Thereafter, he and his family were assaulted by thumpings, tattoos of the drum and other noises. There were also scratchings, panting like a dog, sulphurous and other smells, and strange lights; in addition, objects were thrown around the room, beds elevated, horses lamed and the like. These disturbances continued over several months into 1663, despite the fact that for part of this time Drury was incarcerated at Gloucester on a charge of theft. Meanwhile, the case became well-known, and many people visited Mompesson's house to witness the strange occurrences for themselves.[23]

The story is considered to be an early, well-documented, account of the activity of a poltergeist. There is evidence, such as family letters, that Hunter draws upon in support of it being genuine. However, even if the story was a complete 17th-century fabrication, the overlap with modern poltergeist description and experience gives evidence for such paranormal experience being known about four centuries ago. And even earlier, a quick trawl on the Web and you will find that from way back, to the first-century, there are claims of ghosts and poltergeists:

The great Roman author and statesman Pliny the Younger recorded one of the first notable ghost stories in his letters, which became famous for their vivid account of life during the heyday of the Roman Empire. Pliny reported that the spectre of an old man with a long beard, rattling chains, was haunting his house in Athens.[24]

This item goes on to say the Greek writer Lucian and Pliny's fellow Roman, Plautus, also wrote memorable ghost stories. Moving on a few centuries, to 856 AD, what is believed to be the first poltergeist experience ever recorded happened in a farmhouse in Germany. The poltergeist "tormented the family living there by throwing stones and starting fires, among other things."[25] Sound a bit familiar? It does to me.

My people too were scared with eerie sounds,
A footstep, a low throbbing in the walls.

A noise of falling weights that never fell,
Weird whispers, bells that rang without a hand,
Door-handles turn'd when none was at the door,
And bolted doors that open'd of themselves;
And one betwixt the dark and light had seen
Her, bending by the cradle of her babe.

Extract from The Ring, Alfred, Lord Tennyson, Poet Laureate[26]

My own ghost and paranormal stories

Staying with ghost and paranormal stories for the present; a reason I have taken some interest in such stories, as relayed above, is because I have also been witness to one or two things myself – and also know people who have experienced similar. In a personal way, these have gone into the mixing pot to aid and abet my giving more serious consideration to the overall matter in hand – than I might have done had I not experienced them. I have a couple of experiences that come to mind, and also odd events on the enchanting RMS *Queen Mary*, to share with you. Although, let me add, these are not as disturbing, or potentially as sinister, as some of the experiences listed above.

Nevertheless… back in 1973 I was living in a large three story Edwardian doctor's town house on Thorpe Road in Peterborough. I was there because of my work in archaeology. This hitherto vacant house had been taken over by the NVRC[27] for use as a *dig house* – a place where archaeologists could stay for the duration of excavations in and around Peterborough. At times there were up to sixteen people living in the house and taking up every available space – including, as I well recall, one person choosing to sleep in the cupboard under the stairs and yet another living in the cellar. It was a right odd mix that included diggers from around the UK and from the USA and Canada.

My bedroom was on the first floor at the back of the house. It was next door but one to the bathroom and separate loo. One night, around 3am, I came out of my bedroom to use the loo. All lights were off and it was dark in the corridor. As I came out of the room I clearly heard footsteps coming along the landing, around the corner from me, and heading in my direction. Thinking this was one of the guys from the front of the house, with the same needs as myself, I thought I'd pull a fast one and waited in my doorway to say, "After you." as they walked by – yes I know, infantile. The footsteps stopped however just short of turning down my bit of the corridor. I continued to wait expectantly. Next I saw what I can only describe as a luminous cloudy ghostly image floating in my direction – no footsteps now. I could also only see the top half of a figure of a very stern worried looking man, with a beard. He would have been around six feet tall. Keeping up a brave front, I did quietly try my, "After you" suggestion as this cloud passed me. There was no acknowledgement and as he went towards the loo door he, or the cloud, disappeared. I thought about it and then decided, *what the heck*, nature calls, I couldn't wait any longer – I used the loo and went back to bed.

Had it all ended there, I would at the time have passed it off as my being half-asleep and hallucinating. However when, next day, I happened to mention this event to some of the inmates, it transpired that one of the women said she felt there was an odd presence in the house. She had noticed it outside of the bathroom on the second (top) floor, and had thought best not to say anything. It also transpired that a number of people felt that whenever they were alone in the house they were being watched – I admit I also had felt this.

To add to this little mystery, I and the rest of the team eventually left the house, and it became empty again for a time. Then one summer, a couple of years later, the house was once again used to accommodate diggers. This time it was used for a team down from Manchester University. Sometime after they had left I learnt, from their co-ordinator, that one of the group claimed he had seen a ghost in the house, and had wondered if any of us had experienced similar while living there. Although I tried, I never caught up with this witness to exchange notes. I would have liked to have known if he and I saw anything like the same figure.

And another odd event...

This happened on a trip that a friend and I made over to Grantham in Lincolnshire. I was driving into Grantham, on the outskirts, on the A607. It was getting twilight time and raining. Up ahead I spotted two cyclists riding two abreast with no lights on their bikes. I remember thinking how stupid, two abreast and no lights in this weather. As I drove towards them I was forced to move out towards the middle of the road to avoid them. At that point my passenger got concerned and asked what I was doing, and I replied that I was just avoiding the cyclists. Puzzled, he asked, "What cyclists?" He hadn't seen any cyclists. Sure enough, as I checked back in my rear-view mirror, there was no sign of any cyclists.

This was back in 1968/69 time. I'm guessing, but it wouldn't surprise me to learn that a couple of cyclists had been killed at that spot. Interesting though that he didn't see the cyclists when I clearly saw them, even if in the twilight.

And here's one that happened to a contact of mine

Tim, who I have to say has his feet firmly on the ground and not a little sceptical regarding such matters, was in The Stag Hotel at Redhill in Warwickshire (a lovely hotel by the way, on the A46 just outside Stratford upon Avon), having a meal one evening back in 2011. He told me of this sudden commotion amongst a group of people across on another table. They were up from their table taking photos of a spot near one of the walls. He decided to go and find out what was happening.

The group claimed they had just seen the apparition of a young boy (probably around ten years old) walk through one wall, across the room and then through the wall on the other side. They all saw it. And now they were busy taking photos of what the apparition had left behind. Tim had to see this for himself. He went over to find there were three clear footprints on the floor, near the ghost's exit wall. He described them as looking like chalky footprint marks of child-sized feet.

The Stag, it turns out, has a colourful history. It was once Stratford upon Avon's courtroom and jail, so certainly the place for extremes of experience and emotion. Maybe some joy but one would suspect a whole lot of misery, which has no doubt left its mark on the place. It is a given that the walls the apparition walked through would not have been there in the time that the boy lived – or else there may, of course, have been entrances in the walls at those points. The footprints might also suggest that, at the time of this memory imprint, the boy was walking on a dusty floor in bare feet. Who knows what his fate was back then. You'll find ghosts not only walking through walls but also on floor levels no longer extant. Anyhow an interesting and atmospheric story – and certainly it had left Tim disturbed enough to want to share it with me – and wonder what it was all about.

The RMS Queen Mary – a very spooky ship

Partly out of memory of my father – who worked on the *Queen Mary* – when my partner Annie and I did a tour around California some years back (in 2000) we planned in a visit to Long Beach to stay on the ship for a night. You probably know it is a hotel, and staying there was too much of an opportunity to miss out on in our itinerary. It certainly was a moving sight to see that huge ship come into view as we drove into the car park next to it. On-board it soon lived up to my expectations of getting a sense of the old ship in past times – particularly as we walked down the long low-lit B Deck corridor to find our cabin (B456, as I noted in my diary), one was easily transported back to much earlier times, when it began life – back in 1936.

But oh what a spooky place it is too. On arrival we had no idea that the ship was well-known for its paranormal activity. We only discovered later, during the evening, that a ghost walk was on the list of events for the next day, and also a regular occurrence.

I didn't need to know that however to convince me that things were happening that didn't quite add up. I was to discover that pretty soon after our arrival. Once we had settled into our cabin, I was really interested to take a stroll and explore the ship by myself – to get a feel of this old liner and importantly link with what was my father's old workplace. Annie was quite happy for me to do that. She needed to rest after the drive, and to get a shower. It was going to be a somewhat emotional and contemplative walk around for me – at least that is how I viewed it. It was clear that part of the ship had been updated to hotel status while other parts, presumably, had either been purposely left as they were, to retain the period charm and atmosphere, or were due to undergo updating. Instead of walking towards the main hotel foyer, as most people would for access to other parts of the ship, I decided to go in the opposite direction further down the B Deck corridor into what looked like the less used part of the ship – the lighting got less bright too, or seemed so. It could have been any time from the *Thirties* and very atmospheric.

A bit further towards the aft of the ship I happened on an old lift, very probably as old as the ship, that I thought must be for staff usage. I reckon it would have only carried about three to four adults at a squeeze. My plan was to get to the top of the ship so this was just fine. I got inside, checked the options and selected the top floor. The old lift creaked as it got underway. It then unexpectedly stopped two floors up. The doors opened. There was no one waiting. I thought well they must have taken the stairs instead. The doors closed and next, surprise to me, the lift went down a floor and stopped again, but this time without the doors opening. Pressing the buttons made no difference. The lift sat there for probably a minute – but seemed much longer. I tried to manually open the doors and they wouldn't budge. I could almost hear Corporal Jones (from the UK TV comedy, *Dad's Army*), saying in my ear, "Don't panic. Don't panic."

I pressed the up button again and instead we went down then stopped – probably a floor below where I had started from. Again the doors didn't open while we sat there. Next we were moving on our way up again. This time the lift stopped possibly three floors above where I started from – I was losing track. By this point I was needing to just get off and make other arrangements – like finding the stairs.

The doors opened, I went to get off but immediately outside the lift I met a roped area and two or three workmen working in pitch black with spotlights, and busy on something, using welding equipment. They looked at me askance – like, "Are you really thinking of getting off here?" I reluctantly withdrew back into the lift. The doors closed and this time the lift started going up before I had time to select a button. We went up another floor – or was it two, I was definitely losing track as to where I was. The doors opened and I found myself at the top of the ship, coming out by one of the funnels – "Oh joy, oh for fresh air, oh to be out of there."

I can tell you I felt a great sense of relief to get out of that lift – talk about mind of its own. For all the movement up and down I was the only (let's say physical) passenger on-board for the duration. I certainly felt like I had moved into the twilight zone for a while – but then there was an excitement about it too, and I'd come to no harm. It was a beautiful evening and great being up there on top. Eventually – using the stairs this time – I worked my way back to our cabin. Another bizarre little episode unfolded at this point as the card key to open the cabin door – which had worked fine when we arrived – now refused to work. My partner was inside, but she was in the shower room and didn't hear my knocks. After several attempts with the card, and it continuing not to work, I decided, and also voiced the matter, as no one else was within earshot, that I'd give it one more go before fetching someone to sort the door for me. On this attempt it worked, the lock opened no problem.

The two events together were odd. I was left feeling like my patience had been tested. It was like someone was trying to wind me up – and I admit I was biting a bit, but hey I do have an Irish temperament. With regard to the cabin door, for the rest of our short stay, neither Annie or I had a problem with it. Regarding the lift, I must tell you that I discovered someone else who'd had a similar experience on the ship – on what could actually have been the same lift. I found this on the, *Your Ghost Stories* website. This person regularly visited the ship and obviously liked to go on the lift he describes. For him the lift always took him down to the "Engine

Room" regardless of what he requested. On an occasion, some years after he first discovered it, he even demonstrated the phenomenon to his wife. He took her on the lift and it happened again. When he raised the matter with hotel staff, he was told that the lift going to the engine room, "was not possible because that elevator does not go to the engine room unless you have a key."[28]

I did go on the ghost walk the next day. It was interesting and it took the group into some spooky areas of the old ship. I discovered after our trip that the ghostly phenomena of the ship is well known and has been well documented. The following was taken from Wikipedia (from 2010):[29]

> Ghosts were reported on-board only after being permanently docked in California. Many areas are rumored to be haunted. Reports of hearing little children crying in the nursery room, actually used as the third-class playroom, and a mysterious splash noise in the drained first-class swimming pool are cited. In 1966, 18-year-old engineer John Pedder was crushed by a watertight door in the engine room during a fire drill, and his ghost is said to haunt the ship. There is also said to be the spirit of a young girl named Jackie Korin who drowned in the second class pool and continues to haunt the first class pool room onboard the ship.
>
> A young woman by the name of 'Sarah' was said to have been murdered in the first class women's changing rooms by an unknown man and she also haunts the first class pool with Jackie.
>
> Some visitors say they have seen women wearing early 1930's bathing suits in the pool areas. It is also said that men can be heard screaming and the sound of metal crushing against metal can be heard below decks at the extreme front end of the bow. Those who have heard this believe it to be the screams of the sailors aboard the HMS Curacoa at the moment the destroyer was split in half by the liner.

The latter comment refers to October 2nd 1942, during the last war, when the *Queen Mary* sliced through her escort ship, the light cruiser, HMS *Curacoa*, off the Irish coast, while following its designated zigzag path to avoid German U-boats. The liner was on its way up to

Greenock, in Scotland, from Liverpool. At the time she was known as the *Grey Ghost* (due to being painted grey) and commissioned as a troop carrier – carrying up to eighteen thousand troops in one sail. She was not allowed to stop for anyone. Over three hundred lives were lost in that tragic accident. I know my father was on-board 'the Mary' at the time.

I was interested to learn later that RMS *Queen Mary* is considered being amongst the top ten of the world's most haunted places by the *Times Magazine* (in 2008).[30] Also that the most haunted room on the ship is B340, where, it is believed, the murder of a child took place. This room, by the way, is down the same corridor from where we stayed – and probably close to the lift I used – spooky.

Possible explanations for ghostly paranormal events

Ghost and poltergeist stories, like the ones I've listed, abound I suspect in every quarter of the earth. They come and go – and have been doing so throughout recorded history. Indeed I could easily have filled this chapter with stories from the UK alone, and, in an earlier draft, I had included the Borley Rectory poltergeist (Borley, Essex, reputed by psychic investigatory, Harry Price, to be the most haunted house in England); the Pitmilly House poltergeist (reputed to be Scotland's most haunted house, that was subject to a huge fire in the Forties, and which was legally treated as being caused by a poltergeist); the weirdness of goings on at The (Ancient) Ram Inn (Gloucestershire), and the malevolent activity of the poltergeist at 30 East Drive, Pontefract, West Yorkshire.

> 📖 **BONUS ONLINE CONTENT**: Get the ghost and poltergeist stories left out of the book – and mentioned above. Download the *UK Ghost and Poltergeist Stories* article. Visit the **Free Article Resource** on book's website, **LifeandDeaththeBook.com**

Leaving aside the knee-jerk explanations – such as vivid imagination, embellishment and fanciful story telling – as the cause or causes behind all such phenomena, they represent grounds for reviewing our understanding of life and the world we inhabit. We could consider that some of these events are the result of residual energy, a *playback* of something that has been recorded – usually the outcome of an event emotionally highly charged or tragic – that has seeped into the very fabric and atmosphere of a given location. The playback is then triggered when conditions are right or possibly on a particular time or date. Resulting apparitions, like the one I saw in the house in Peterborough, are as video playbacks and cannot be interacted with. Some ghostly sightings, on the other hand, can be intelligent and interacted with. They could be actual visitations of the departed – back to somewhere they are fond of – or worse they could be actually grounded in a situation they have never really left. My view is that, on the other side of death, we are likely to be no different in our habits and behaviours as we were in physical life – at least not in the immediate aftermath. We most probably attempt to hold to what was familiar – still needing what physical life brought to us. Some of us may refuse to acknowledge (or we simply don't know) we are in a different state, that we have died and passed over, and by that we may not easily accept, or trust, any help offered to us to move on. And some of us, who have led a manipulative, shady, selfish or unloving life, might well find it difficult dealing with what could come next – I'll talk more about these matters in *The Other Side* chapter.

I might just mention an attendant phenomenon here that links with the above and challenges our understanding of life. This is where psychics and paranormal investigators talk of observing *vortices* – or vortexes. These are generally invisible to the naked eye but arguably are picked up on camera. They look like other kinds of vortices, such as caused by wind (dust devils, whirlwinds, tornados) on a comparatively small scale (although some would argue the well-known Sedona vortices are huge). But, if real, these are whirling fields of energy, some call it *spirit energy*, that may suddenly show up and disappear just as quickly – usually in places known for paranormal activity, so can be observed in buildings, in natural structures and landscape. You will find lots of examples of this phenomenon in pictures on the Web. Like so much of paranormal phenomena, they are controversial as no one seems entirely sure what they are. They could be whirling energy, many balls of spirit orbs moving quickly, or an issue with the camera itself. One theory that ghost hunters, mediums and psychics – such as British medium Derek Acorah – subscribe to, is that these vortices are a kind of portal allowing souls to enter and exit the atmosphere of a given location. If this is the case they could be both a concern – as they may allow all kinds of traffic, wholesome and unwholesome, to come and go – and an area for increasing our understanding of energy, spiritual movement, and of the possibility of inter-dimensional movement such as considered as an explanation for some UFO and alien sightings.

With regard to poltergeist activity: Theories abound to explain it from elemental spirits, or souls, coming from the lower regions, or psychokinesis (most often being linked to children, or one child in a family, and reaching puberty with their energies not yet orchestrated), to pheromones, static electricity, electromagnetic fields, ultrasound, infrasound, and a host of other explanations including, of course, fraud. It could be a combination of some of these and include, what I would describe as, a *call for action*. Offence being the best form of defence, it is like someone, or something, has decided to take up residence, and manipulate the physicality around it, in order to not just scare any human residents but to also live off the fear thus generated. Certainly one can say there is usually an associated negative charge or energy imbalance in the location, or in the ether, where it is manifesting – coupling with signs of immaturity, intelligence, cunning, trickery and rage, often triggered by human involvement. And maybe too, a dollop of ignorance and denial, that has helped to keep it running.

In a number of cases, poltergeist activity has been observed to last a few months before ending. A reason why the Enfield Poltergeist generated much interest was because of its long, fourteen months, timespan of observation. But even that is short when compared with the goings-on at 30 East Drive, or the Mackenzie story. Short of a tortured soul explanation, such as the Bill Wilkins personality, of the Enfield Poltergeist, I'm inclined towards the psychokinesis theory as being the explanation, or at least part of it – with energy being manipulated at a subconscious and/or possibly at a disturbed level by us humans. I'd also throw in stress, anxiety and body changes as a cause or contributory factor.

Effects resulting from psychokinesis can be very innocent and perhaps would explain an effect I've sometimes had when using the radio. At certain times I find I am either blocking or sometimes improving reception. When in this state I may walk towards the radio and the volume will increase with reception becoming crystal clear, or if I walk away, or at an angle, the quality may drop away becoming muddy and off-station. I've particularly noticed this effect at times when I'm under some kind of stress, angst or exhaustion – indeed it has occasionally served to notify me that I am under more stress than I'm otherwise aware of. Also the psychokinesis theory might help explain the sudden loud creaking noises I sometimes hear in the furniture around me when arousing from sleep. This may be one quite loud noise that puts me on alert, while at other times creaking sounds in quick succession. It can be quite disturbing. While it might be suggested that this could be the result of changes in room temperature, I believe it is mostly not so in this case, as it can happen regardless time of night or time of year. So far I've never found any damage to the furniture resulting from these noises.

But the psychiatrist Carl Jung did experience such a phenomenon where there were resultant breakages. He wrote in *Memories, Dreams, Reflections*,[31] how he heard a loud bang coming from the dining room at his home. He was in one room and his mother was in the dining room. He described the sound as "a report like a pistol shot." He rushed in and found his mother startled. The top of the round walnut table, next to her, had "split from the rim to beyond the centre, and not along any joint; the split ran right through solid wood." Drying wood couldn't account for it; the table was seventy-years-old and although it was summertime it was a relatively humid day. One might however argue a natural explanation for this event, had it not been for what followed next...

Two weeks later came a second incident. Returning home in the evening, Jung found an agitated household. An hour earlier there had been another "deafening report" – this time coming from a large sideboard. No one had so far discovered what had produced it. Jung inspected the sideboard and couldn't find any split in it. However he found the answer inside, where they kept the breadbasket, bread and bread knife. He found that the knife had shattered into four pieces, with a piece of the knife neatly placed at each corner of the basket. The knife had been used earlier for tea, and then put away, but no one had touched it, nor opened the cupboard since. When he took the knife to a cutler, he was told that there was no fault in the steel and that someone must have broken it on purpose. He kept the shattered knife for the rest of his life as a reminder of the existence of paranormal phenomena.

Concerning RMS *Queen Mary*, I have a theory, that you'll probably laugh at (and decide this is where this book and you go separate ways), as to why the paranormal phenomena appears to have started, in earnest, when she became permanently docked. Bear in mind this is a big regal and proud ship, built in Scotland for the high seas. In 1966 she was sold off to become the hotel she is today – rather than be scrapped, which was of course a good thing that she was saved. However in context with being permanently docked much was taken out of her: It, "required removal of all the boiler rooms, the forward engine room, both turbo generator rooms, the ship stabilisers and the water softening plant. The ship's now empty fuel tanks were then filled with local mud which would keep the ship's centre of gravity and draft at the correct levels, as these critical factors had been affected by the removal of the various components and structure. Only the aft engine room and 'shaft alley,' at the stern of the ship, would be spared."[32] If you think about it this is drastic. It was a decisive moment in her existence as an ocean going liner. She was reduced to this; for all the service she had given, particularly during the war years. There was no turning back to sea. Indeed, one could go further and say she could no longer get home, to where she was built, nay born, and she was now trapped. She had had her heart removed and could no longer carry out the job she was originally designed and built for.

To accept this, of course, you have to believe that machines we build are given some kind of life-force – the *ghost in the machine*. Maybe, I muse, machines are given life by their makers and this becomes more noticeable in big machines like steam engines, oilrigs, aeroplanes and ships – and likewise they become unhappy and morose when they can no longer do what they were originally designed for. Okay bonkers or what? Except, once one can accept that all matter is energy many things may be possible to envisage and be acceptable – possibly even true.

The elephant in the haunted room

In some context I want to add that while the information I am presenting to you here serves my purpose to indicate we don't yet fully comprehend the whole life and death picture – that there are forces at play that we need to get to grips with – I'm also aware that, although arguably not in every case, haunted places generally are the outcome of unhappiness, tragedy, sadness, abuse of power, abuse of people, fear, insecurity, unfinished business, unwholesome events, places of misery, indeed a wounding. There is usually a rift in the balance of energies, something dark and fear-ridden and in need of healing. If, for example, a person (or persons), carries out a vicious act against another person (or persons), it will not only leave a mark, a wounding, on the person but on that place, on the atmosphere. Like any wounding it needs attention, cleansing and healing, except that using our normal senses we don't see such a wounding. Time may heal but if left unhealed, left to fester, and if indeed further atrocities also occur in the same place, the atmosphere can eventually become rancid and turn into an opening allowing for all manner of traffic. It can become a real challenge to heal such a wound once it is established.

Sometimes too this imbalance may be the outcome of dark intention on a mass scale that fractures the atmosphere and can attract souls of a very dark or of lower negative vibration – lower even than the fictional Voldemort. Here I am thinking of places such as Auschwitz, which we all know of, or indeed the less well known island of Poveglia,[33] near Venice which, if stories are to be believed, is another one of the most haunted places on the planet. Such is the stuff that vortices can be made of. As such, although I'm aware there is commercial opportunity in such places, and that such commercial ventures can also help to raise public awareness of paranormal phenomena, I'm inclined to the view that locations as these, and locations discussed above, should never be used purely for entertainment purposes – which is only likely to perpetuate the discord. Rather I see them as places of learning and research towards a better understanding of what is going on – and eventually with the outcome of the place or land being made well again. This could possibly be achieved by, what I'd call, *psychic cleaners*; literally people who would clean up the atmosphere and help stuck souls move on – probably making full use of sound and music, in the cleansing process. This should especially be so where there is every intention to sell on (or rent out) such, otherwise, infected dwellings to unsuspecting buyers.

Of course the *elephant* in the haunted room creating all of this light or darkness is, bottom line, ourselves. How we live and how we die can leave a powerful emotional imprint on our world. If you think about it hauntings are mostly linked to the human condition. On the topic of elephants; spectres of animals are said to occur in hauntings but these are most often in association with people. If the death and suffering of animals were to be the criteria for hauntings then we would have animal ghosts in a huge number of locations, and especially places like abattoirs would be amongst the most haunted of places. Fortunately for us, regardless of our sometimes use and abuse of their lives, most animals, indeed most sentient beings, hold nothing against us – unlike the situation we human souls find ourselves in, within our waking state, where *forgiveness* is, by nature, a conscious decision.

Everything points to our needing to be more careful, aware and awake, in our *here and now*, of what we are putting onto the atmosphere around us, with our thoughts and actions – the situation being more dynamic than we might suppose. And this is why spreading love and happiness is so important too. On a positive note, from our Other Side existence we may, if we have learned how, still visit loved ones and return to places that we have loved or felt good in during our physical lives on the earth. It could possibly be helping to bring joy back to such situations and places – helping to retain goodness. We may truly be able to help make the world a better place than how we found it – from either side.

Near-Death Experience (NDE)

So what is death? Do we have to change our concepts about death, not only based on what has been thought and written about death in human history around the world in many cultures, in many religions and in all times, but also change our concepts about death based on insights from recent scientific research on NDE?

Pim Van Lommel, cardiologist, author, researcher into NDE[34]

Let's now move on to some really exciting evidence for the likelihood of survival beyond death. Back in the Seventies I got hold of a book that gave me a bit of an eye opener – you will no doubt have heard of it, and very possibly have read it. Here was a writer from a respected medical background who had written a radical book to help revolutionise our thinking about death. By this time I was opening up to spiritual perspectives, had attended workshops dealing with such matters and had read a number of books for, and against, our survival of death. One particular writer, Elisabeth Kubler-Ross, inspired me. Her name cropped up a lot in discussions and articles about death, dying and counselling the bereaved. Her books – for example, *Death: the Final Stage of Growth*[35] – have been a huge source of nourishment for me. It was partly the fact that she did the foreword for the book, that I'm about to mention, that encouraged me to go out and get it. This was *Life After Life* by Dr Raymond Moody JR[36]. The cover on this version of the book reads:

> The astounding bestseller that offers true experiences of those people declared clinically dead... descriptions so similar, so vivid, and so overwhelmingly positive that they may change mankind's view of life, death and spiritual survival forever.

In case you are not that familiar with near-death experience (NDE), this is when a person dies through cardiac arrest and is brought back to life some time later. Actually *near-death* is a misnomer as most people who experience this have actually died, however briefly. For obvious reasons NDEs will usually occur in hospitals, where there is every chance of resuscitation, and therefore for people to report what they experienced. In simple, matter of fact, terms a given person has a cardiac arrest, is pronounced clinically dead, and is then later resuscitated. It may be minutes (somewhere between five to twenty minutes is the general area) but it has been hours later, as in the case of Paul Eicke[37] who was clinically dead for over three hours – and whose story is relayed below.

Although reports of NDEs go back to the 19th-century, [38] possibly earlier,[39] public interest in this fascinating field of study really only began with the writings of Jess E Weiss' book, *The Vestibule*,[40] featuring Elisabeth Kübler-Ross and George Ritchie. Also George Ritchie & Elizabeth Sherrill's book, *Return from Tomorrow*,[41] and, of course, Moody's book.

It is fair to say that prior to Moody's work all previous evidence for survival of death had been anecdotal: individual stories, experiences, offering little by the way of searching for consistency or statistical evidence that researchers might get their teeth into. One could, of course, argue the cases that Moody listed were also anecdotal, except he discovered that a lot of people reported having similar kinds of experiences, and so common themes or stages began to emerge that could be identified, and even anticipated in the NDE.

In his book, Moody outlines ten possible stages in the near-death experience. These have since been researched, revisited and to some degree revised or added to – now up to sixteen pointers. Broadly these stages include:

The ill person *hearing they have died*. This is where some people describe overhearing themselves being pronounced dead by a doctor or surgeon. The person, once resuscitated, may accurately report back on conversations they heard, and/or observations they made while dead. The hearing stage can be accompanied by a sense of *well-being and painlessness*, or a sense of peace and removal from the world.

Another stage experienced may be, being pulled or drawn through some kind of dark space, or what Moody described as a *dark tunnel*, which is often concurrent with *noise* of some kind – these are not necessarily nice sounds. The tunnel has been variously identified as being like, but not limited to, a cave, a well, a funnel, a tunnel, a vacuum, a void, or a sewer.

A possible *out-of-body* stage can occur, where the person experiences being alongside their physical body, or where they may report being up at the ceiling looking down on surgeons working on their body.

Meeting others is another possible stage involving the person experiencing other beings in their vicinity. As discussed, in *The Other Side* chapter, these visitors can be unknown to the person, or can be loved ones, friends, family members who are deceased. They will turn up to help with the transition, or maybe their role will be to tell the person that their time to die has not yet come and that they must return to their physical body. Another person may alternatively meet loved ones at a later stage in the NDE process.

Another stage, in the experience, may be what is associated with a *being of light*. This is one of the most common stages that people report back on, and an experience that can have a truly profound effect on their lives. Moody comments that, for many, it doesn't, "hurt their eyes, or dazzle them, or keep them from seeing other things around them" – perhaps because at this point they don't have physical eyes to be dazzled. The latter ties in with reports that registered blind people can have the same experience. Also, according to Moody, "not one person has expressed any doubt whatsoever that it is a being, a being of light ... [having] a very definite personality," and further the, "love and warmth which emanate from this being to the dying person are utterly beyond words, and he [she] feels completely surrounded by it and taken up in it, completely at ease and accepted in the presence of this being."[42]

For some there may be a *life review* stage, or even being given knowledge of life and the universe. This stage, involving the dead person being shown a review of their life, and provoking reflection on one's life thus far, appears to be most often carried out by the being of light.

There is then a *border* or *limit* stage that is also a common experience. A number of people report, in their NDE, that they seemed to be approaching a border or limit of some kind. It could be a fence, a wall, a body of water, a grey mist, or a door. This is a ring-pass-not between going over – completely disconnecting from one's physical body – and returning back.

And then, it follows, there is also the *coming back into the body* stage. What is sometimes reported is that, in the early stages of the near-death experience, the person wants to get back into their body as soon as possible – which is totally understandable. In the later stages, however, when resuscitation is having effect, people commonly report that they do not want to come back – they like being where they are – but are coming back often for the sake of others. The NDE can commonly leave people with vivid memories and less fear concerning their eventual death – and this may remain in place for the rest of their lives.

Note that a person going through a NDE may only experience one or two of these common stages. On the other hand, all, or most of these, could be experienced in a full NDE. It has to be said, too, that this list represents what one would describe as the positive experience side, or outcomes, of a NDE. As if dying wasn't difficult enough, a few people have reported experiencing negative NDEs.[43] There may be a link between these experiences and the hellish void that I will pick up on in *The Other Side* chapter. Describing three types of NDEs, IANDS (International Association for Near-death Studies) write regarding the negative NDE experience:

> The third and rarest type included hellish imagery such as an ugly or foreboding landscape; demonic beings; loud, annoying noises; frightening animals; and other beings in extreme distress. Only rarely have such NDErs themselves felt personally tormented.[44]

Today, following the work of authors like Kubler-Ross and Moody, interest in near-death experience is a global phenomenon. Whole groups of people are interested in the topic, and are delving into this matter. A number of studies have been (and are being) made, and researchers are now working with sixteen possible stages of experience (as mentioned above) using the *16-item Greyson NDE scale,*[45] which has developed out of Moody's ten. Explanations as to how the experiences may occur: being caused by the dying brain – as opposed to any kind of spiritual experience – have become more sophisticated too. Close on the heels of Moody's work came the aforementioned IANDS in 1981. IANDS is an organisation that encourages scientific research and education on the physical, psychological, social and spiritual implications, and ramifications, of near-death experiences across the globe.

It is worth noting that on the IANDS website[46] they say that in over eight hundred cases of NDEs, that they have on their database, a quarter of the people, "were not close to death" when they experienced elements of a NDE. Rather they were, "in emotionally intense situations, praying or meditating, sleeping or in ordinary states of consciousness when this phenomenon occurred." IANDS call these "near-death-like experiences" or NDLEs for short. Maybe you are one of the twenty-five percent who have had such an out-of-body experience...? If you are, you might consider contacting IANDS (iands.org) to let them know.

NDE Research

Research in this area has mainly been carried out by the disciplines of medicine, psychology and psychiatry. Notably there is, at the time of writing, little interest from the neurosciences (that address psychological functions in context with the neural circuitry of the brain) to get involved in studies into NDE – which, I might add, makes the book, and NDE, of Dr Eben Alexander (a neurosurgeon, whose comments I will be drawing upon in *The Other Side* chapter), all the more spectacular. In the research that has been undertaken two notable studies stand out for me: These are; Dr Pim van Lommel's study published in 2001, in *The Lancet,* [47] and then the *AWARE (AWAreness during REesuscitation) study* led by Dr Sam Parnia, published at the back end of 2014.

Dr Lommel's study took place in the Netherlands. It involved three hundred and forty-four heart patients, resuscitated after cardiac arrest.[48] All patients had therefore been clinically dead at some point during their treatment. The aim was to, "investigate the frequency, the cause, and the content of a NDE." The study involved carrying out interviews with patients and scoring them on their NDE components. They found that a large number of people (eighty-two percent of the group) couldn't remember anything either of their cardiac arrest or during the period that they were unconscious. Sixty-two people from the group, however, did report having a NDE. Of these, over forty had a high score – a score of six or higher in the interviews was considered high. Within this higher score group Lommel also found twenty-three patients (seven percent overall), reported having a, "deep or very deep experience," recording a score of ten or higher.

These "deep" experiences followed a similar pattern to what had been observed by Moody. Overall they involved: *awareness of being dead*; *positive emotions*; *out-of-body experience*; *moving through a tunnel*; communications with *the light*, or *observing colours*; *observing a celestial landscape*; meeting with *relatives who are deceased*; having a *life review*; having experience of a *border* before returning.

Lommel's original study took place in 1988. He and his team took this further by taping interviews, with survivors, over periods of two and eight years after their cardiac arrest. This was to assess, "whether the loss of fear of death, the transformation in attitude toward life and the enhanced intuitive sensibility is the result of having a NDE or just the result of the cardiac arrest itself." He concluded from this research that, "Only patients with a NDE did show [such a] transformation." And added that the, "long lasting transformational effects of an experience that lasted only a few minutes was a surprising and unexpected finding."[49]

Lommel's study was a great success and greatly endorsed the findings of Moody's work. Let's look at the other piece of research now. The *AWARE study*,[50] began in 2008 (the pilot began the year before) and ended in 2012. This was a huge undertaking and is literally the world's largest NDE study so far published. It was the first study launched under the flag of the Human Consciousness Project,[51] and run by Dr Sam Parnia, with a team of over thirty people, and carried out across fifteen medical centres in the UK, USA and Austria. It essentially looked for evidence of awareness in patients during cardiac arrest and resuscitation. Similar to Lommel's study, a big part of this research involved interviewing survivors, but only those who also met with certain criteria to be considered for interview – which discounted a large number from the interview process.

Altogether the study involved over two-thousand patients. Of these, a hundred and forty people went on to complete a first stage interview, and from these a hundred and one went on to complete the, more involved, second stage of interviews.[52] Nine percent of this group were reported as having a NDE. Two people out of the group, "described awareness with explicit recall of 'seeing' and 'hearing' actual events related to their resuscitation." One of the two "had a verifiable period of conscious awareness [up to three minutes] during which time cerebral function was not expected."

What I find most notable in this study is that fifty-five of the group, who went on to participate in the second stage interviews, responded positively to the question, "Do you remember anything from the time during your unconsciousness." This represents a good size (thirty-nine percent, of all survivors who completed *stage one* of the interview process), and should give us cause to reflect on it providing evidence for signs of consciousness when supposedly we are meant, by all physical measures, to be unconscious, indeed dead. Although, for me, this piece of research didn't quite deliver against all the excitement, hopes and high expectations, it nevertheless provided a very encouraging outcome for further research into the exploration of NDE.

What we can say from NDE studies so far is that, across various researches, in hospitals over a range of countries, it appears that around ten percent of those who clinically die, and are then resuscitated, have a NDE. In the AWARE study it was nine percent. Some research findings have been as low as four percent, others higher, up to eighteen percent – as in the findings of the Lommel study. It does, however, suggest that, across the board, somewhere

---

　　　　　LIFE AND DEATH: MAKING SENSE OF IT

between eighty or ninety percent of people, who die and are resuscitated, do not experience or remember a NDE. From this the question naturally arises as to what is really going on to produce such an effect.

This concern, of course, has not gone unnoticed with researchers. Lommel explored possible reasons why only a small percentage of people experienced a NDE in his study. He could find no one cause to be at the root of it. He found a number of possibilities that might have influenced the outcome, such as; a NDE is, "more frequently reported at ages below 60 years," or more likely to be experienced by, "patients who had experienced a NDE previously." He concluded that having a, "Good short-term memory seems to be essential for remembering an NDE."[53] Parnia meanwhile disputes whether the high percentages, of people who don't recall anything, are really accurate. He says, "It could be that a far higher proportion of people have near-death experiences but don't remember them."[54] He makes a similar comment on the AWARE study findings and there pinpoints, "cerebral inflammation and, or sedatives on memory consolidation and recall" as possible reasons for people not remembering. On a less traumatic level, it occurs to me that I can rarely recall my dreams from one day to the next but that I, like a great number of people, probably dream four or five times a night, if REM (rapid eye movement) is evidence that one is dreaming. It is quite possible therefore that we simply do not remember – or not remember immediately, or not remember without being triggered in some way – in our waking state, even though the event or experience did actually happen.

A Day-Return ticket

We live in exciting times. A real breakthrough in what we know about our situation after-death is imminent. As mentioned in the last chapter, the time delay between being pronounced clinically dead and being brought back to life safely, with less risk of brain damage, is set to get longer, possibly could be up to a day. This forecast has been made by Dr Parnia who is suggesting that this development could happen over the next twenty years, with the way resuscitation technique and technology is heading. When Parnia was interviewed by the German, *Der Spiegel*,[55] weekly magazine he had this to say on the matter:

> In the past decade we have seen tremendous progress. With today's medicine, we can bring people back to life up to one, maybe two hours, sometimes even longer, after their heart stopped beating and they have thus died by circulatory failure. In the future, we will likely get better at reversing death. ... It is possible that in twenty years, we may be able to restore people to life twelve hours or maybe even twenty four hours after they have died.

And this being the prognosis, what amazing life after death accounts may we encounter when that technology is with us. Possibly a lot more in the nature of the account that follows...

Paul Eicke story

To complete my comments on NDE, I want to pick up on the Paul Eicke story I mentioned above. This story was reported in *The Daily Mail*[56] and elsewhere back in 2010. It is about a boy, aged just three-years-old at the time, who had, by all accounts, drowned and then came back from the dead. It happened in Germany.

Paul fell into the pond at his grandparents' house when the family were visiting. It is believed that he was in the pond for several minutes before his grandfather saw him and pulled him out. His father then gave him heart massage and *mouth-to-mouth* during the ten minutes it took for an ambulance helicopter to arrive.

Paramedics then took over and Paul was taken on a ten minute journey to the hospital. Doctors then tried to resuscitate him for hours. They had just about given up when, three hours and eighteen minutes after he was brought in, Paul's heart started beating again under its own steam.

Professor Lothar Schweigerer, director of the Helios Clinic where Paul was taken, said he had never experienced anything like it. He said, "When children have been underwater for a few minutes they mostly don't make it. This is a most extraordinary case." *The Daily Mail* version of the story quoted statistics from America that showed in the majority of children, who survive drownings, ninety-two percent, are discovered within two minutes following submersion. Also, that nearly all children, who require cardiopulmonary resuscitation, either die or are left with severe brain injury.

In this case it is thought that the temperature of the pond helped Paul to survive for longer. The water was very cold and the boy's core temperature had dropped to just 28° Celsius, compared to the normal of 37° Celsius. Cold temperatures slow the metabolism – which can allow the body to survive for longer without oxygen.

According to Schweigerer, if the temperature had been higher, the team would have stopped trying to resuscitate after forty minutes because the boy would definitely have been brain dead. Instead, they carried on with the chest compressions to stimulate Paul's organs, which had shut down after he breathed in the cold water.

The Professor said: "My doctors were close to saying 'we can do no more' after two hours of thorax compression. This was because the chances of survival had gone and the little lad must have been brain dead." He continued, "But then suddenly his heart started to beat again ... it was a fantastic miracle." And he added at the time, "I've been doing this job for thirty years and have never seen anything like this. It goes to show the human body is a very resilient organism and you should never give up."

But now let's consider the NDE part of this story... If Paul's survival was not profound enough, in itself, there was another aspect to this young person's story that bears some similarity to the common stages in the near-death experience. While unconscious Paul claims he saw his great-grandmother, "Emmi," who turned him back from a gate, urging him to go back to his parents. Paul said: "There was a lot of light and I was floating. I came to a gate and I saw Grandma Emmi on the other side."

She asked him what he was doing there. He said that she told him to go back to his mum and dad, and that she would wait for him over there. He said, "I knew I was in heaven. But grandma said I had to come back home. She said that I should go back very quickly." He added that, "Heaven looked nice" but he was glad to be, "back with mummy and daddy now." Paul indeed went back home, to Lychen, north of Berlin, with reportedly no sign of brain damage.

Children's recall of previous lives

> Children's past life memories is a phenomenon with far-reaching implications for every person who is curious about the truth of reincarnation and wonders about their own past lives.
>
> Carol Bowman, therapist, past life researcher and author[57]

Following the Paul Eicke NDE story, this is a good moment to continue with the experience of children...

Memory is an odd thing isn't it? I've already mentioned above, with regard to remembering my dreams, but to keep it on a more mundane level, what I remember of last week can already be fuzzy and yet my long term memory can be vivid with names and places popping up as I contemplate a given time in my life. This is particularly so if I sit quietly and contemplate on an earlier period in my life. If however you were to ask me *off the bat* for names of the people I knew, in say my twenties, I would probably struggle to give you more than one or two of them. In fairness, I find that generally I remember faces better than names.

One of the arguments often set against a belief in reincarnation is that we don't remember our past lives and so, it naturally follows, that we most likely didn't have any. It is a bit of a generalisation of course. From what I've said already, you'll anticipate this *not remembering past lives* comes as no great surprise to me. Memory is indeed odd – or how easy we can access it, or not, is odd. On a subconscious level we can argue that every experience is registered and nothing lost. Particularly what we do or what we experience in childhood firms up our potential and influences our direction whether towards good and healthy or even dysfunctional outcomes.

If you think about it, it is hard for us to remember really early in our development as children. If you can remember back to when you were two or three-years-old that's quite a feat I'd suggest. If however something dramatic or traumatic happened back then you may have powerful recall of that moment. For example, I have some recall of a moment when I was less than three-years-old. I remember it because I had a serious accident. My mother was then looking after a presbytery and took me to work with her each day. While she was getting on with her duties, around the priest's house, she had taken her eyes off the ball (me) for a moment and I had found my way into the kitchen. Being inquisitive I wanted to find out what all the bubbling noise was about. The cause of the bubbling noise was an old-fashioned tin bath boiler, sitting on a gas ring and bubbling away washing clothes. I somehow got up to it, and, holding onto the side to look over, I rocked it, and water came splashing over and scalded my arms – causing burns up to my elbows. The trauma must have been life-threatening. I don't remember anything else after that moment but I learnt much later, from my mother, that the hospital doctor thought I was going to need a skin graft, as my burns were so bad. But anyhow I didn't have a graft; my arms healed and are today still scarred but only faintly so. Even so the bit I can remember lives on as if it was yesterday.

I suspect, in context, we are more likely to remember events that have been shocking to us in some way – for either nice surprises or not nice reasons. It can of course have the opposite effect; that we blank out traumatic moments. But the point I wish to make is this: the reason why some of us may remember a past life, when others don't, is due, in part, to something shocking about it – probably how we lived, and particularly how we died. Sudden death can leave us incomplete, without closure, without time to resolve our affairs – with our plans, and those we have left behind, at the forefront of our mind.

Imagine this for example: It's today, now, you're by yourself in the comfort of your home getting on with your life. You have a lot on your mind, things to do. A lot of stressful concerns and changes have been going on for you recently that have made you frankly unhappy and exhausted. Your partner or family are out for a while. There is a knock on your door. You answer it. There is a taxi outside. Someone has come to collect you. It's a surprise, and you are given little choice in the matter. The next thing you know you are being whisked away, to a place, who knows, perhaps many thousands of miles away.

In no time it seems you arrive at your destination. Now okay, this place you have been taken to turns out to be a beautiful and inspiring place, with very friendly faces to greet you. Initially you went along with this, but are you really noticing what a nice place it is right now? Most probably you are getting really confused and upset. Someone tries to explain why you have been brought to this place, but are you listening? Most probably you are too preoccupied, too much in shock to listen. All you want to do now is get back to your home, back to your life and activities, back to sorting out those issues demanding your attention, back to your family and friends – indeed you are now demanding to be taken back…

Dying in a sudden manner can set up a powerful yearning to get back with the people you love, to carry on with things. There may be an urgency to get back to where one left off – even though in the real scheme of things none of us can really go back to where we left off just like that, for obvious reasons. But we may pretty quickly go that step to get back if things are that urgent or important to us… Re-entering the physical world from this state can provoke a strong enough recall for us to remember what happened, or to have an inkling of being driven, by some urgent matter needing to be resolved.

I've read a number of accounts regarding children recalling previous lives. The amazing thing is that children have no investment in trying to hoodwink anyone, or prove a point, when they say they remember things, and have knowledge they couldn't otherwise have access to. So while it may be possible to dismiss an adult claiming to have had a past life, it is more difficult to dismiss such recollections with children – and particularly when those recollections stand up to scrutiny.

According to children's previous lives investigator, Carol Bowman, children as young as two-years-old can, without prompting, describe memories of former lives. And if her findings, together with the late Dr Ian Stevenson's findings, are anything to go by, this memory in children could be more common than we might presuppose. Stevenson, internationally known for his research into past lives of children, and author of, *Children Who Remember Previous Lives*,[58] documented (over a forty year period), more than three thousand cases of children who offered, in his words, "undeniable evidence" for their memories being real and, by deduction, linked to past life experience. Children with such recall will supply names of towns, describe the place where they lived, their relatives, their occupations and relationships that, in cases from across the world, are unique to the individuals who have died. Although it is quite possible the past life being recalled by a child is that of being a member (albeit former member) of the same family they are with now, it appears the lives children describe, in most cases, are not known to the child's present family.

James Leininger's story

One such past life story is comprehensively relayed in the book, *Soul Survivor*.[59] This is about James Leininger (a six-year-old at the time the book was written) who has powerful recall of a plane crash that occurred off the Japanese coast during World War II. This was a plane crash in which he is believed to have died as fighter pilot, James Huston Jr., back in 1945 – he even has the same first name in this life. This is about a boy who at two-years-old was fascinated with aeroplanes. It is about a boy who, at two, was experiencing nightmares so regular, up to four times a week, and so frightening, causing him to violently kick and scream, that his parents, Bruce and Andrea Leininger, became very concerned for his health, his safety and indeed his sanity.

When details of planes and war tragedies, no small boy could know about, also began to emerge, his parents racked their brains about the source of the disturbing information they were hearing. They had always tried to create a healthy atmosphere, for their child to grow up in, and had been careful to keep violence away from his sight. At first they began to analyse their lifestyles for clues, their dinner conversations, what James was watching on television, and other things that could possibly have influenced him. Of course, at two-years-old, he certainly wasn't getting it from reading. All *normal* explanations drew a blank on anything having this kind of influence. Neither at first did they even cotton-on to the aviation links he was expressing – as they weren't themselves involved in aviation in any way.

While Andrea, at a later stage, and with some family support, began to entertain the idea of James possibly recalling a past life (and then decided to contact Carol Bowman for expert opinion on this), his father, having a strong orthodox Christian faith, could not accept any such notion and went to great lengths to kick this view into the long grass. He set about looking into the background of the information, his son was providing, to demonstrate it was anything other than a past life. The notion of anyone having a *past life* couldn't exist in his view. His research was intensive – leaving no stone unturned. However, the further he delved into it the more he was faced with the possibility that his son might just be telling the truth – certainly more than could be put down to a young child's fantasy world.

This very brief overview only scratches the surface of the huge amount of content in the book. You must read it to find out the lengths James's father actually went to, to demolish any notion his son was a reincarnated fighter pilot – and whether or not he eventually came to terms with what he discovered. Carol Bowman, who wrote the foreword to the book, begins it by saying, "The story of James Leininger is the best American case of a child's past life memory among the thousands I've encountered." The book certainly makes a milestone contribution to providing evidence of a past life; and, in my opinion, easily helps to put past lives and *reincarnation* on the table for serious debate.

And there are many more cases. For example, check out the stories on Bowman's website[60] and in her book, *Children's Past Lives*[61] where you will find examples such as the following two:

Past Life as a Nun

Bowman relates the story of a little girl named *Elspeth* who, before she was even two-years-old, spontaneously recalled becoming a nun.

"I'm going to take my vows," she suddenly told her mother while being bathed one day – and remarkably too, this comment was the first full sentence she had ever uttered. When she was later questioned on this, she told her mother, "I'm not Elspeth now. I'm Rose," and then added, "but I'm going to be Sister Teresa Gregory." This small person even described some of her convent duties, including milking the goats, making cheese and saying prayers. She even described her own death as a nun.

The Sewing Sailor

In another anecdote, from Bowman, five-year-old *Tommy Hibbert* somehow knew how to sew a button back on his pants. "Tommy went and got a needle and thread," his mother recalled, "threaded the needle, and sewed that button on, so expertly, that I couldn't believe it. I had never taught him to sew and he had never even seen me do it." Amazed, she asked him as to where on earth he learnt to sew on buttons. He told her, "Well, we used to do it on my ship all of the time." When she asked him if he was a sailor, he replied, "Oh, yes." He then told her about how his ship would creak in the night while he was lying in his bunk, in what he described as, "an old sailing ship with tall masts and many ropes." It turns out too that, when Tommy grew up, he actually joined the Navy.

There are a lot more stories like these in the book and on the website mentioned, where you will also find much discussion and advice particularly on children's past lives, and past lives generally. But before leaving this section I couldn't help but add in the following Sujith and Sammy story of a past life, as investigated by Dr Ian Stevenson.[62] If you are in doubt that reincarnation can exist, this story, like the James Leininger story above, should help you to allay that doubt and give serious reconsideration to what you believe.

Sujith and Sammy

This remarkable story is of a young boy, *Sujith Lakmal Jayaratne* – who was born on August 8, 1969 in Sri Lanka – and his recall of his life as *Sammy Fernando*, a real person who had died six months earlier on January 29, 1969.

When he was barely old enough to speak, Sujith began to tell his family of a previous life as a man named Sammy. He told them that Sammy had lived in the village of Gorakana – eight miles to the south of Sujith's current home. He told them that in his life, as Sammy, he had worked on the engines of trains and how he also got fired from this railroad job. Stevenson investigating this case was, from early on, impressed that Sujith had recalled Sammy losing his job on the railroad; which occurred when Sammy was twenty-five years of age – a gap of over twenty-five years had transpired to the point when Sujith was now reporting this event. There was much more to follow…

Sujith gave a lot of detail about his life as Sammy, where he went to school, how his teacher was named *Francis*, how he used to go to Kale Pansala (using the actual name – which translated means *Forest Temple*) where two Buddhist monks lived, and how he gave them money for the temple. He was able to name one of the monks as *Amitha*, which checked out. All of this was checked out in the life of Sammy, through Sammy's surviving relatives. We learn how, before Sujith learned to talk, he tried to express that someone had fallen and had become lame – he did this by imitating a person limping and using a cane. Later, when Sujith was able to converse, he told his mother that the person who fell and limped was his younger brother, who he called *Milton*. Sammy, it transpired, did indeed have a brother called Milton Fernando, who had had the misfortune of falling from a train and as a result had incurred a serious injury to his back, and who then walked with a limp and had to use a cane for the rest of his life.

Sujith also frequently referred to his father, who he said was named *Jamis* and who had a "bad right eye." Stevenson discovered that Sammy's father was Jamis Fernando, who had a defect of his right eye, in which the lens was opaque. It was noted that when Sujith was describing his life as Sammy he had a tendency to speak in the present tense, for example saying, "Jamis is at Gorakana," whereas in reality, Jamis had died in September 1970 just a year after Sujith was born. He also repeatedly asked to be taken to Gorakana which he claimed was his home.

Speaking to relatives, Stevenson uncovered that in the life of Sammy Fernando, after losing his railway job, he took up bootlegging *arrack* (an alcoholic drink consumed in Sri Lanka). He learnt how Sammy was very good at his craft and his arrack was in high demand. The production of arrack however was illegal, and it transpired Sammy was imprisoned, at least eight times during his life, because of this. Stevenson found out that he married *Maggilin Alwis*, whom he called *Maggie*. In 1972, in this amazing story, Maggilin visited the young Sujith – who, at the time of her visit, was under three-years-old. He recognised her and called her Maggie. He also told her he loved her and indeed it was clear, from his comments and advances, that he treated her as his wife and wanted to move back with her. He also challenged her saying, "Look what you did to me. Look what you did to me." which was explained as blaming her for what happened to him regarding his death.

Linking to Sammy's death: From an early age, Sujith had a marked fear of lorries. The family didn't initially understand why he had this fear until one night he woke them up to tell them that he was, "run over by a lorry and that is how I died." In context with this part of the story, in the life of Sammy, the young Sujith also had a strong liking for arrack, and even went to lengths to get it from neighbours – we're talking about a four-year-old at this point asking for an alcoholic drink. When instead he was given a soda to drink he would act as if he were intoxicated. Similarly as bizarre, Sujith had a strong liking for cigarettes. None of his family drank or smoked so there was no home influence to encourage this. The drinking and smoking however are important components in this story of Sammy Fernando, and particularly how he died...

It transpired that Sammy and Maggie lived in her house, which was on the main highway between Colombo and Galle. The road was a major thoroughfare and commercial vehicles made full use of it, often driving at high speed. It emerged that Sammy was often drunk and had violent rows with Maggie. She would often run out of the house to get away from him. On this occasion Maggie left the house and Sammy followed her, with his brother-in-law, *Martin Alwis*, in tow. On their way Sammy and Martin then stopped in a shop to purchase cigarettes. As Martin was making payment, Sammy, in his drunken state, had walked out of the shop, onto the road... and BAM.

Sujith, now, taking up the story of Sammy's death, described how, after he had had an argument with Maggie, he went to a shop to get some cigarettes. When he stepped out on the road he was killed when a lorry struck him. Sujith would even imitate the posture that he was in on the road after being struck. He would lay on the ground, on his back, with one arm stuck out. Sammy's brother-in-law confirmed that this was how he was found, after being hit. Sammy had died shortly thereafter. He was fifty-years of age.

It should be noted here that Sijuth's family had never been to Gorakana and hadn't known anyone that fitted Sammy's description. There are many more details left out of this brief account, such as Sujith correctly identifying the name of Sammy's daughter *Nandanie* and his niece, *Kusuma*. Indeed the investigation by Stevenson, confirmed as many as sixty, of the details of the life of Sammy Fernando, were as given by Sujith. The case was also investigated by a Buddhist monk after the family, also Buddhists, initially contacted him. This also helped some of the details to emerge. It is considered to be one of the strongest cases of reincarnation on record.

Additional note

I have every belief that as young children, we can more easily access information from previous lives than we can as adults. Carol Bowman, for example, found that children, before the age of three, can more easily recall previous lives than after that point. Such memories then begin to fade by age five. By age seven and onwards any such memory is now getting overlaid with current life experience, and therefore a lot less easy to access – other than in dreams, via our intuition, or when under hypnosis – which conveniently links to the next section.

Past Life Regression (PLR)

One could say that past lives are the major concern of past life regression (PLR) procedure. There is more to it than that however. If you are new to this then let me just say that PLR is a therapy where people are believed to be able to access previous lives, under hypnosis, to help resolve issues in this life. This is not a *New Age* philosophy in action by the way – although you might think it as a recent development. Dealing with past lives through some means of regression has been around for a very long time – from as early as the 2nd-century BC it is generally claimed. It is mentioned in the Upanishads and in the Yoga Sutras of Patanjali of ancient Indian literature.[63] In more recent times it has gained new popularity through the works of Madame Blavatsky, during the 19th-century, but in the 20th-century, following the Fifties, it took on new interest within areas of medicine, in psychology and psychiatry – and in the holistic therapies movement generally.

In PLR, the practitioner will use hypnosis, suggestions, and questions, all designed to help the person undergoing the regression treatment to relax, regress back through their years, to before they were born – which then allows for past life memories to surface. Visualization techniques are often used, such as having the client envision a peaceful setting, maybe a garden or meadow. The person, once relaxed, will then be encouraged to see themselves crossing say a footbridge, or going through a gateway. As they cross the barrier, scenes from past incarnation/s, past life memories, may then surface.

The therapy aspect of this is designed to help individuals deal with painful and unresolved irrational fears or phobias (e.g. a fear of drowning, or perhaps a fear of lorries as in Sujith's case) that can't be linked to experiences or memories from their present lifetime. The possibility arises that a given phobia may be stemming from a past life experience (often associated with how the person died in that life) and that, by revisiting the previous life, there is the opportunity for the cause of the fear, or phobia, to be faced again, but this time within a supportive atmosphere. The intention is that, by revisiting the situation, the individual is better equipped to understand and control, heal, or move on from, whatever experience and fear they have had.

For the purpose of this section, my interest lies in discussing PLR in context with providing evidence for the existence of past lives. I do believe that PLR, in its most rigorous and professional form, can help provide insight and answers to philosophical questions regarding life and death. It has to be said however that PLR is considered a controversial form of treatment, not just within orthodox psychology and psychiatry but even among those who research into, and accept, past lives and reincarnation. Dr Ian Stevenson, introduced above, for example, was an advocate of it but also cautious, as he made clear in comments from his *Hypnotic Regression to Previous Lives*:

> I am not now engaging in experiments with hypnotic regression to 'previous lives.' … I do not approve of any hypnotist who makes promises to clients that suggest they will certainly return to a real previous life under his direction. I do not approve of anyone who charges fees for acting as a hypnotist in such experiments.[64]

I suspect one of the reasons he was concerned is because more or less anyone, at the time, could set themselves up as a PLR therapist, with a minimum amount of training. This is now in the process of changing through organisations such as *The Earth Association for Regression Therapy*[65] and *The Past Life Therapists Association*[66] that aim to improve the professionalism and practice of PLR. Given that, Stevenson's main concern though was, rather than be tapping into a previous life one could, using this method, be tapping into, or generating a new personality (or a number of *previous personalities*) from the release of subconscious parts of the mind. These, in effect, through use of the imagination, write their own narrative and may in turn be very plausible to the person having the experience. If the person has been instructed by the hypnotist to go back to another place and time, or be given some similar suggestion, the new personality may *appear* to be of another period of history. Stevenson writes:

...nearly all such hypnotically evoked *previous personalities* are entirely imaginary just as are the contents of most dreams. They may include some accurate historical details, but these are usually derived from information the subject has acquired normally through reading, radio and television programmes, or other sources.[67]

Stevenson further describes how the person under hypnosis, may not remember where they obtained the information they are giving, as a different personality; but later this may change through further sessions designed to search out the sources used in making up the personality. Other explanations for what is perceived to be a past life may instead be the result of suggestion, paramnesia (distortion of memory), cryptomnesia (forgotten memory returning and perceived as something new), false memory syndrome, possession, psychiatric illness, or multiple personality disorder. Given such variable explanations, and in context with the subconscious wherein all personal and long forgotten experience will tend to be archived, it is indeed a minefield to establish that a true past life is being tapped into, during PLR therapy.

One of the most famous cases of PLR (shown to be unreliable in providing evidence for a past life) is that of *Bridey Murphy*. Virginia Tighe, an American, was hypnotically regressed by another American, businessman Morey Bernstein, on a number of occasions. In these sessions she became Bridey Murphy. Bridey we learn, was born in Cork, Ireland, in 1798. She was the daughter of a Protestant barrister called Duncan Murphy and his wife Kathleen. She had a brother, Duncan Blaine Murphy, who had married an Aimee Strayne. She had another brother who had died in infancy. We learn that, at the age of twenty, Bridey married a Brian Joseph McCarthy, a Roman Catholic. They had a protestant ceremony. Brian and Bridey then moved to Belfast, where, through pursuing his studies, Brian eventually taught law at Queen's University. We are told Bridey lived there until she died, at age sixty-six. She had no children.

Morey Bernstein wrote a book on the matter, first published in 1956; *The Search for Bridey Murphy*. The book was also made into a movie.

On investigation of the case it transpired that none of the details Bridey claimed regarding her birth, her family, marriage and death, or the wooden house she is supposed to have lived in, could be verified. Some other details did however tally well. For instance, her descriptions of the Antrim coastline were very accurate. So, too, was her account of a journey from Belfast to Cork. The young Bridey also shopped for provisions with a grocer named Farr, and it was discovered that such a grocer had existed at the time claimed. But her account also included inaccuracies. For example she claimed she went to a St. Theresa's Church. There was indeed one where she said there was, but it was not built until 1911.

Sceptics claim the Bridey Murphy personality to be a case of cryptomnesia, that she can be explained as a memory of Virginia Tighe's long-forgotten childhood. There are some good grounds for this assessment, and this case is considered closed. Although Tighe had never been to Ireland her parents were both part-Irish. She had lived with them until the age of three and was then brought up by a Norwegian uncle, and his wife. It also transpired there was an Irish immigrant named Bridie Murphy Corkell (she died in 1957) who lived across the street from Tighe's childhood home, in Chicago, Illinois, and that this was the most likely source for the name.

The Bridey Murphy story is a prime example of how careful one has to be of the pitfalls in establishing a link to a previous life while using PLR. Even so there have also been one or two remarkable PLR accounts that are less easy to explain away, other than by invoking a *past life* verdict. To look at a couple of these who better to turn to than Stevenson; for although he had his concerns with PLR he didn't dismiss it out of hand and did research some claims, with interesting and, where past lives are concerned, encouraging results. One of the most convincing aspects of PLR is where a person being regressed begins speaking in a foreign language, and likewise provides verifiable data regarding their identity and their history. The following two examples are taken from articles, by Walter Semkiw MD, writing on investigations by Stevenson.

TE and Jensen Jocoby

This case (investigated by Stevenson in 1958),[68] involved a physician (practising medicine in Philadelphia, Pennsylvania), and his wife. The wife underwent hypnosis by her husband. The husband had learnt to use hypnosis, back in 1954, and was experimenting with PLR. His wife turned out to be a good subject and he carried out experiments with her over 1955 to 1956. To keep their identity private, Stevenson used their initials KE, and his wife TE, in his investigation.

Once under hypnosis, TE's voice deepened to one that was distinctly male. The personality that emerged spoke English that was peppered with Swedish words. She declared, in broken English, that she was a man, a farmer named *Jensen Jacoby*, who lived in the 17th-century. After six hypnotic sessions, TE was talking exclusively in Swedish. We need to keep in mind that TE was actually born in Philadelphia, with English being her native language. She and her husband swore they knew nothing of the Swedish language. Also no one in the family had ever been to the Scandinavian part of the world, let alone Sweden, and they knew no one who could speak Swedish.

In the process, TE's husband arranged for a number of Swedish persons to witness the phenomenon of his wife speaking Swedish. As Jensen (a *he*) she was able to converse fluently with them. They confirmed that he was speaking an older form of Swedish that would have been spoken at the time he said he had lived. Regarding his life; Jensen described how he lived in a village, "Morby Hagar," near the harbour town of "Havero," and another town, "Torohaven." He raised, "cows, horses, goats and chickens." He, "baked bread and made goat's cheese," and sold his produce at Havero. Then at times:

> ... his family would eat salmon, which presumably came from the harbour town. ...he was one of three sons. He had a wife ... Latvia,

---

who made poppy seed cakes and poppy seed juice. The couple had no children. …he built his own stone house… he hunted for bears and he liked to drink at a tavern. …he worshiped Jesus Christ.[69]

He knew of Swedish things from his period. He could identify a model of a Swedish 17th-century sailing ship, as a *skuta* or *skute*. He also correctly named a Swedish container used to measure grain, and correctly named a wolf in Swedish. He described how he had a hatred for warfare and, when asked how his life ended, he said he was, "engaged in some type of fight with enemies, was forced into a body of water and received a blow to the head," which apparently killed him.

Worth noting that in TE's first hypnosis session, she felt she was being hit on the head and experienced severe head pain. At the time, due to her suffering, KE took her out of the hypnotic state. She reported that she still experienced head pain for the next two days and repeatedly felt her head, looking for a lump.

Stevenson studied the case in meticulous detail. He had three Swedish people, on separate occasions, sign statements confirming that the language TE was speaking was indeed Swedish. In the statements, it was noted that the accent was that of a, "natural Swedish speaker." He also had transcripts and tape recordings analysed by Swedish linguistic experts, who confirmed that TE was speaking Swedish in a conversational manner. These experts also testified that an, "excellent Swedish accent was being spoken and that the language was an old form of Swedish, identified as Middle Swedish." Stevenson counted a, "vocabulary of over 100 Swedish words" spoken by TE. He also had both take lie detector tests to rule out fraud; which they passed.

Stevenson, firmly believed in the legitimacy of the case, and rejected that any fraud was involved. He concluded that, "Jenson Jacoby had once lived on the west coast of Sweden, near Norway, in the 17th-century." He commented that the case, "represented strong evidence for the survival of personality after death."

DJ and Gretchen Gottlieb

Another case that Stevenson investigated[70] was that of a lady, whose initials are DJ, with her husband's initials being CJ. CJ was a Methodist Christian minister who started to practice hypnosis in 1954. This was initially to help people get relief from chronic pain. In the Sixties, he started to experiment with PLR.

During 1970, DJ was having back pain. CJ conducted a hypnosis session with the aim of relieving his wife's pain. While under hypnosis however CJ asked DJ if her back hurt, she replied in German, "Nein" (No). In another session, DJ said, in German, "Ich bin *Gretchen*" (I am Gretchen).

In further sessions, over the following period, Gretchen appeared repeatedly and spoke only German. After ten such sessions, a native German speaker was brought in to have a conversation with Gretchen, in German. In a later session DJ wrote forty words in German during a manifestation of Gretchen.

The article author, Walter Semkiw MD, notes that, "Of interest, the handwriting of Gretchen was different than the handwriting of DJ. This infers that handwriting does not necessarily stay the same from one incarnation to another." Having studied handwriting analysis I would tend to agree that this could be so. Handwriting is unique to the individual. It is an expression of personality, and even though it may superficially alter with mood, stress, and self-conscious construction, the deeper components of the strokes (such as pressure, the width or narrowness of characters, how characters are linked, and zonal emphasis) will remain intact. A different personality will most likely tend to express a different form of writing.

What interested Stevenson, to investigate, was that DJ had never learned German, and did not understand or speak it in her normal waking state. As it happened Stevenson knew German and was able to participate in a session, speaking the language. As in other investigations, he also enlisted other people who spoke the same language to have conversations with the subject. At a later time, in

1974, DJ went to Stevenson's laboratory, at the University of Virginia, where he and a colleague had conversations with Gretchen, again in German. They transcribed conversations spanning nineteen sessions – six of which were tape recorded. These transcripts totalled three hundred and forty six double-spaced typewritten pages. What Stevenson found was that:

> Gretchen spoke 237 different German words in these transcripts. She used 120 specific words before anyone else had said them, which indicates that she was not just mimicking conversation. In one session that was taped, Gretchen introduced 96 German words that were not previously spoken by interviewers, 21 of which neither Gretchen, nor interviewers, had ever spoken before. Stevenson had three different German speakers sign statements that Gretchen was truly speaking German.[71]

Stevenson had DJ undergo a lie detector test which she passed – vouching that she had not learned or known German prior to Gretchen emerging. He also interviewed DJ's parents, as well as her sister. All three signed statements that no one they knew spoke German, and that there were no German speaking individuals in the area where they lived.

In the life of *Gretchen Gottlieb*, she lived with her father, whose name was Herman. She described him as old, with white hair. Her mother, Erika, had died when she was eight-years-old. She had no brothers or sisters. She said her father was the Mayor of Eberswalde, Germany, where they lived – and that they lived on a street called Birkenstrasse. Gretchen described Eberswalde as a small town with a bakery, butcher shop, church and a college. There was a forest and river outside the town. She also spoke of the cities, Worms and Wiesbaden.

She said that a housekeeper, named Frau Schilder, came to their home to cook and clean. Frau Schilder would bring her four children with her and Gretchen would play with the children – of which the youngest was three-years-old. Gretchen was raised as a Roman Catholic and knew that the Pope was the head of the church. She was opposed to the Protestant Reformation and she referred to Martin Luther, several times, as a troublemaker. She repeatedly showed fear, and even paranoia, when she talked about the Bundesrat (Federal Council 1871–1919). Due to this statement, Stevenson assumed that Gretchen lived in the late 19th-century in Germany. She was dead by the age of 16, due to a serious illness, with the primary symptom being headache. Overall, Semkiw writes:

> Stevenson saw no reason for the [couple] or their family to make false statements and he believed this to be a legitimate xenoglossy case [as in the case above; where an individual can speak a language that was not learned by normal means]. If reincarnation is indeed accepted as the explanation, we see how talents, including the ability to speak a language, can be conveyed from one incarnation to another.[72]

There are many more cases that we could have looked at in this section. For example the well-known *Bloxham Tapes*[73] of the Seventies, involving the story of Jane Evans's remarkable six previous lives – particular her highly detailed life as *Rebecca* that was also reviewed in a more recent article by Ian Lawton.[74] Or the case of *Carroll Beckwith* who emerged through Robert Snow, a retired Captain of the Indianapolis Metropolitan Police Dept.[75] Or, from Rick Brown's book, *The Reincarnation of James the Submarine Man*,[76] which covers the case of Bruce Kelly (under hypnosis with Rick Brown) having vivid recalls of a past life as *James Johnston* – who died in a depth charge attack on the Submarine U.S.S. Shark in WWII.[77] All provide convincing evidence that these are genuine people tapping into real previous lives.

So in answer to my request for PLR providing some, "sound evidence for the existence of past lives," I would say that it clearly can but one needs to be very cautious for all the reasons given above – and I'd add, only trust a professional therapist. The more I've looked into this the more I'm of the view that this is an area for promising research.

Past lives comment

> All the world's a stage
> And all the men and women merely players
> They have their exits and their entrances
> And one man in his time plays many parts...
>
> From As You Like It by William Shakespeare

Just to raise a point for the sake of clarity, on PLR (and the general semantics used throughout this book): I would suggest that while I am seeking to engage you into considering you will also have had past lives and will live again, beyond death, it is only in the broader sense that I am using the word, *you*, to aid ease of understanding. In truth though it is not really you, as you know yourself, that I am addressing here, rather it is your soul.

You see there is no way that I, as *Francis*, can regress and fully experience the dynamic of a true previous life, as if it were my own, because, put simply, Francis hasn't had a previous life. Francis is the name given (by my parents) to what is my current soul situation (and the personality that has developed with it), so another situation, another name and another personality – or aspect thereof. In other words one needs to hold in mind that it is your *soul* that is implied in such comments where I am making them. And paraphrasing Shakespeare I'd say, your soul plays many parts, is the actor, the traveller, and each new life is, as it were, a drama and chapter, in your soul's unfolding story.

Communications through Psychics and Mediums

Communications through psychics and mediums also convince me there is more going on than meets the eye. How can a person, who describes him or herself as a medium, relay information about a loved one that they themselves couldn't possibly know or glean from the person they are talking to at the time? Well okay we are perhaps all aware of how easy we can be deceived by trickery and illusion. Research into this area often describes the accuracy, or inaccuracy, of the information being exchanged as being only as good as what is gleaned from *cold reading* cues of the exchange. In other words such research may deduce that there is no evidence for communications with the dead, rather good intuitive, sometimes telepathic, communications with the living.

Regarding research into mediums and psychics you would be advised to visit the websites of *Society for Psychical Research* in the UK[78] or USA.[79] Also the *British Psychological Society*[80] conducts such research work.

It is very easy to dismiss all psychics or mediums as fakes or entertainers, particular if one has never had a one-to-one, or never been to one of their meetings, demonstrations, or shows. Annie and I have attended quite a few demonstrations in and around Cheltenham, Evesham and Stratford upon Avon, in the UK. As you will find in a later chapter I have also spent some time with two mediums, friends of mine, and learnt a great deal from the experience.

Admittedly the information that comes up in demonstrations can be somewhat uninteresting, and sometimes even banal or gossipy, unless, of course, you happen to be the person, or persons, who the communication is directed towards. The information itself however can be very detailed.

For example here's one that I noted down, from one of the shows I've attended: The medium says, "I have someone called *John* here." My ears pricked up as my father's name was John. He continues,

"John died recently in a tragic accident, looks like a motoring accident from what he is showing me. Does anyone relate to John?" This no longer had any link with my father but, anyhow, three hands go up in the audience of about a thousand people. The medium goes to each in turn to find out if they have definitely lost a "John" from their lives recently. One of the people responding says she lost a, "Jonathan, a year ago in a car accident." The medium asks if he ever called himself "John" for short, to which the reply was, "No, never." The medium comes back saying, "Sorry I'm hearing it is definitely John who wants to talk," and he leaves the situation open with that person for the time being. He turns to the other two people still with their hands up. These people also happen to be in the right area of the audience. A number of mediums, perhaps all, get a strong sense of where in the audience the communication is intended for – sometimes the actual person will be targeted without any request for a response from them. The medium needs further help at this point and draws on what, he claims, John is telling him. John is telling him he has a sister called, what sounds like, "Mel" or "Melanie." He checks if that makes any sense to either of the two people with their hands up. One person had a brother called John, but she's called "Maureen." This is pretty close but not what the medium is looking for. It turns out that none of the three people are familiar with, or know of a Melanie in John's life. On further exploration with Maureen the medium was unhappy with this possible link.

In such a situation the medium may decide to leave it hanging at that, and go onto another communicator, but rarely do they give up so easily from what I've observed. I've seen the likes of Colin Fry, Gordon Smith and Derek Acorah really push the point, in a particular area of the audience. Often in a big audience people are just too shy, or even too disturbed by what they are hearing, to respond, and they sometimes have to be coaxed into holding their hand up. So it was in this case. The medium didn't give up and pursued the area of the audience where he felt the message was intended for. After some embarrassing waiting, and gentle goading by the medium, eventually a person put their hand up. She was very

---

softly spoken. She said that she had lost her brother in a motorcycle accident, and that her name was Melanie. The link was looking good. At this point the medium did some further identification, "John is showing me that he is wearing a blue jumper with a zigzag pattern. He says it is a favourite of his, he wore it a lot – and you'll remember it." Melanie replies that he did wear such a jumper a lot, and indeed, "wore it the day he died," as she so remembers. "Well, he's telling me it looks as good as new now," the medium replies. Further information was exchanged, such as John not being married and having no children, but loved visiting Melanie, and seeing her children. All such detail helped to confirm the identification of John for Melanie.

Through the medium, John says he has visited Melanie's house since the accident, and has some comment to make about changes that have taken place in the home. He expresses concern about one of her daughters, who is not spending nearly enough time on doing her maths homework, and this is because she is struggling with it and needs help. Melanie admits to knowing this and is also concerned. In the normal run of things the medium will usually have a message to get across for the person on the receiving end. In this case the message was to reassure Melanie that her brother is still very much alive and happy, and she is to get on with her life. John tells her, "Don't keep looking at photographs of me with such sadness. You are often looking at the one you took where I am leaning against my motorcycle outside my flat – and you cry a lot. Please put it away for some time. Everything is okay. I'm fine." At this point John sends his love and signs off through the medium.

In a one-off like this a sceptic might suggest that the person, calling herself Melanie, could have been planted in the audience. Without having proof to the contrary this has to be considered as a possibility. During a show though there may be possibly ten or so similar exchanges, all natural, all exploratory and differing in detail which, if contrived, would be a lot for any one person to remember. Annie, or myself, have also been involved in at least three of these types of exchanges so we can say we know from first-hand experience it is kosher. Admittedly the medium is there to make it interesting and entertaining too. In a large audience a lot of people will be there for a message but will miss out, and yet will want to go away with something. What a good number of people will go away with is witnessing exchanges that amount to good circumstantial evidence of life after death. If they are sceptic or agnostic regarding such belief then they will be witness to something of a spectacle that might make them think differently about the matter.

One-to-one session example

To complete the round on psychics and mediums, here is an example of a one-to-one session – shown on British television.[81] This is an extract from a session between G (a woman in her mid-fifties) and spiritual medium, Colin Fry.[82] During the session Fry picks up on a number of matters that he could not have known about before the reading. G did not even know all of this herself – until, that is, she checked back with her mother. As will become clear in the reading, it follows too that Fry could not have wangled this information out of G by fishing for what to say. The only means by which this makes sense to me is that someone, I believe G's father, was communicating with Fry. Once you allow for that possibility then it all falls into place. There is no smoke and mirrors here, just good communications with the Other Side.

Fry begins by saying, "Right, I've got a gentleman starting off trying to connect to me. He's giving me the feeling that he had far too much energy for a man of his age than was good for him. I do feel that he reached quite a reasonable age but he always seemed to have this exuberance of energy more or less right up until the end. ... I'm either talking about your dad or father in law; and I feel I've got to say, your dad."
G: Yes.
Fry: A fiercely independent old boy wasn't he?
G: Yes.
G [post the reading, talking to camera]: My father was very independent. He liked to do things his way, the way he wanted to. ... He would

always do his best for us, that was all that he was concerned about, his family.

F: Dad's showing me quite striking images of India.

G: Yes (pauses...). Yes.

F: Almost like vivid postcard images, picture cards of India. He doesn't want to tell me why. He won't explain to me why. He's just asked me to mention about India and that you would understand the reason why he asked.

G: He was in Burma during the War and he went through India.

F: I think it must have had quite an impact on him.

G: He came home with polio so that had quite a big impact on him.

G [post the reading, talking to camera]: He didn't see a very nice side of India, only the worst bits but he was always telling us the story about going to India and obviously coming home after he had polio – whereby the other soldiers who had polio died and he was the only one that survived.

F: ... he's showing me an image of someone who had lumber punctures or injections into the spine. I know you are in a wheelchair but was that you?

G: Yes.

F: Right. They mucked it up completely.

G [post the reading, talking to camera]: I was diagnosed with MS five years before my hospital visit where I had a major attack. And while I was in intensive care the doctors were trying to tell me I had meningitis whereas I knew I'd got multiple sclerosis. And I told them this, but no they were quite sure that I had meningitis. I was quite angry about it. And I used to tell my dad about this ... this was a real mess-up.

F: Look this is going to sound ever such a strange thing but I've got to say it. Do you have a recurring dream about dancing?

G: Yes I do.

F: He's just told me that he has to tell you: he sees you dance in your dream.

G: Yes I do...

F: That is the only way I can understand it.

G: And skating as well.

F: Like ice skating and like very...

G: Yes.

F: Yes.

G [post the reading, talking to camera]: I get this dream quite frequently that I just stand up out of my wheelchair and I dance, mostly on skates. I did skate as a teenager. And it is so easy and I just glide across the ice.

F: You've got an appointment to see a consultant at the end of June or the beginning of July.

G: Not yet.

F: I can't alter it. I can only tell you what your dad is showing me...

G [post the reading, talking to camera]: Two days later I got two letters from the National Hospital of Neurology that I wasn't expecting, and they were giving me an appointment in June, and another one in August. Alright so that wasn't 'July' but I don't think the NHS ties up with psychic readings.

F: This is ever so strange. Did your dad have strange toes?

G: Do you know, I don't know. I'll have to ask my mother.

F: He's making a joke about, particularly the right foot, not so much the left foot. And all he keeps on showing me is the toes ...

G [post the reading, talking to camera]: I didn't realise my father had strange toes but when I mentioned it to my mother she said yes he did. On both feet the fourth toe sort of grew under the others towards the big toe. I was quite surprised about this because I had never heard of it.

F: Really, really nice guy. I feel he just wanted to come and say hello to you.

G: Okay.

F: And with that I'm going to leave your dad's love with you.

G [post the reading, talking to camera]: I thought the whole reading was wonderful but I was so surprised that he brought up the India connection, the meningitis connection, and the dancing in my dream connection. Blew me away really...

Fry carried out a lot of these filmed one-to-one readings during 2002–2004 and the one's I've seen are very accurate, as endorsed each time by the person on the receiving end.

Making allowances

There is no doubt that mediums vary in their abilities, and the individual medium may vary from day to day regarding what they can tap into when they *open up*. It is also the case that the person trying to communicate from the Other Side may not be all that skilled in the method of communications needed. Some communicators will need, what Fry calls, *enablers* to help them to get their message across. This is someone who knows how thought impressions work in order to do the job. But yet always the pressure is upon the medium, the messenger in this case, to be accurate with everything they say. We have to bear in mind that mediums are people who have, naturally, or by training, fine-tuned their intuition, listening and holistic abilities to receive and interpret telepathic impressions, but who are still very much *over here* within the physical boundaries and limitation of earth life – which means it may not always be so easy to maintain a clear reception with the Other Side.

Indeed, as the radio has already cropped up in one of my comments above, let me draw on it again here, to make an analogy with mediumship. You'll know when tuning a radio you may have to move the dial backwards and forwards until you find the right spot. Sometimes you can think you are in the best spot, as you are getting good reception, but then it begins waxing and waning, even breaking up a bit, and so you nudge the control a little, either way, until you get it nice and clear. It is the same for a medium tuning into the right spot – just off and the link is bitty. Given the limitations of the human condition, I'm surprised there are not more off-station psychics or mediums than there are – or by the same token, it is not surprising how few good ones there are.

I do hope that this *fringe benefits* overview will have given you food for thought, indeed some insight and evidence that there is a lot more going on in life than we may wish to acknowledge from inside our bubble of normality. Importantly, I hope, that this overview has also provided cause for optimism that we too are *a lot more* than the assumed limits of our physical bodies.

Notes & references

[1] Elizabeth Kubler-Ross quote from the Elizabeth Kubler-Ross Foundation http://www.ekrfoundation.org/quotes/ [Accessed 18/01/2013].

[2] Albert Einstein quote from https://www.pinterest.com/pin/390335492679201202/ [Accessed 11/03/2016]

[3] Playfair, G. L. (2007) *This House is Haunted*. The History Press.

[4] Quoted on many websites. Example: http://en.wikiquote.org/wiki/Talk:Bertrand_Russell [Accessed 20/02/2014]

[5] Deborah Hyde, Managing Editor *The Skeptic* magazine. From interview on *This Morning* ITV programme shown 06/02/2012 with Philip Schofield, Janet Winter (formally Hodgson), Guy Lyon Playfair, and Deborah Hyde. Video also on Web entitled, The Enfield Poltergeist.

[6] Maurice Grosse was the main researcher, joined later by Guy Lyon Playfair.

[7] Playfair, G. L. (2007), op. cit.

[8] Ian Gardner quote from http://blog.gaiam.com/quotes/authors/ian-gardner [Accessed 17/02/2012]

[9] Quoted from Goodreads http://www.goodreads.com/quotes/117915-there-are-no-mistakes-no-coincidences-all-events-are-blessings [Accessed 17/02/2012]

[10] Rogo, D. S. (2005) On the Track of the Poltergeist. Anomalist Books.

[11] Geller, U. (2001, 31 December) *When Uri met David*. The Telegraph

[12] Visit website http://en.wikipedia.org/wiki/Enfield_Poltergeist. [Accessed 17/02/2012].

[13] Playfair, G. L. (2007), op. cit.

[14] From interview on This Morning ITV programme shown 06/02/2012 with Philip Schofield, Janet Winter (formally Hodgson), Guy Lyon Playfair, and Deborah Hyde.

[15] Find out more about the Covenanters at http://www.covenanter.org.uk/ [Accessed 18/03/2014]

[16] Stevenson, R. L. (2011-03-30) Edinburgh Picturesque Notes. Kindle Edition.

[17] Henderson, J. A. (2010) *Edinburgh: City of the Dead*. Black and White Publishing.

[18] Quoted from http://www.cityofthedeadtours.com/the-mackenzie-poltergeist/ [Accessed 17/02/2012].

[19] Fortean Times magazine – visit website http://www.forteantimes.com [Accessed 17/02/2012].

[20] Fort, C. (1973) *The Book of the Damned*. Sphere Books Ltd (Abacus paperback series). Note, The Book of The Damned is now in the Public Domain.

[21] Ibid., p 186

[22] Ibid., p 185

[23] Hunter, M. (2005) *New light on the 'Drummer of Tedworth': conflicting narratives of witchcraft in Restoration England*. Birkbeck University of London.

²⁴ Source: History.com. http://www.history.com/topics/halloween/historical-ghost-stories [Accessed 28/09/2014].

²⁵ Ibid.

²⁶ The Ring. Source: Public Domain Poetry. http://www.public-domain-poetry.com/alfred-lord-tennyson/ring-685 [Accessed 20/02/2015]

²⁷ NVRC: Nene Valley Research Committee.

²⁸ Visit http://www.yourghoststories.com/real-ghost-story.php?story=16440 [Accessed 14/10/2013]

²⁹ Check out *RMS Queen Mary* on Wikipedia - http://en.wikipedia.org/wiki/RMS_Queen_Mary [Accessed 08/06/2010] Note, this commentary, taken from June 2010, has since been edited, possibly a number of times. One concern I have with Wikipedia is that any person, or organisation, can present facts, comments, reviews, information, on controversial matters (I'm thinking of fringe topics here), to support an *agenda* that may not be motivated around fair representation but nevertheless is well-written, cross-referenced and meets the otherwise excellent editorial standards.

³⁰ Time Magazine (2008, 30 October) Top 10 Haunted Places http://content.time.com/time/specials/packages/article/0,28804,1855221_1855285_1855252,00.html [Accessed 18/01/2013].

³¹ Jung, C. G. (1972) *Memories, Dreams, Reflections*. Collins Fontana Library.

³² *RMS Queen Mary*, op. cit.

³³ As a tourist you would find it difficult to get anyone to take you to Poveglia from Venice, even though it is just across the water. Such is its reputation. The island has been the focus for many wars from the 9th century onwards and that by itself could account for paranormal activity reported there. But there are many more layers to consider in this matrix. For example the Romans placed their plague victims on the island. Prisoners were also retained on the island over certain periods. There is also the more disturbing news of people dying of bubonic plague being taken to, and left on the island to die. It is believed that upwards of one hundred and sixty thousand people went through this horrible and frightening death and were left to rot with no proper burial – but then who would do such burials? There is also the story of the psychiatric hospital built there in 1922 (abandoned in the 1960s), where a doctor is said to have performed horrific acts on his patients. Any wonder the island gained a dark and sinister reputation for being cursed and why people even today steer clear of it. Interestingly it may have had this reputation for many centuries too. The island had remained uninhabited for a number of centuries when, "in 1527 the doge [Venetian leaders] offered the island to the Camaldolese monks, but they refused the offer," and then in "1661 the descendants of the original inhabitants were offered to reconstruct their village on the island, but they refused to do so." [Quotes from Wikipedia http://en.wikipedia.org/wiki/Poveglia - accessed 16/10/2013].

[34] Van Lommel, Dr P. (2006) *Near-Death Experience, Consciousness, and the Brain: A New Concept About the Continuity of Our Consciousness based on Recent Scientific Research on Near-Death Experience in Survivors of Cardiac Arrest*. World Futures, 62: pp134–151.

[35] Kubler-Ross, E. (1975) *Death: the Final Stage of Growth*. Spectrum Books.

[36] Moody JR, Dr R. (1977) *Life After Life*. Bantam Books.

[37] Paul Eicke NDE story. Visit http://someinspiration.com/bit-of-a-story/nde-story-paul-eicke/ [Accessed 18/01/2013].

[38] Possibly earlier judging by Hieronymus Bosch painting circa 1490, the Ascent of the Blessed which is often cited as depicting the tunnel as seen by people undergoing NDE. Also not forgetting that the spiritual philosopher Emanuel Swedenborg (1688-1772) described out of body experiences that have remarkable parallels with NDE - visit http://www.swedenborg.org.uk/emanuel_swedenborg [Accessed 28/09/2014].

[39] A study by Gregory Shushan who analysed the afterlife beliefs of five ancient civilizations found implications to suggest that the authors of these ancient religious texts were familiar with NDE or similar. He found references to the nine most frequently recurring NDE elements. Shushan, G (2009) Conceptions of the Afterlife in Early Civilizations: Universalism, Constructivism and Near-Death Experience. Continuum.

[40] Weiss, J. E. (1972) *The Vestibule*. Ashley Books Inc.

[41] Richie, G. R. and Sherrill, E. (1978) *Return from Tomorrow*. Revell books.

[42] Moody op. cit. p59

[43] Atwater, P. M. H. (2007) *The Big Book of Near-Death Experiences: The Ultimate Guide to What Happens When We Die*. Hampton Roads Publishing Company. Provides a comprehensive guide to NDEs.

[44] Found on IANDS website - http://iands.org/home.html [Accessed 16/03/2013].

[45] Greyson 16 item NDE Scale. Visit http://iands.org/research/important-research-articles/698-greyson-nde-scale.html [Accessed 27/11/2014] to find out more. Note, this scale was probably also used in Lommel's study; Greyson is referenced but use of the scale is not stated.

[46] Ibid.

[47] Van Lommel, Dr P. (2001) *Near-death experience in survivors of cardiac arrest: a prospective study in the Netherlands*. Find at http://profezie3m.altervista.org/archivio/TheLancet_NDE.htm [Accessed 16/03/2013].

[48] Van Lommel, Dr P. (2006) op. cit., Research and quotations drawn from this article.

[49] Van Lommel, Dr P. (2006) op. cit., Research and quotations drawn from this article.

[50] Parnia, S. et al. (2014) AWARE – AWAreness during Resuscitation – A prospective study. Resuscitation journal.

51 Human Consciousness Project. Check out the Nour Foundation website www.nourfoundation.com also Horizon Research Foundation website www.horizonresearch.org for more information.

52 The study report highlights that of the 2060 only 330 made it to hospital discharge. For various reasons given, of these, 140 survivors completed stage 1 of the interview process, with 101 people going on to completed stage 2 interviews – the other 39 that didn't were suffering mainly from fatigue.

53 Van Lommel, Dr P. (2006) op. cit., Research and quotations drawn from this article.

54 Dr Sam Parnia comment on NDE, on Wikipedia – visit http://en.wikipedia.org/wiki/Near-death_experience [Accessed 11/03/2013].

55 Parnia, Dr S. (2013, July 29) *Back from the Dead: Resuscitation Expert Says End is Reversible.* Der Spiegel Online. Interviewer Marco Evers.

56 Daily Mail newspaper reported this Paul Eicke story on April 19th, 2010.

57 Carol Bowman quote taken from http://www.carolbowman.com/childrens-past-lives/ [Accessed 21/02/2015].

58 Stevenson, Dr I. (2000) *Children Who Remember Previous Lives: A Question of Reincarnation.* McFarland & Company.

59 Leininger, B. A. and Gross, K. (2009). *Soul Survivor.* Hay House.

60 Carol Bowman's website http://www.childpastlives.org/ [Accessed 11/03/2013].

61 Bowman, C. (1998) *Children's Past Lives: How Past Life Memories Affect Your Child.* Bantam.

62 Stevenson, Dr I. (1977) *Cases of the Reincarnation Type, Volume II, Sri Lanka.* University Press of Virginia, pp. 242-243.

63 To get a good account of the history of PLR check out http://en.wikipedia.org/wiki/Past_life_regression [Accessed 11/03/2013].

64 Stevenson Dr I. *Hypnotic Regression to Previous Lives.* University of Virginia, School of Medicine. http://www.medicine.virginia.edu/clinical/departments/psychiatry/sections/cspp/dops/regression-page [Accessed 27/07/2012].

65 The Earth Association for Regression Therapy http://www.earth-association.org/ [Accessed 11/03/2013].

66 The Past Life Therapists Association http://www.pastliferegression.co.uk/pltahome.html

67 Stevenson Dr I. *Hypnotic Regression to Previous Lives.*op.cit.

68 Information drawn from an article by Walter Semkiw MD. *The Xenoglossy Reincarnation Case of Jenson Jacoby | TE. A Physician's Wife Starts Speaking Swedish under Hypnosis.* http://www.iisis.net/index.php?page=semkiw-ian-stevenson-xenglossy-reincarnation-past-lives [Accessed 27/07/2012].

69 Ibid.

70 Information drawn from an article by Walter Semkiw MD. *The Xenoglossy Reincarnation Case of Gretchen Gottlieb/Dolores Jay*

http://www.iisis.net/index.php?page=semkiw-ian-stevenson-xenoglossy-reincarnation-past-lives-gretchen&hl=en_US [Accessed 27/07/2012].

[71] Ibid.

[72] Ibid.

[73] Iverson, J. (1976) *More Lives Than One? The evidence of the remarkable Bloxham Tapes.* Souvenir Press, London.

[74] Lawton, I. (2008) *The Bloxham Tapes Revisited - Why Cryptomnesia is not the Complete Explanation* http://www.ianlawton.com/plr1.htm [Accessed 27/07/2012].

[75] Snow, R. (1999) *Looking for Carroll Beckwith.* St Martin's Press.

[76] Brown, R. (1989) *The Reincarnation of James the Submarine Man.* Rick Brown publisher.

[77] Check out a review Rick Brown. The Reincarnation of James the Submarine Man. Visit http://www.ial.goldthread.com/brown.html [Accessed 11/03/2013].

[78] Society for Psychical Research UK. Web address: http://spr.ac.uk

[79] American Society for Psychical Research. Web address: http://aspr.com

[80] The British Psychological Society. Web address: http://www.bps.org.uk/

[81] Courtesy Colin Fry. Shown on LivingTV (2002-2004) *Sixth Sense with Colin Fry.* Re-shown on Pick TV 2013.

[82] I was saddened by the death of Colin Fry (25th August 2015). He will be missed by a great many people who consider him to have been Britain's most loved spiritual medium. I was fortunate enough to have seen him perform at a number of venues and indeed to briefly chat to him when he visited Evesham in 2014. This was in order to get his blessing on using the one-to-one transcript in this chapter.

CHAPTER 4

OUT OF THE GARDEN

> What is the meaning of human life, or of organic life altogether? To answer this question at all implies a religion. Is there any sense then, you ask, in putting it? I answer, the man who regards his own life and that of his fellow creatures as meaningless is not merely unfortunate but almost disqualified for life.
>
> Albert Einstein, physicist, philosopher[1]

Staying with Einstein's thoughts on the matter, is life, as we know it, really a random chance outcome, the product of blind evolution, a hit or miss affair? Alternatively could there possibly be a plan, an intelligence operating behind it? Are we human beings any different from the rest of the animal kingdom, and if so in what way are we different? And in that context just what did happen, dramatic by evolutionary standards, around fifty thousand or so years ago, that changed our direction and led us to where, and what, we are today?

This chapter will endeavour to answer these questions by taking a look at the development of life, and particularly human development. It'll be raising one or two obvious factors here that we really need to take on-board before buying into the orthodox view of ourselves being simply *animal*, an outcome of evolution, that could just as easily have gone in a different direction. Paradoxically I believe these same factors implicate a bigger purpose lurking in the story of life on Earth which argues that all lifeforms are being urged to head the same way.

The apes aren't building cars or measuring the stars

Not yet at least. It surely goes without saying that all life, animals and plants, hold a crucial place in the scheme of things here on Earth. Indeed, as we know, all contribute to the eco-balance of the planet and help to make it an amazing and magical world to live on. From an environmental and economic viewpoint I'm inclined to see nature a little bit like a market place. There is the law of supply and demand operating here don't you think? What I mean by this is that where there's a niche gap emerging in the system, someone, animal, insect, plant, bacteria, virus will come along, will evolve, to fill it – and beat the competition off where it can.

Let's say there's an opening for a tree to live in cold climates, thousands of feet above sea level, and along comes the evergreen conifer, dividing into varieties to meet different local conditions. Sticking with trees, there's an opening for someone to help break down dead wood lying on the forest floor, and along comes the saprophyte (fungi) to take that job on. Ants do good work to help to improve the nutrients of soil, and support higher levels of the food chain, but where they get over-abundant they can have a negative impact on other insects, due to their predatory, aggressive and territorial behaviour. In Central America this has gotten out of control and there are a number of jobs going, right now, to help steady the ant population. Only anteaters need apply. I think you get my drift. It's not all as simple as that maybe, and I'm not a zoologist or botanist to assume I can make a professional judgement, but then one doesn't have to be that kind of expert to see there is a balancing act going on – often with symbiotic outcomes, with one lifeform helping or benefiting from another directly or indirectly. And let's add that maintaining this situation surely takes intelligence too.

Given this situation, no plant or animal interacts with the world in quite the complex way that we humans do – for better or worse let's say. With our desires, intentions, needs, yes and instincts, interests, natural inquisitiveness, ability to adapt, and the adeptness and creativity of our minds, we stand alone amongst the rest of the flora and fauna of the earth. I'm saying this as an observation rather than an arrogant statement about our place in Nature. Our nearest relative, the chimpanzee, may be our equal in activities we have in common, as in caring for its young. It may be our superior in others, as in its climbing and mobility through trees, and dealing with heights. But no matter how we look at it, the life of a chimp is much simpler than living in our human jungle. Our cousin is likely to be aware of the dangers of living in the wild, and survive in a sometimes riskier environment than we would, yet the chimp is going to be much more accepting and unquestioning of his or her lot than we are. These might be considered qualities of wisdom, but, the point I would make here is that, if it is wisdom, then it is wisdom coming from a *state of innocence.*

Living in innocence

Here let me suggest that, at this time at least, all our fellow plants, animals and insects live in a state of innocence – with varying degrees of consciousness attached. Not having our level of awareness, our ability to reason and make choices, they also do not carry quite the same responsibility for their actions as we do. A lion may hunt and kill in a world of apparent savagery to us but at the bottom line it is simply doing what all lions do. It does the job it is designed for. It fills a niche in the market place as a predator. It kills to live. And because of its power it may also hurt or kill other lions, or be killed by other lions. It could also be killed by other animals bigger and stronger. By the same token, if it kills a human being, by doing its *job*, it has not committed a crime, a murder; simply a kill. In such circumstances we may label it as a *man-eater* and seek to destroy the animal because of what it has done – while of course seeking to protect ourselves against further killings. But there is no guilt involved here, the lion remains in a state of innocence – simply following its natural remit. Okay it may come to like the taste of human flesh, but that would be no different to our deciding we prefer the taste of mackerel to beef.

If we could have a conversation with the lion we know there is the every likelihood that it would not be able to reason that it has done any harm by killing one of us. Rather, if it could reason, it would probably say it was doing what it could to establish its territory, or find food for itself, or help feed its family. Granted it might feel different if it saw us as a friend or family member. It is possible of course that it did it in self-defence, a case of kill or be killed. It is not however the same as a human being killing another human being – whether for self-defence or otherwise. I think we all get this, we, and the rest of the flora and fauna, are not in the same boat.

Well let's suppose we do get this now. Believe it or not, during mediaeval through to the post-mediaeval Europe – and I'm talking up to the 18th-century – we didn't always get this. Animals could be tried and sentenced for crimes just the same as people. Farm animals could be tried for maiming or killing people, in a full-blown criminal court proceeding. Cats could be tried for heresy, deeds of witchcraft, or acts against people, in an ecclesiastical court system. There are records to say even small animals – mice for example – were convicted for eating crops and other dastardly deeds. It was believed that insects that crawled around the ground – such as ants or woodlice – could be easily influenced by daemonic forces, turning them into colonies of vermin.

Much of this madness grew out of a literal translation of the Bible, being embedded into legal practices and culture at the time. Professor of Criminology, Piers Beirne, whose work – *The Law is an Ass: Reading EP Evans*,[2] *The Mediaeval Prosecution and Capital Punishment of Animals* – I draw on considerably here,[3] writes how in mediaeval times the authorities...

> interpreted literally the Hebrew injunction in Exodus that goring oxen should be stoned to death. Additional biblical support for the prosecution of offending animals was found to lie in the

prescription in Genesis (9: 5) that animals are accountable for the shedding of human blood...

In getting across the seriousness of the matter, Beirne also reminds us of the context in which such animal trials took place in Europe – that being within the feudal system with its hierarchical structures of the male God at the top followed by:

> His earthly representatives and interpreters (Church and State), then by the multi-tiered social strata of feudalism, all of which in their respective positions in the human hierarchy sat atop the nonhuman animal kingdom in theirs – primates, quadrupeds, the 'lower' animals and vermin, and vegetative and plant life.

And bizarrely sentencing of guilty animals was rigidly adhered to, following established procedures. These could include, "a reprimanding knock on the head, the curse of an anathema, excommunication or even, in the case of the larger quadrupeds, such as pigs and bulls, capital punishment."[4]

Berne also flags up that while animals seriously injuring or killing a human being could receive capital punishment; it was not so much because of the action in itself, or the likelihood of their doing it again, but because of the implications of the act being against a human being. As the human being was considered closer to God, than any animal, such an act, "threatened to turn upside down the divinely ordained hierarchy of God's creation."[5]

Today we know better – well we should – the animals, insects and vegetable life, are innocent every time. People can still be inhumane and cruel to animals, as we know, but for reasons other than superstition – or maybe not.

Leaving the Garden

Along with elephants and whales, dolphins are considered highly intelligent beings, and, it would seem, by some people's view of them, that they are all of a higher spiritual level and value than we.

Yet for all their intelligence we learn that dolphins (and sea lions) have been trained to work with the military for good or ill.[6] Even, so the story goes, learning to plant bombs onto the hulls of ships. And why not, we might say, for providing they like their friends, which could just as easily be the military as anyone else, they will learn and perform such acts without conscience, or a questioning of the morality of being involved in either protecting humans from other humans, or helping humans harm other humans. They don't appear to discriminate in that way. It seems they can have an affinity with us, and think the best of us, no matter what we might be up to.

I'm arguing then that at this time, apart from ourselves, the flora and fauna of the earth remains in this state of innocence. They are still in the Garden of Eden, or in a state of being unconscious or semiconscious, living by instinct, either pretty much closed or, to a greater or lesser degree, open to individual learning and wakefulness. We, however, are no longer in that same Garden. We know the (Judeo-Christian) Bible version of how we came to leave. And it carries one or two useful clues to our state of being...

From within, the Garden of Eden, God had warned Adam and Eve not to go near the, "tree of knowledge of good and evil," growing in the middle of the garden, for that way lay certain death. We then learn of the serpent that gets in on the act. The serpent has the ear of Eve and encourages her and Adam to eat of the fruit.[7] To fast forward to the punch line of this part of the story; they then do indeed eat the fruit, from, "a tree to be desired to make one wise" (Genesis 3:6), with the result that, "the eyes of them both were opened, and they knew they were naked" (Genesis 3:7).

In the next part of the story God comes walking through the garden calling for Adam. When eventually he finds him, out of his hiding place, Adam says, "I heard thy voice in the garden, and I was afraid because I was naked; and I hid myself" (Genesis 3:10). At this point God asks Adam as to who told him he was naked, and quickly answers his own question, by asking another, "Hast thou eaten of the tree, whereof I commanded thee that thou shouldest not eat?" (Genesis 3:11). Adam owns up to his misdemeanour, that he did indeed eat some of the fruit, but pulls in Eve to take the rap for it. The story culminates with God banishing Adam and Eve from the Garden of Eden with the passing shot of, "cursed is the ground for thy sake; in sorrow shalt thou eat of it all the days of thy life." (Genesis 3:17).

Now conventional Christian wisdom tends to see what happened in the Garden as the beginnings of Original Sin – which we consequently all carry. God placed conditions on Adam and Eve and they broke those conditions. They broke God's trust by taking something they were expressly forbidden from taking. This allegorical story probably has many connotations, including the important relationship between our heavenly home and entering into the physical world, but I want to focus on one that I believe is closer to the reality we exist in, as human beings, and thereby closer to our truth. One of the fundamental driving forces of our existence, and to a great extent the measure of our lives, is our inquisitiveness and appetite for knowledge. We have a need to nourish ourselves, a need to know, a need to find out... Don't tell us not to do something, as we will probably go and do it, sometimes regardless of consequences. Coupled with knowledge though is something bigger, and that is our wakefulness, yes our level of consciousness.

Let me put this to you: What happened for Adam and Eve was, I believe, intended from the outset. It was all in God's plan, if risky. For *serpent* read encouraging inquisitiveness, desire to know, to take risks, to break through boundaries – and to improve on one's lot let's say. Through eating the fruit of the tree of knowledge they left *innocence* behind and became awake, they became conscious. They had always been naked but now they knew they were naked, now they could see their situation. Made of the, "dust of the ground" (Genesis 3:7), they were always going to die and their bodies return to dust, but now, in becoming awake, they knew they would die. And that, I believe, is what is meant when God warned them not to touch or eat the fruit – "lest ye die" (Genesis 3:3). They died that very day as they became awake to their own mortality – and to the duality they, and we, live in. Consciousness comes at a price. A big part of that price is the *knowing*, knowing the difference between right and wrong, light and darkness, between good and evil, knowing our mortality and the implications this has for us. You eat of this *fruit of knowledge* and your innocence dies all right.

It is this *knowing* that now sets us apart from other creatures, and stops us from – as the song goes – "getting back to the Garden." We can't. Actually I'm thinking the Joni Mitchell song is more about getting back to the Garden on a spiritual, conscious level[8] – and to get there in that state we have to go forward at this point. Forward into consciousness that will, I believe, eventually allow us to return to the Garden, but not as inmates, rather as custodians. Either way we can never go back to the innocence our fellow creatures and plants currently live in – we are out of that box for good or ill.

For my money it is consciousness that is at the root of our being different to other creatures on the earth, at this time. It is consciousness that causes us to be no longer a fully paid up member of the animal kingdom. While we may be subject to the same laws of evolution, physical needs and desires as our animal counterparts, for us it is not so written in stone, clear cut and predictable as for most of our cousins. With consciousness comes greater emphasis on individual differences, on uniqueness, on personality and character, on self-awareness and collective responsibility – again not so abundant with other species at present.

Okay, so we can see certain animals, or individuals in species, that jut out from the rest, from the herd. We know apes have some personality, and certainly character, but comparing ourselves with apes, due to our similar genetic makeup, is not in any way a fair comparison. It falls short and probably will do so until the apes are running their own farming communities, living in towns and cities, and talking across the Internet. We need to end this madness of seeking to understand ourselves through dumbing ourselves down, to common denominators with other creatures – measuring ourselves by where we sit with other species in our genetic makeup. Lifting other creatures up to us, discovering how the ape or dolphin might become more awake, now that is going to be a different story…

Life – who'd have thought it?

On the face of it, from an evolutionary and biological standpoint, from the standpoint of our being treated as part of the animal kingdom and survival of the fittest, there is surely no rhyme or reason for us needing to become conscious – or to become this conscious let's say. From an animal perspective there is no obvious need for it for survival. If it was necessary for that purpose alone then we might expect more, or perhaps even most, animals might well be "eating of the fruit" and arriving at a similar state to ourselves. Was it then something that was inevitable on the path we have been travelling or could we say it is just another random chance thing, for want of a better explanation, an oddity, a freak of Nature? Could we not have had pretty good lives just continuing on in a state of innocence – like everyone else? Certainly it was looking like that anyhow for a long while.

When I listen to experts, talking about the evolution of life on our planet, it makes a lot of sense for most of the story – even though it appears to be difficult to pin down just how it all got started. Theories for the origin of life abound but in the round it does look to have arisen precariously. It was a very random and chance happening by all accounts; and in particular, for starters, our planet being in the right location from the Sun with just the right (earth, air, fire and water) essentials for life to occur. From inorganic matter to molecules to nucleic acids, amino acids that became organised into proteins, that then started to reproduce, which – allowing for big gaps and debate on these matters being conveniently bridged or bypassed by my ignorance – eventually, and over a very long period, gave way to single-celled organisms – prokaryotes, or bacteria, and certain types of algae, having no nucleus, to eukaryotes, fungi, and protozoa having a nucleus. These in turn are thought to have kick-started life, with a *capital L*, and thus began the journey into more complex multi-cellular life; and then to the living creatures that we see in the fossil records. This of course happened over a huge period of time – we're talking billions, not millions, of years.

It is estimated that, including simple organisms, there are around ten million animal species and several hundred thousand plant species on the earth.[9] So from all that primordial sludge back then we have all this life-stuff now. Of course the big players mentioned, the bacteria, algae, fungi and protozoa, are still very much with us today. The development of more organised life (animals and plants), as we would recognise it, is thought to have taken up the last fifteen percent or so of time in the development of life – with the development of the big players taking up the bigger eighty-five percent chunk of time.

The Missing Links

The story of how we humans came about begins with... Well that bit is less certain. Often popularised as the *Missing Link*, current thinking anticipates a number of transitional links, or streams that fed into the development of the human form. Primates are the obvious quoted; which can be traced back 65-million years – give or take a million or two. It's a chicken and egg thing though as there is no certainty with current records whether for instance the chimpanzee was our direct ancestor or a cousin of ours from a common ancestor (the latter most probable), so the lineage is not entirely clear and is still being argued out.

Timeline out of Africa

Let's get to something recognisable. Let's go to, what has come to be called, the *Hominidae* family. This is the biological family of which we humans are a registered member, along with the great apes and chimpanzees. In this *hominid* arrangement our more direct ancestors are the *australopithecines* – and it should be added they are now extinct. Knowledge of our links to the australopithecines came about with the help of pioneers, like the anatomist and anthropologist, Raymond Dart and palaeontologist, Robert Broom, from the 1920s into the 1930s. They were followed by Louis and Mary Leakey[10] picking up the ball and running with it, from the Thirties onwards.

Other members of the Leakey family have continued the work up to the present day. The investment put in resulted in the discoveries we have with us today, particularly in the Olduvai Gorge,[11] in Tanzania, where a number of ape-man fossils were found.

Australopithecus africanus was first coined by Dart in 1925,[12] and the root towards bipedal beings, that used tools to some extent, was being established as beginning in Africa. It looks like the australopithecines broke away from other primates around five-million years ago. By around three-million years ago these ape-man creatures are found coming in different shapes and sizes. Homo habilis or "nutcracker man" – evidenced to be short with long arms so more ape-like – is seen as the first to arrive. S/he made simple stone tools. It is followed by Homo erectus (by then being found in Asia, Africa and even Europe). As the name implies, H. erectus was upright. S/he was also a hunter-gatherer. These creatures made use of tools, and there is also evidence that they used fire. H. erectus is considered to be at the root of later adaptions and early human-like forms such as Homo ergaster and Homo heidelbergensis (having a brain capacity almost the same as the human brain capacity). H. ergaster is said to be the more direct ancestor from which Homo neanderthalensis (Neanderthals) and Homo sapiens (or wise man), which is nearly ourselves, is thought to have emerged. This outcome looks to have started anywhere between 2.3-million and 500-thousand years ago – depending upon which source or scheme one draws the timeline from. However, if we consider the recent Homo naledi find in South Africa (possibly 2.5-million-years-old),[13] plus a transitional H. sapiens jawbone found on the Afar rift valley of Ethiopia and dated to 2.8-million-years-old,[14] then the trend could be towards an earlier start for ourselves than previously thought. If so, this could put a spanner in the works of a neat linear system. It could possibly suggest our ancestors may have begun to develop away from their ancient australopithecine links much earlier than previously thought. The question then arises as to whether they might even have been living alongside their australopithecine ancestors. Maybe the transition was less linear and rather more experimental and deviating.

Keeping to what we currently know, it is believed that H. sapiens reached the form that looks like ourselves (anatomical modernity) around 200-thousand years ago. Evidence, from another find in Ethiopia, supports this, indicating that the earliest H. sapiens were there at least 160-thousand years ago – with three fossil skulls recovered from the same Afar region. Some experts had not been so sure that it all started in Africa. Rather it was considered that the australopithecines (eventually giving rise to H. sapiens) were possibly originating in other parts of the world more or less at the same time. This Ethiopia evidence gives, "credence to the theory that modern humans evolved in Africa before spreading around the world." [15] The fossils included two adult males and one child. They were found among stone tools and butchered hippopotamus bones. Cut marks on the skulls suggest an early form of mortuary practice too.

Cro-Magnon, Upper Palaeolithic culture, and Modern Humans

And so the story continues… Things plod along it would seem, from the scant records, for at least another 100-thousand years. But then something very interesting had started to happen, and going by the previous slow fossil record timeline it was rather radical too. Here we are considering around 50-thousand years ago. Enter what's known as *Cro-Magnon man*.

Cro-Magnon[16] is so named because he was first discovered by French geologist Louis Lartet, in 1868, in the caves of Cro-Magnon at Les Eyzies, in the Dordogne area of France. Cro-Magnon belongs in what's known as the European Upper Palaeolithic (old stone age) jutting into the Mesolithic (middle stone age) period – this was during the last Ice Age, the Pleistocene epoch. There is general agreement amongst palaeontologists that Cro-Magnon represents the earliest *Homo sapiens sapiens*, or modern humans, not just in form but now in behaviour too, which of course means that by then, we, as recognisable human beings, had arrived. There is a point to all of this so bear with me.

Increasingly what was found at Cro-Magnon caves was also found to be widespread and became linked to *Aurignacian culture*. This name stems from another site found in France, at Aurignac. We can easily call Cro-Magnons, *Aurignacians*, indeed we do. The term Cro-Magnon has been dropped from being used so much today. The modern term preferred (including divisions and cultures that followed such as *Gravettian* and *Magdalenian*) is *European Early Modern Humans* (EEMH) and therefore to make life easier I'll stick simply to *early modern humans*, as in any case this stretches beyond Europe. These early modern human stone-age, hunter-gatherer cultures lasted for many thousands of years, into the Neolithic period (stone age and beginnings of settled farming) with evidence of their being found in France, Germany, other parts of Europe; and also outside of Europe – in Asia and Africa too.

The early modern human remains found at Cro-Magnon have been radiocarbon dated to 28-thousand-years-old, but elsewhere there are much earlier remains, for example found in Grotta del Cavallo, Italy, going back some 45-thousand years. Our early human ancestors, with their larger brain and ability to think and speak, had arrived. We were back then already very different to the other kids on the block.

Although in the intervening period coming forward our brains have developed further, not necessarily in size, to cope with the enormous pressures we have placed on ourselves – through cultural developments, wars, communications, technological advances, the increase in our populations etc – nevertheless it is argued, at least on the basis of design, that if we could bring these early humans into our modern world then they would be anatomically equally well equipped, for coping and learning to fit into it, as we are.

According to what we understand, our ancestors lived alongside Neanderthals. As mentioned above Neanderthals could be the forebears of early modern humans, or they could be cousins. One view is that the emerging H. sapiens in Africa are thought to have given rise to both early modern humans and also to Neanderthals; although who can really say for sure who came to the party back then. Neanderthals appear, from what finds of theirs have survived, to have been less sophisticated and less adaptive to their environment than our ancestors. They are thought to have died out as a line during the Ice Age – although it is also considered[17] that they and our ancestors may have interbred and genetically, at least, they are still with us today as a percentage of our DNA.

The Awakening

The evolution of humans can not only be seen as the grand total of their wars; it is also defined by the evolution of the human mind and the development of the human consciousness.

Friedrich Durrenmatt, Swiss author/dramatist[18]

But in any case, let us get to what I consider the exciting bit… Our early modern humans were nomads, hunter-gatherers who made their own tools. By then there was nothing special in that development; although they now had access to flint and were able to make more refined tools. They also made use of fire to keep warm and most likely to cook food. Fire was already being used as early as H. erectus for keeping warm, while the design of early H. sapiens teeth suggests there was less need to tear raw flesh – and thereby food was most probably being cooked back then. The early modern humans also buried their dead in rudimentary graves, but which, by that period, was not necessarily new – that had already been done too by Neanderthals if not before.[19] Burying the dead to reduce the attraction of predators and remove bad odours, from one's locality, could be argued a near instinctual reaction and therefore probably started very early in our development, possibly stretching back to australopithecine times. Honouring the dead, and the placing of grave goods, well, it's fair to consider that that would've been a more recent development of the period I am discussing…

Okay, but now stand by for a very new evolutionary factor. This is in the form of art and imagination. Early modern humans culture is known for its *Venus figurines* and other sophisticated developments. These include figurines of extinct mammals such as, "mammoths, rhinoceros and tarpan [or wild horse], along with anthropomorphised depictions that could be inferred as some of the earliest evidence of religion."[20] Suggestion of a musical instrument, a possible ivory flute, has also been found. They clothed themselves in animal skins, used finely made bone needles to sew the skins together. They used beautifully made harpoons to hunt for fish.

> By the beginning of the Upper Palaeolithic period (50,000 BP), full behavioural modernity, including language, music and other cultural universals [i.e., behaviours or traits that occur universally in all cultures, and good candidates for evolutionary adaptations] had developed.
>
> *Human*, Wikipedia[21]

Even more astounding they are attributed with the truly amazing cave paintings of animals, human figures and abstract designs and signs, notably at caves in France and Spain – Lascaux probably being the most famous in France, and Altamira the most famous in Spain. The cave paintings at Lascaux are estimated to be around 20-thousand-years-old, at Altamira up to 34-thousand-years-old. Rock art has also been found in Africa with the *Apollo 11 stones* from Namibia which are thought to be around 28-thousand-years-old. Even older, a piece of, "ochre decorated with a delicate geometric pattern" was unearthed in Blombos Cave on the southern Cape coast. Professor Chris Henshilwood (Cambridge University), who announced the find, dated it, "conservatively at 77-thousand-years-old … and could be as much as 100-thousand-years-old."[22] That could indicate the beginnings of early modern human culture to be much older than the currently accepted time frame. But, even if so, a radical shift was taking place – and this is the real point I'm making.

So what's all this new *human* form, the new model, and the corresponding change and shift in behaviour and culture about? Seemingly from out of nowhere, by geological standards, we have us … modern human beings.

He was not in the least ape-like. On the contrary, he was fully human – only more so. Above average height – the males approached six foot six – he was shown to have a broad high forehead, prominent cheek-bones, and a pronounced firm chin. His skull capacity was above the average for modern Europeans.

Geoffrey Bibby, prehistorian, archaeologist[23]

No one knows for sure why this happened. It is very tempting and easy to brush over it as if a bit of speeded up evolution had taken place, but this was a leap if it was anything. I have a suggestion to make – actually more an argument - but let's explore a bit more first. The paintings found in the caves depict a range of animals from bison, auroch, wild horses, bears, to mammoth, to woolly rhinoceros. See what you think to Herbert Kuhn's description of these paintings – taken from, *On the Track of Prehistoric Man*:

> The bumps on the walls take on movement and life. One of the lumps carries the figure of a standing bison, another swelling bears a beast crumpled up. The prehistory artist has utilized the irregularities of the surface to convey the impression of relief. Thus the pictures are paintings and relief work at one and the same time, and as such are impossible to render well on paper.

Kuhn's description is infectious:

> Here, for instance, is a hind. It measures about four and a half feet long, is masterly in execution. And over there is a bison as if struck by a spear, a remarkable picture, quite unforgettable; it is marvellous to see how the beast sinks its head, its hind legs double up, and its coat shines like that of a living animal, and how the figure stands out and the colours have been applied despite all the difficulties presented by the surface... We are used to thinking of the beginnings of art as stiff and formal – but here we are confronted with paintings that are absolutely natural, which breathe, live and speak.

Herbert Kuhn, prehistorian, archaeologist[24]

Note his comments on paintings that are, "absolutely natural, which breathe, live and speak." Kuhn was clearly impressed and moved by them.

The animal bone carvings, and cave paintings, found in these places were not the result of people just having discovered art, or having time on their hands and little else to do. No there was intention behind the work – probably along the lines of sympathetic magic, suggesting a shamanic culture. Herbert Wendt comments that, "cult and magic played a significant role in the lives of their creators [as] is evident from many of the paintings to be found in these caves. The pictures found in the halls of the Tuc d'Audoubert cave show quite clearly that early hunting tribes had used this place for initiating their adolescent children into adulthood, a custom still practiced by many primitive tribes today..." He continues, "High up in the cavern of the Les Trois Freres cave we find the strange picture of a sorcerer dressed in an animal skin, also indicating that rites of some sort were performed there, probably hunting rites. The manner in which the animals are depicted makes this highly probable: arrows are flying in their direction, their bodies exhibit open wounds, while blood can be seen gushing from a bear's mouth." [25]

Kuhn describing his first impressions of the cave of Font-de-Gaume said:

> ...When you stand in the midst of it, look all around and take in the chamber in its entirety, you are immediately aware that you are in a sacred place, a cult place, where Ice Age man underwent his religious spiritualisation. [26]

All these indicators point to a growing cultural awareness that included, with burial practices, an awareness of the significance of death, and real hints of concerns with honouring the dead.

So, to recap, starting with the australopithecines, our broad timeline has run like this: Enter the australopithecines five million years ago; giving rise to H. sapiens, or early human form, from around three million years. This form continues to around fifty thousand years ago, when we have the arrival of H. sapiens sapiens or European Early Modern Humans (that I abbreviated to *early modern humans*). Up to this point our lineage stretching back all those millions of years has been hunter-gatherers, ape-men, making rudimentary stone tools to do the job. But by around this fifty thousand years mark – okay so possibly twice as long in real terms – there is evidence of a sophisticated human culture and civilisation taking form. Human beings had arrived in what, on a geological and evolutionary time frame, is a sudden leap forward. We should also consider this to be a leap in *wakefulness* or awareness – not just in intelligence, in the survival instinct and manipulation of one's environment, but actual self-awareness had started. What I am getting at is that this was a *leap in consciousness*.

The palaeontologist or the anthropologist seeking more evidence and from further afield, might resist the temptation to get excited about this, but even allowing for gaps in the artefact, or fossil, records across the board – which is hardly surprising given the huge time frame we are talking about here,[27] this was a leap with no precedent in the rest of the animal kingdom. This was a leap that was then built on speedily and one that brought us eventually to our *here and now*. Once it got going, it got going with all the hallmarks of a major evolutionary step forward. This was a step forward that was to take us out of that state of innocence towards awareness and taking responsibility for our actions. We definitely had eaten of the fruit and were out of the Garden of Eden by then.

In our *here and now*, when at our highest and most emancipated – because as we know so well, having all this wakefulness by itself does not necessarily make us angels; on the contrary it is very risky to venture outside of innocence – we find ourselves having effectively risen well above our animal past in how we apply ourselves to the world. Meanwhile, at our lowest we are capable of achieving a depravity that no animal would sink to. Hardly surprising the animal kingdom, on the wild side at least, does not trust us that much.

Why the sudden change?

> Why did humans lose their body hair? Why did they start walking on their hind legs? Why did they develop big brains? I think that the answer to all three questions is sexual selection.
>
> Richard Dawkins, biologist, ethologist[28]

We really need to ask ourselves what brought on this sudden change of direction, this cultural development, this consciousness – what was it, what was behind it? Here are three suggestions that might provide us with a clue:

❖ It was a relative speeding up of evolution, a series of quick steps being made that brought about exponential changes to the early H. sapiens form. It was due to environmental and cultural changes (or maybe as Dawkins describes above), and possibly being pushed along by a number of eureka moments or mistakes, in a process that continues today. We and consciousness therefore happened by accident rather than by any design.

❖ Or our ancestors were visited by a more advanced civilisation – from elsewhere in our Milky Way galaxy. Possibly through genetic modification and/or interbreeding they made changes to the hominid design. The changes ultimately raised new levels of awareness, creativity and application as a result.

❖ Or, this development is something that was, and is always, on the cards. It just needed a little push or opportunity in the right direction to manifest. It is something that all of life is ultimately seeking and struggling for. This is what might be described as *proactive evolution*, or evolution with direction and purpose. The change came at the right time for wakefulness to happen. In spiritual terms, what happened was that the soul, the source, residing in the proto-human form, began to proactively stretch and change the appearance and nature of that form to help awaken it to consciousness. That this process of awakening probably began in earnest from around 200-thousand years ago (with the appearance of H. sapiens), and then leapt forward in the arrival of early modern humans (H. sapiens sapiens) some 100-thousand to 150-thousand years later – around the 50-thousand years mark.

What do you think to these suggestions, for explanation of our lot? I'm guessing, on the face of it, would it be fairly easy to dismiss the latter two suggestions and not dignify them with further consideration? I suspect most of us would plump for the first suggestion as a most likely candidate. It is a practice well-known in science; and in archaeology I did similar. I learnt one always looks for the simplest explanation or solution to a given set of problems or circumstances of how things developed. It's similar to getting to the root of a problem with one's car: You don't start removing the cylinder head and valves when that misfire could simply be caused by spark plugs that have passed their use-by date. Rule the *simple* out only if or when it doesn't fit the solution. And if and when the simple explanation doesn't suffice, then start to look for a more complex, oblique or speculative interpretation and explanation.

> I fully believe we are not alone and have for many years. Even though at the time I went to the Moon it was the conventional wisdom both in science and theology that we were alone in the Universe... We have been visited.
>
> Edgar Mitchell, former Moon landing astronaut[29]

Plumping for the simplest explanation may satisfy our curiosity, and allow us to move on, but does not necessarily mean we've hit on the right answer. Maybe there is a fourth possibility that I don't know about, and have subsequently left out. Even so let us not be so hasty to dump the second and third suggestions here. This is so often our problem with seeking to understand ourselves, we forget where we are. Certain considerations can be immediately scoffed at, discounted, or even seen as ridiculous, because more often than not we have been told, by our upbringing, our culture, what to take seriously and what not to take seriously. It isn't necessarily based upon the clear light of reasoning. We'll often only entertain such *off the wall* suggestions or theories, like being visited by a more advanced civilisation, if they have started to get popular (shades here of Eric von Daniken),[30] out of hand or threaten our established worldview. Well maybe we need our established worldview to be shaken around and updated somewhat.

You may have heard of *Area 51* in Nevada and its links with UFOs. As I understand it, interest in the area began with the revelations by physicist, Bob Lazar, back in the Eighties. I should say, from the bat, that not everyone thinks Lazar is kosher. He is a controversial figure. He claimed he worked in *S4* an additional area associated with Area 51. He says he actually saw a saucer-shaped vehicle in one of the hangars there – even stepped inside it. But let's leave that aside and consider his comments on alien visits. He claims while working at the establishment, as part of his induction, he was expected to read a number of top secret documents. In these documents he read about aliens (popularly known as the *greys* these days) and some of the technology they brought with them. Lazar comments:

> This technology... was brought here by some alien beings from *Zeta Reticuli 1* and 2 star systems. These stars are located in the constellation of *Reticulum*, which can only be seen from the Southern Hemisphere. ... located approximately thirty light years from Earth. These beings said that they had been visiting Earth for a long time and presented photographic evidence which they contended was over 10-thousand-years-old. [They] said that Man was the product of externally corrected evolution. They said that Man as a species had been genetically altered sixty five times. They refer to humans as 'containers' yet I don't know what we're the containers of...
>
> Robert Lazar, Senior Staff Physicist S4 Nevada, 1988-89[31]

I might just add here that the notion of our having had visitations, from Zeta Reticuli, was already being discussed from back in the Sixties; with the very controversial, but believed, abduction story, of

Betty and Barney Hill – that was investigated by J. Allen Hynek.[32] Also the latter query by Lazar here, can, I believe, be easily answered: our bodies are the containers of our *souls*. I'll say more on this in the next chapter. But let's deal with his main comments here: is this too bizarre to believe?

Could it have been the folk from Zeta Reticuli who helped to bring us on into the human form? When placed in context, with our *nine to five* normality, it all sounds crackers, I'll grant you, but before we bin this possibility let us again just remind ourselves of where we are. You and I are living on a planet that even a hundred years ago was a very different place. Can you imagine, with the speed of development in our sciences and technology, that in, say, a thousand years from now (it could be a lot less time) we might be visiting some distant planet and be genetically modifying life there ourselves – helping it to advance forward in its development and wakefulness? Is it really that impossible to conceive? Is it really that bizarre to consider that life from elsewhere, more advanced than us, could have been visiting us, from many thousands of years ago, perhaps much longer, with a similar intention – and very possibly are still visiting us, even living amongst us today? I'll hold my hand up and say that I buy into the latter two bulleted suggestions as more likely explanations for our development. Either we brought about our development, as conscious beings, entirely through our own (soul) volition or else we got some outside help, some intervention to help the process along.

If we approach getting to grips with this sudden evolutionary change from the more orthodox view, we will have to reason that somehow the rise of consciousness was a natural, even freakish, evolutionary step that mankind made; being born out of survival in the wild. Consciousness is born out of vulnerable people having to scavenge for food, or work together to hunt huge animals for food, and also eke out shelter. We might give good argument for the benefits of our wakefulness once we have it. For example, an increased perception on things, our being in a better position to plan ahead, to be proactive, anticipate consequences of our actions, carry through pre-emptive strikes on our game or enemy, being more cunning, more manipulative of our environment. But this argument is not all that unfamiliar to existing predatory species that hunt in packs. It reduces the potential of consciousness back to the near-instinctual and I have to say such an explanation only beggars the question again – was consciousness all that necessary a requirement? Aren't all, or most, other creatures getting by perfectly well without the level of consciousness we have acquired? Do baboons or crocodiles have it? Bears can spend time in caves so why aren't they drawing pictures? Is it just a lack of motivation or something else?

If we could but counsel the rest of the animal kingdom, and for that matter the plant kingdom, on this matter, and ask them would they take on *being conscious* if they could have it, with all that this entails either way, would we get a resounding *Yes* or a *No way*? At this point I suspect we would get the latter. I mean what animal in their right mind would want to be awake to all this scary life stuff? It would mean being awake to having to make individual sense of life – and rely less on one's instinct. It would involve having a sense of *self*. It would involve having to find reasons for why one gets up in the morning. It would involve making sense out of the forces in nature, also naming things, having thoughts and feelings, having memories – where we are directly involved or as an onlooker – having responsibilities, or feeling a sense of love or hatred towards others in one's species. It would involve being aware of one's own limitations and mortality, and having to earn money and start paying taxes. Ah well, when it's put like that. "No," they'd say, "leave us in the state we are already in, and let it all happen when it happens." I sometimes think that a lot of us would also like to return to that innocence, indeed do our damndest to get back there, but for all the wrong reasons.

So, joking aside, why, I might ask, isn't consciousness one of the building blocks of nature? Well this is where I am playing a sort of *devil's advocate* for I believe it is, and more besides, but it is dependent on conditions arising to allow or coax it to happen within lifeforms. In context with time everything appears on a slow burn.

Some of what is going on isn't necessarily that obvious or visible for that matter – I believe it is operating, at what I would call, a *soul level*.

Intelligence and consciousness

We perhaps need to make a distinction between intelligence and consciousness at this point. Defining intelligence is a bit of a minefield and one that, for the most part, I intend to steer clear of here, as I wish to stay within a more general description, or definition, to suit my purpose. But before going onto that let me at least give you a flavour of the debate. And before I do, I should say that the definition of intelligence being described here is really a definition of human intelligence.

The traditional or general definition of intelligence is based upon the view that *verbal-linguistic* and *logical-mathematical* abilities – being good at words, languages, logic, abstractions, reasoning, numbers and critical thinking – are the gauge by which we measure intelligence. These are seen as the abilities we need for making headway in the world, and especially to do well in our education. Need it be said though that not all of us have this edgy *out of the blocks* intelligence on the *get-go*. Some of us, at least, are less well-equipped for travelling at speed from the bat. So does this mean we are less intelligent? Arguably some of us just take that bit longer to gather and apply our intelligence in order to get there. But could it be that those of us in that position are possibly better suited to applying our intelligence differently? Could it be that possibly we operate from a different kind of intelligence? Back in 1983 the American psychologist, Howard Gardner (with his book, *Frames of Mind: The Theory of Multiple Intelligence*[33]), challenged the old definition when he proposed up to seven types of intelligence. These being: the Verbal-linguistic and Logical-mathematical of the conventional view, plus *Visual-spatial* (spatial judgment and the ability to visualize with the mind's eye), *Musical* (having a sensitivity to sounds, composition, rhythms, tones, and music), *Bodily-kinaesthetic* (body awareness, control of one's bodily motions as in gymnastics/athletics, and the capacity to handle objects skilfully), *Interpersonal-social* (sensitivity towards others – their moods, feelings, temperaments and motivations, and ease of cooperation), and *Intrapersonal* (capacity for introspection and being self-reflective). He later (1995) added *Naturalist* (having a good, and productive, handle on the flora and fauna or on one's natural surroundings) to this list. His argument being intelligence can vary by context: "It's not how smart you are but how you are smart." And we each have a propensity to apply our smartness in what best suits us.

The criticism of this *multiple intelligences* approach is that it is more a list of abilities and of aptitude than intelligence. This list could be added to as we consider other possible avenues of application, and we are then obliged to include those – such as *Existential* and *Moral* intelligences, which have since been included. The proponents of multiple intelligences, on the other hand, argue the traditional definition of intelligence is too narrow – which I would agree with. And the debate continues...

Leaving this debate to one side, I want to talk about a broader intelligence, to make a distinction with consciousness. As I see it *intelligence* is in abundance from the lowest to the highest lifeforms. I'm sure you would agree that Nature, as we lump all life together, is astoundingly intelligent. For the most part this intelligence and design is placed at the level of the instinctual, the visceral, operating at the level of the unconscious or semiconscious, whereby a given individual plant or animal seeks to fulfil itself without necessarily needing to know much about what it is up to. Its needs, activities and routine are more organically mapped out. It uses its design, and the tools that came with the package, without much need to think about it. A moth, for example, doesn't need to be told or taught it can fly – that comes with the package. The spider doesn't need lessons or a manual on how to build a web – it has its own online manual inside its genetic makeup. The more complex the lifeform the more there is needed the opportunity to *learn* – such as cubs and chicks learning from their parents for example. But all of this is intelligence, learning the ropes the old tried and trusted ways. It can, and perhaps will, lead to consciousness, becoming awake, but it is not consciousness in itself.

Let us, for example, look at another species for a moment – one that is often alluded to, with regard to our own behaviour. We can study the evolution and behaviour of wolves, how they developed out of early carnivores, the *Miacidae*, some 50-million years ago. The *Miacids* are seen as the ancestors of wolves, coyote, dogs and foxes. By comparison to the great time of development, the grey wolf itself has only been around for about a million years. We can look at how they hunt in packs of up to forty in number, how they each have a strict social order, with an *alpha* leader (male or female) who is recognised by their aggressive and dominant behaviour, and, at the other end of the chain, the more timid *omega* wolf who effectively takes a lot of flak, but acts as a safety-valve for the pack, for release of aggression – keeping it *within the family* so to speak. We can learn how wolves live for only a few years in the wild (up to ten years, and longer in captivity) and how they may travel great distances hunting for food.

We might well make comparisons of some of our findings to our human behaviour and describe how we too tend to live like wolves. We live gregariously in groups, in our towns and cities, have our alpha leaders and have people at the other end of the scale who, unfortunately, take a lot of omega abuse. We may consider that we experience this type of relationship more prominently in our working lives, or perhaps in context with the customs, policies and rulership of the given country we live in.

But given we have explored and compared all the aspects of being a wolf and being a human being, we would fall a long way short if we were coming to a conclusion that the drivers behind the behaviour of wolves are the same, or similar, drivers operating behind our own culture and civilisation. We are hugely more complex. At our best we care. We care not only for our young but for our disabled, sick and elderly. At our best we make choices about who we work with, and what country we live in. At our best we are emancipated, free to participate or not participate. At our best we create – we write music, books, draw and paint pictures, build skyscrapers, roads, cars, ships, spaceships and aeroplanes. At our best we are not pack animals but individuals making choices (not always conscious) regarding our collective participation, and regarding who we live with and befriend. It is indeed our differences, our diversity that is our strength. At our best we are coming to realise we have a duty of care for each other and our world.

There is much debate regarding the whole issue of consciousness, of what it is and its levels, amongst philosophers and psychologists. For my purpose I'm discussing this in context with soul, and more so with spiritual endeavour and awakening as this book unfolds, but I'm wishing to keep this simple at this point, as consciousness is something we humans all experience to a greater or lesser extent – and, I believe, we all have to capacity towards the *greater*. Right now I am writing this piece of text and am aware that I am doing so – aware of being in the act of writing, and for that matter what I am saying. If you are right now reading it, you are now, with my mentioning it, aware that you are in the act of reading it. You will have learnt to read and make sense of what you are reading. You, like me, will no doubt find you can easily switch your attention to other things happening in your immediate environment, be aware of what is around you (even possibly at subtle levels) and how you feel in context. You can switch your attention to other concerns, think about matters, easily reflect on the past seven days and probably, using your imagination, be able to anticipate some aspects of what the coming next seven days will bring – possibly even what the next year will bring, or you hope, or plan, it will bring. Using your imagination, you will be capable of thinking laterally, outside the box, putting yourself in another person's shoes perhaps. You are a member of the human species but you are also an individual and unique, in your own right and potential – you are awake or in the process of awakening.

Well I'm still writing and right now I'm considering just how awesome this life stuff is – that here we are amongst the myriad lifeforms that surround us. It really is so easy to be blind to what is actually staring us in the face. I've talked about people experiencing events that we in turn describe as paranormal, but if we step outside of our constructs, on normality, for a moment we might consider the whole caboodle is paranormal, or amazing, beautiful and strange. None of it should really be taken for granted. This is part of our awakening, to become awake to this strange situation we may now find ourselves in and need to make sense of.

Of Sludge and Slime

One of the reasons we fail to see how strange our existence really is, is because of time. The changes we are considering here, in evolutionary terms, with the flora and fauna, have taken a long time to be arrived at, and this comparatively slow process masks what profound changes have actually been taking place. If we were to squeeze time down though, so that the journey of life out of effectively nothing to ourselves took say a thousand years, we would see starkly the magic that has unfolded. Just because it has all been done in slow motion doesn't make it any less profound. Another reason, for failing to see the wonders around us, is of course because we live in it every day; we've grown up in it; we're used to it, and more so we can easily take it all for granted – so something along the lines of *familiarity breeds contempt*? Well not quite, in my mind it is more a case of *familiarity breeds normality*.

We have to be careful though not to presume that, *Add a drop of water to sludge and slime + right conditions x time = human beings, mice or elephants,* "just like that." (as the late UK comedian, Tommy Cooper, would say), and that somehow knowing the equation itself has it covered, with no further explanation really needed – and with that knowledge we are free to go back to sleep or continue on with our busy lives. What I mean here is that we use the word, *evolution* or the description, *evolution of a species* as if by using it, we somehow conjure an explanation for the origins, the process and objectives of a given species. It's a bit like we use the word *gravity* to explain why things fall back to the earth, and because we all know what the word implies, somehow that is enough, in itself, to explain what gravity is – when we know it really isn't. We're only naming a law, a force, dealing with matter attracting other matter, that is ever present in our lives, and one that we can describe and predict but that we have yet to fully understand. For instance are there different types of gravity – such as the gravity of matter and the gravity of sub-atomic particles? What is the relationship of gravity with electromagnetism and nuclear forces – is it all the same? Is anti-gravity possible by shifting the polarity of an object or vessel to being the same as the earth's pole – as can be simply demonstrated by using two magnets and their like poles repelling each other? Is gravity in any way linked to the Law of Attraction, a different kind of pulling power – in resonance or vibration? Questions like these might be asked – and hopefully answered.

With *evolution*, comments or descriptions such as *nature red in tooth and claw*, the *survival of the fittest*, *natural selection*, all help to clarify some of the process and possible immediate objectives in the flora and fauna, but it falls a long way short of telling us what it is all about. Why are we, this life stuff, doing this? We've given the life process a name, to explain what we observe, and while we may be able to throw up a chart, a genealogical tree to explain how dogs developed from the grey wolf, or to demonstrate that the horse shares a common ancestry with tapirs and rhinoceroses, we are only tracking the *how* it is happening but not the *why* it is happening – other than, in fairness, explaining the short steps of the process itself.

> Because it is possible to trace evolutionary paths, sometimes in surprising detail, it is difficult to avoid sensing an underlying purpose in the history of life. Nearly all specialists on evolution resolutely turn their backs on what is effectively a religious question, but it may be possible to find some sort of middle ground...
>
> Simon Conway Morris, palaeontologist[34]

Could we but contemplate Morris's "middle ground" we might discover something important in our assumptions. Who was it who said; "Creating all of this flora and fauna out of random chance selection is like throwing bricks and mortar out of an aeroplane and expecting them to have landed as a building?" Well, no matter who it was, the implication is that there has to be more to this than random chance occurrence at play. In context *evolution* as conventionally applied does not provide an answer. Think on this: Evolution as a study does not provide any explanation for the origins of life. It allows us to observe mutations and adaptions in creatures and allows us to comment on how this or that development took place in order for a given species to survive and prosper, within its environment, but it ignores any aspect of what we might call, *proactive evolution* – evolution with direction. Any suggestion of intelligent purpose, intentional progress or, heaven forbade, *design*, to creep into the equation is *not on* as that could invoke a *designer* and that will almost inevitably lead us into the supernatural – and a potentially huge problem for the *mechanistic paradigm* upon which so much of our science hangs.

Evolution, as we conventionally view it, is blind. It doesn't predict beginnings, directions or end points, rather it describes what is immediate or mostly deemed necessary to survival. For example, following the discovery of the archaeopteryx, proto-bird, it is now accepted that some dinosaurs of the Jurassic and Cretaceous periods developed feathers, which were used later for flight, as they became birds. The reason they developed feathers is explained, by palaeontologists, in terms of being developed for insulation (for warmth) and only later then adapted to flight. The argument here being that lots of birds have feathers and yet don't fly or spend much of their time off the ground (the chicken, the ostrich or indeed the penguin being prime examples) and feathers keep you warm. But what if *flight* itself was an intended evolutionary path for some dinosaurs, an entering into a niche market, and feathers were developed in advance of that shift? Would that be *by design* rather than *reaction to* the need for survival, creeping in? Just imagine that moment, that shift, when someone thought they could spread their wings and fly. Was that a moment of consciousness, on behalf of a very brave dinosaur, a case of, "Let's give it a go," off the top of a conifer, or did it come with (at the time), the latest update or package? Was there already in place, in Nature, if you will, an intention to get off the ground?

Accepting evolution at the level of *process* allows us to stay within the scientific remit of reporting on what we can trust through our observations rather than constructing theory that cannot be substantiated. I fully get this from archaeological excavations. On prehistoric (Neolithic, Bronze and Iron Age) excavations for example, with less evidence surviving and no records or history to draw from – apart from comparative sites where similar structures or artefacts may have been found – one comes to rely on one's detective abilities, one's knowledge and imagination to fill in the gaps in the unfolding story. While it is very tempting then to follow through with what one has construed, it is a different matter when getting down to the nitty-gritty of reporting on one's findings. At that point the ideas or suggestions arrived at (unless they can be substantiated), will take a backseat and what is observed, and can be established with some certainty, is what is written up. It is then left to others to draw comparisons and interpret as more evidence comes to light from similar excavations – and a reliable picture can then begin to emerge. This serves, in other words to sticking to what we can know for sure rather than, as in this case, flights of fancy - literally.

I'd suggest it is the same with talking of *evolution*. But given we can observe and know, or have a good stab at the *how*, regarding how certain developments have taken place, how some lifeforms get from A to B – whether by legs, by tail, by flight or by car – one cannot ignore returning to the philosophical *why* and invoking an obvious question such as: Why the big urgency about life? Why are all these species going to so much bother to adapt and survive – for what purpose? Is it simply to survive, to reproduce and protect offspring so that the offspring can adapt and survive and in turn reproduce and protect their offspring, who it turn adapt and survive to reproduce and protect their offspring, like an endless treadmill? If so, it is sort of meaningless isn't it? Good reason, of course, for lifeforms not being too awake to what they are up to. Anyhow, this explanation doesn't really answer it for me – well certainly not in every case, ourselves in particular. As I see it that's only keeping the kettle boiling and I'm left asking the same question in the round.

All the fauna and flora on the planet want to survive and thrive. Is it so daft to ask, why this is so. Okay, is it all so obvious that we shouldn't really need to ask? If we do ask we probably need to be careful of who we ask, as asking the wrong person puts us in danger of cycling back to the ready answer of, "That's evolution for you," which only leads to everything explained in terms we all think we understand – like *gravity*.

Well not being in the straitjacket required for scientific reporting let me forward an idea for the suggestion box: I think we, and the rest of the fauna and flora, are up to something – and it is more than just adapting and procreating. It is something big that draws on the collective intelligence of life. It does, I believe, have direction and an end game. It is evolution with direction that hooks into *consciousness*. It is exciting, profound and its implications huge. It ties in with my discussion on *The Soul Question* in the next chapter.

Notes & references

[1] Einstein, A. (2006) *The World as I See It*. Citadel Press Books

[2] Evans, E. P. (1906)(1987) *The Criminal Prosecution and Capital Punishment of Animals*. London: Faber & Faber. Beirne based much of his discussion on this book and Evans writing in general.

[3] Beirne, P. (1994) *The Law is an Ass: Reading E P Evans, The Mediaeval Prosecution and Capital Punishment of Animals*. Society and Animals, Vol 2., No1. The White Horse Press, Cambridge UK

[4] Ibid., p31.

[5] Ibid., p30.

[6] United States Navy Marine Mammal Program. Find on https://en.wikipedia.org/wiki/United_States_Navy_Marine_Mammal_Program [Accessed 11/05/2014].

[7] Have you ever asked yourself how we first came to know we can eat the foodstuffs we eat? It occurs to me that in some ways this story is allegorical for the risks and

possible dire consequences our ancestors may have experienced when first testing out plants and fruit as sources of food. Arguably there are not too many plants (like Hemlock) and fruits (like the little apple of death) on the planet that would kill us off on a small testing mouthful, but it is still amazing that in each case someone took the risk to find out.

[8] Song, *Woodstock* by Joni Mitchell.

[9] Sweetlove, L. (2011, August 24) Number of species on Earth tagged at 8.7 million. Nature journal. http://www.nature.com/news/2011/110823/full/news.2011.498.html [Accessed 15/10/2011].

[10] Leakey, L. S. B. (1960) Adam's Ancestors: The Evolution of Man and His Culture. Harper & Row.

[11] Find out more via The Olduvai Gorge Research Project - http://www.olduvaiproject.org/ [Accessed 07/10/2014].

[12] Dart, R. A. (1925, February 7) Australopithecus Africanus: The Man-Ape of South Africa. Nature journal. See also Dart, R A (1982) Adventures With the Missing Link. Better Baby Pr.

[13] Homo naledi is estimated to be 2.5 million years old - visit https://en.wikipedia.org/wiki/Homo_naledi [Accessed 12/09/2015].

[14] Wu, B (2015 5th March) The Science Times http://www.sciencetimes.com/articles/3687/20150305/ancient-human-jaw-bone-evidence-earlier-evolution.htm [Accessed 06/03/2015].

[15] National Geographic http://news.nationalgeographic.com/news/2003/06/0611_030611_earliesthuman.html [Accessed 11/05/2014].

[16] Cro-Magnon. Visit Wikipedia for more information. http://en.wikipedia.org/wiki/Cro-Magnon [Accessed 11/05/2014].

[17] Neanderthal culture on Wikipedia - http://en.wikipedia.org/wiki/Neanderthal [Accessed 11/05/2014].

[18] Friedrich Durrenmatt quote on BrainyQuote - http://www.brainyquote.com/quotes/quotes/f/friedrichd404245.html [Accessed 11/05/2014].

[19] Burial practices, on Wikipedia - http://en.wikipedia.org/wiki/Burial [Accessed 11/05/2014].

[20] Aurignacian culture on Wikipedia - http://en.wikipedia.org/wiki/Aurignacian [Accessed 11/05/2014].

[21] Human. Visit Wikipedia for more information. https://en.wikipedia.org/wiki/Human

[22] Chris Henshilwood – see http://www.bradshawfoundation.com/africa/oldest_art/index.php [Accessed 11/05/2014].

[23] Bibby, G. (1956) *The Testimony of The Spade*. Alfred A. Knopf.

[24] Kuhn, H. (1958) *On the Track of Prehistoric Man*. Arrow Books.

[25] Wendt, H. (1972) *From Ape to Adam*. Omega. pp 110-111.

[26] Ibid., p106.

[27] The author has excavated Neolithic sites, going back only some five-thousand years, and has been pleased to get even scant returns of artefacts.

[28] Holt, J. (2004, 1 December) *The Man Behind the Meme: An Interview with Richard Dawkins*. Source: A Good Atheist Secularist Skeptical Book Collection.

[29] Edgar Mitchell quoted from (2013) *Former Astronaut Explains The UFO Cover-up*. YouTube video https://www.youtube.com/watch?v=7AAJ34_NMcI#t=333 [Accessed 26/10/2014]

[30] Erich von Däniken is a Swiss author of several books which make controversial claims about extra-terrestrial influences on early human culture. They include the best-selling Chariots of the Gods? published in 1968. Von Däniken is one of the main figures responsible for popularizing the 'paleo-contact' and ancient astronauts hypotheses. The ideas put forth in his books are largely rejected by scientists and academics, who categorize his work as pseudohistory and pseudoarchaeology. Notes from Wikipedia [Accessed 11/05/2014].

[31] Lazar R,(2010, 20 November) *UFOs & Area 51 - The Official Bob Lazar Video - Alien Technology Revealed*. UFOTV® The Disclosure Movie Network https://www.youtube.com/watch?v=IJolFbj8nc4. This is a remake of an earlier film.

[32] Hynek, J.A. (1972) The UFO Experience: A Scientific Inquiry. Henry Regnery Company. ISBN 0-8094-8054-9.

[33] Gardner, H. (1993) Frames Of Mind: The Theory Of Multiple Intelligences. Basic Books (first published 1983).

[34] Morris, S. C. (1996) *The History in Our Bones*. BBC Education.

CHAPTER 5

THE SOUL QUESTION

Does such a thing as the soul exist? If so what is its nature and where is it? And further, if given each one of us has, or is, a soul, what does that mean in context with life and death?

For this chapter I will be drawing on orthodox Christian and esoteric (Theosophical and Rosicrucian) perspectives on the soul, and equally how the soul ties in with the concept of *karma*. The chapter challenges, what I believe to be, misconceptions regarding what the soul is, and its place in our lives. Or, as I will argue, it is not so much about *place* as the fact we are souls, and finding our way through the situations we generate. The focus here is on providing an answer (or answers) to the soul question – which is then expanded upon in the remainder of the book.

I've chosen to draw on Christianity, in general and Roman Catholicism in particular, for reasons that it is the religion I have most experience of, that also holds with the existence of the soul. Also, for it being the largest of the Abrahamic group of religions, it shares common ground, and overlaps, with Judaism, Islam and Bahá'í faiths. It is this group however that I also have most concerns with regarding some of the accepted beliefs about soul, and life and death. In writing about karma, this chapter also inevitably touches more broadly on Eastern beliefs too.

The Soul and Christian teachings

Here's a short poem, **Timeline**, to get the ball rolling:

One grows and grows
Until another knows
And grows alongside
On lines
That twist and curl
Accelerate vertical and parallel
Then eventually divide
And fade into dashes
And fade into ashes

I wrote *Timeline* back in my early twenties. I've put it in here because it reflects a time when I had become very disillusioned with my Christian upbringing and religion in general. You can probably pick up the cold starkness in my words. They were an honest reflection of what I believed. I had reduced life down to a simple nihilistic, and for that matter geometrical, observation.

I'm not in that same place now – as, I trust, is coming across in this book. Let's say there has been too much challenging water under the bridge. Back then I saw death as final and hadn't considered what might be on the other side of those "ashes" – a *phoenix* perhaps? Nor had I given any consideration to what part of me (even if there was such a part), that could possibly survive such an event. Yes I had learned, with my upbringing, that I was supposed to have a soul but I had no real idea as to what this was or where located – was it in my head, my heart, the soles of my feet? Rather I drew on the obvious: a "fade into ashes," to which line I could have added a *full-stop* terminal, intended to serve as more than simple punctuation. I didn't, in other words, really believe there was such a thing as a soul. This disbelief in there being a soul, or its immortality, of course remains true for a great number of us. We see endings happening to each other and, likewise, to all forms of life on our planet. If we rely solely on the physical evidence, it is pretty conclusive and far easier (certainly in our more advanced and sophisticated cultures), to believe there is nothing beyond death than to believe there is some kind of continuity.

Given this position, I think you'd probably agree, that it can take a bit of a leap of faith (especially if we haven't really experienced or explored supportive evidence) for us to go against the tide and believe we could survive death after all. Of course those of us sticking with a more secular or humanistic view of death, will explain away such *faith* as somewhat misguided, naïve, as conjured up to meet our need for some kind of comforting explanation to help us face what is an inevitable end.

> I regard the brain as a computer which will stop working when its components fail. There is no heaven or afterlife for broken down computers; that is a fairy story for people afraid of the dark.
>
> Stephen Hawking, physicist, cosmologist[1]

The conventional alternative, for probably the majority of us, is that we turn to religion in the hope of getting sustenance, clarity and answers on the matter of soul, and, of course life and death. It is what it is there for. We know our great religions encompass faith in life after death without question. Yes well, but here's the thing, what I partly mean by saying this is that there is often little or no questioning of the wisdom presented. Rather we are inducted into what is given as fact to us, usually at a young age, and with wildly differing interpretation regarding what we are, where we go or don't go, and what it's like after we die.

Look, let me lay this route to understanding on the line for your consideration: Anyone, like myself, raised as a Christian, but who has not questioned or explored spiritual issues for themselves, is reliant on church doctrine for their knowledge and, as a result, will have come to rely on beliefs and explanations that are, through centuries of tinkering, difficult for some educated minds to now accept and swallow. From where I stand these are indeed shot through with myth, distortion and inaccuracies. One necessarily buys into a virgin birth and the life and times of a spiritual man, who because of how he was born, to Mary, was nothing like that ordinary guy next door – I'm thinking of the Monty Python movie, *Life of Brian*[2] – but the son, indeed, we are informed, the only begotten son, of God. This leaves the rest of us outside in the cold of this special relationship. We are of course also born sinners, through our links with Adam and Eve, and, of consequence, deemed not worthy of such a relationship with God.

An outcome of this near non-relationship is that, accepting this viewpoint and judgement, we are very dependent on the Church as the go-between for our eventual salvation – through its lineage and links with Jesus, and having the ear with God. Of course, while the Church describes Jesus as the, "Son of God," it is important to note that if Jesus called himself anything, it was the, "Son of Man" (Mark 2:10, Matthew 26:63-64), which has a very different connotation altogether, in my book, regarding how he viewed his own identity. It opens the situation up to other interpretation, other possibilities, that could include all of us – a point that I will pick up on again when discussing the views of Origen, one early Christian Father, below.

Body and Soul intertwined

Christianity, and Abrahamic doctrine generally, has had a huge influence on our being aware of, and accepting the concept of the soul – for which it should be applauded. Equally as important, but possibly less well known or fully considered, it has influenced how the soul and physical body are seen to be related or intertwined, resulting in, what I argue, is a disturbing and even frightening scenario for those that buy into it.

What I am talking of here is the belief, in its various forms, in the resurrection of the physical body. As indicated, this is not just peculiar to Christianity but, in differing forms, across the Abrahamic belief systems. In the Christian tradition this concept is now a well-established foundation stone and without any *get-out clause*. Particularly, this is the case following the story of the events after Jesus's death – as given to us by the gospels.[3] Let me briefly take you through it.

The narrative goes (in all four gospels) that Joseph of Arimathea took charge of Jesus' body and placed it in a tomb, hewn out of solid rock. A large boulder was placed at the entrance to this tomb. Now crucial to how this story is played out, we are informed that Jesus had told his disciples that, after three days, he would rise again from the dead. The authorities, who had condemned him, were also aware of this and were concerned that neither he, nor anyone else for that matter, would be in a position to enable Jesus to carry out this threat. For obviously should he do so it would be an embarrassment, proving he probably was what was claimed of him. Matthew (28:62-64)[4] records:

> ...the chief priests and Pharisees came together unto Pilate, saying, Sir, we remember that that deceiver said, while he was yet alive, 'After three days I will rise again.' Command therefore that the sepulchre be made sure until the third day, lest his disciples come by night, and steal him away, and say unto the people, 'He is risen from the dead,' so the last error shall be worse than the first.

To avoid such a catastrophe Pilate consequently had the tomb sealed and guarded, so no one could get in or out. Cometh the third day, we learn one, or two (depending upon source), angels do however intervene to alter the balance of this situation. In Matthew's version (28:2) one angel arrives as an earth tremor; scares the pants off the guards, rolls back the stone and sits on it. When Mary Magdalene then visits with Mary (who we know to be the mother of Jesus, and also arguably mother of James, Joses, Judas, Simon, and also unnamed sisters – Mark 6:3), and Salome (Mark 16:1-2) to bring spices for the body, the angel tells them that Jesus is not there – that he has been, "raised" (Mark 16:6-7). The angel invites them to take a look and then tells them to pass this news onto his disciples.

According to John (20:1-18), this bit is different as Mary Magdalene appears to visit the tomb by herself. The stone covering the entrance had been rolled back. Inside, the body had gone. She next runs to Simon Peter, who's with a second disciple, and she tells them. They ask why she is crying, and she replies, "They have taken my Lord away, and I do not know where they have put him." The three then run over to check the tomb. Sure enough all that they find is the linen wrapping, and a cloth that had been wrapped around Jesus's head. The disciples go away at this point and Mary is left by herself, crying outside the tomb. She then sees two angels who ask her why she is crying – and she tells them. She then turns around to see the silhouette of another figure standing there, who similarly quizzes her regarding why she is crying. She initially thinks this person is the gardener and asks what he has done with the body. But then she discovers it is actually Jesus. I imagine, if an accurate account, that it would have been a very poignant and powerful moment for her, for sure – no doubt a life changing event.

At this point Mary goes to embrace Jesus but he tells her not to. The reason given is because he says, "I have not yet gone back up to the Father." This doesn't make a lot of obvious sense, but I read it that he was telling Mary he was appearing to her but not in physical form, rather in etheric form, and she frankly would have held onto nothing physical had she tried.[5] After seeing Jesus, Mary next goes off to tell his disciples of her experience.

Now in context with the events described we might want to take note of two things here: Firstly the story suggests that at least one of us (collectively speaking that is) has survived death – even if, from the Christian viewpoint, Jesus wasn't one of us, he certainly lived in human form. Secondly the missing body from the tomb, served to evidence Jesus had done what he said he would do. The physical body had to be out of the tomb to prove that he had *risen*.

And this is how the story, from the Christian perspective, needed to unfold with the tomb opened, by divine intervention, and the body (the evidence) gone – with Jesus then appearing to witnesses afterwards. But then there also needs to be some spiritual reason or purpose for the body having left the tomb. And the answer to this is found in the resurrection of the body, which, if not already well embedded via the roots of Christianity, drawing from Judaism and biblical references (e.g. Job 19:25-26), it certainly would have been once this story got around.

This *body resurrection* concept is argued to be relayed down to us via Paul (1 Corinthians 15:42-44), with the Church subsequently holding to this acceptance, of the body and the soul being ultimately inseparable. Article 11 of the *Catechism of the Catholic Church* begins with, "I believe in the resurrection of the body"[6] with the following sections helping to clarify:

> 364. The human body shares in the dignity of 'the image of God': It is a human body precisely because it is animated by a spiritual soul, and it is the whole human person that is intended to become, in the body of Christ, a temple of the Spirit.[7]

> 365 The unity of soul and body is so profound that one has to consider the soul to be the 'form' of the body: i.e., it is because of its spiritual soul that the body made of matter becomes a living, human body; spirit and matter, in man, are not two natures united, but rather their union forms a single nature.[8]

> 990. The term 'flesh' refers to man in his state of weakness and mortality. The 'resurrection of the flesh' (the literal formulation of the Apostles' Creed) means not only that the immortal soul will live on after death, but that even our 'mortal body' will come to life again.[9]

I have no great truck with the general sentiment of articles 364 and 365, but, and this is where I find it gets bizarre, because of the rigidity of this body-soul belief, as expressed in 990, Christians are tied into a physical resurrection. And for it to occur, we are told, it will require Jesus to return to Earth and physically raise all those who have died – on Judgement Day. To put a label on it, this is known as *Christian mortalism*, incorporating the belief that, "the human soul is not naturally immortal and may include the belief that the soul is uncomprehending during the time between bodily death and Judgment Day resurrection."[10] Or in other words at death the soul goes into *soul sleep* a kind of hibernation, until its eventual resurrection and judgement. It is somewhat confusing however as in other respects, at death, the soul is believed to be sent to heaven, hell

---

or purgatory – which rather pre-empts further judgement except for those in purgatory. Regardless, on that day all the departed souls will be awakened, reunited with their bodies, and then face judgement. This is a double-edged sword too for if you buy into this you are depending on the Church safeguarding your body until that time arrives, so hence ideally you need to be also buried in what is deemed sacred, consecrated ground (the church graveyard being the obvious place, if not in the church itself), to ensure your ticket for the big day.

Now this belief may be fine when a dead person is buried six feet under and no one sees the body again, thus believing it could, for all intents and purposes, remain in a fairly pristine form, as it looked at the point of death, but who believes in that anymore? When one has seen what physical remains look like, after being buried for even a relatively short period of time, it doesn't hold water – of course not. Through excavations I know first-hand this to be a fact. I have dug up skeletons anywhere between five-thousand-years-old to relatively recent (19th-century), with some of the *recent* actually being excavated within a church cemetary,[11] and where the flesh had gone while bits of coffin still remained with the skeleton. Let me tell you, it leaves nothing to the imagination. Once one has seen such evidence the notion of the resurrection of the body soon goes out of the window. It would not surprise me to learn either that this binding together of body and soul was further made concrete during the Church council debates of the 6th and 7th centuries when dealing with the topics of Monothelitism[12] (concerned with establishing the human and divine nature and wills of Jesus) and Origenism (the teachings of Origen) with the result that earlier Christian writings were adjusted to comply.

Transmigration of the Soul

By contrast to mortalism, the older notion of the immortality and transmigration of the soul – having any number of bodies on its journey (through reincarnation), offers a very different perspective, and one that I suspect Jesus was well aware of – through, if nothing else, exposure to the Eastern traditions carried by people passing through Nazareth. Indeed I would go further to suggest that judging by his parables[13] and comments such as, "I am telling you the truth: no one can see the Kingdom of God unless he is born again" (John 3:3), he most probably did believe in reincarnation. You won't need me however to tell you, from what has been discussed, that modern Christianity doesn't (excuse the pun), hold a candle up for belief in rebirth or reincarnation. Well certainly not within its orthodox arm – believing as it does that the soul and body are made one at the same time by God. But this wasn't bought into by everyone in its early development. The early Christian Church did consider, and tolerate to a degree, a belief in the pre-existence of souls and thereby reincarnation. Certainly one (3rd-century) well respected theologian, indeed now seen as the first early Christian Church Father of the established church, Origen Adamantius (c184-c254)[14] made an argument for what he saw as both the pre-existence and transmigration of souls.[15] In other words he argued the soul did not depend upon the body, that it was there before the physical world or body, and it was able to have more than the one body. I think we can assume he didn't hold with the accepted view – that of the resurrection of the body.[16] His school and teachings were widely known of, and embraced by a number of influential and politically important Christians in his time. But then…

> Three centuries later his very name was stricken from the books of the Church; yet in the monasteries of the Greeks his influence still lived on, as the spiritual father of Greek monasticism.
>
> P Schaff, The Anathemas Against Origen[17]

It has to be said that in his own time Origen's ideas were considered radical – partly for being associated with pagan beliefs, and even extending to the notion of the Devil eventually making reparation for sins it committed. He was roundly challenged for his beliefs. His teachings certainly caused more than a problem for the Church in its infancy and development towards orthodoxy. This, to the point whereby during the 6th-century Origen's ideas (and his followers, the

Origenists) had been anathematised – making it politically incorrect for anyone to have any association with his teachings, or with them. As a result a great deal of his work was destroyed or revised. A number of Church Fathers had attacked his ideas over the intervening years but it was Patriarch Mennas of Constantinople, possibly in the pocket of Emperor Justinian, who finally stuck the boot in and made support for his ideas, heresy.

And why was this so? Well for the reasons given above but I venture this had more to do with power and political correctness than spiritual clarity. After all, the Church would have argued that if people start to hear and believe in Origen's ideas, then they might start to believe that they, too, were souls first and humans second. Knowing that might lead, by simple deduction, to seeing themselves as, like Jesus, sons and daughters of God. Arguably all people could start believing they are souls working their way back to God, through many lives. If that got accepted by the flock, Jesus would no longer be seen as God's, "only begotten son" but more as a spiritual teacher, one who clearly had travelled further; and who, like perhaps a scout on TV's Wagon Train, or Rawhide, had returned to let us know what is up ahead, to give direction, to point the way home, or to better lands. "I am the way, the truth, and the life; no one goes to the Father except by me" (John 14:6), would take on a different meaning: Jesus could then be talking about the path of the Christ that he also followed. He would be speaking of the journey that we all need to take if we are to be closer to God, to the source, to Love.

Had the Church accepted this it would have risked losing power and sway over people. It doesn't take much to reason that the Church would no longer have been such a necessary requirement or intermediary between God and the individual, or people – the people could choose to seek God by other means. If Origen's ideas had been fully accepted, the Emperor likewise could also have been challenged for assuming himself as a God, or next to God. Rather he too would be regarded as, bottom line, a travelling soul like the rest of humanity, and could risk losing his divinity as ruler. Well that's my take on the matter.

Whatever the acceptable version of reasoning, on this it looks like the Emperor acted fast, and, at the Synod of Constantinople, of 543, Patriarch Mennas made his move – accompanied by the edict of Justinian[18] which was then ratified at the Fifth Council of Constantinople, in 553. Justinian had forced his hand with the Council, and Origen's teachings were declared anathema. This was subsequently carried through by three further ecumenical councils. And so it was that all references to the ideas, of transmigration of souls, were removed from Christian Church doctrine, and the whole matter ever so neatly tied up with *body and soul* as one entity that, save the camel, not even a flea could get through the eye of that needle.

Being told of past lives

In developing out this discussion, on the nature of the soul, and for that matter in context with Origen's beliefs above, I'm going to bring in a little personal experience at this point, that has helped me towards my understanding of the soul. This is driven by being told of past lives – which I will share here.

Back in the Seventies I got invited up to Hull to visit the mediums Andrea and Alan Grieveson. I'd met Andrea some years previously at an astrological conference and we'd kept in touch. In their work they ran fortnightly meetings locally as well as giving talks around the UK. Unlike the focus of many mediums being to pass on messages, their group of communicators were concerned with spiritual health. Andrea writes, in *A Series of Past Lives*, how they talked on spiritual matters, answered questions and offered healing:

> The spirit communicating gave a little talk on some interesting subject and then invited questions. There were some lively discussions and then ... Patian, or some other Tian healer, would come along and give group healing. These group-healing sessions were very good and people liked them. Although one healer was

using Alan's voice, the others were also present and helping people whose health problems were different.

Andrea Grieveson, astrologer, medium[19]

What they were doing interested me to find out more, and so I was excited to meet up.

The day we arranged to meet up was, as it turned out, to be the same day as my father's funeral. We'd made the arrangement a couple of months or so before he died and, although I could have easily cancelled the trip, I decided not to – the two events being closely related in my mind. So that particular weekend comprised of attending the funeral in Leicestershire[20] and later travelling up to Hull to meet up with them. When there, and talking to them in their mediumship capacity, it was an opportunity to enquire after my father as the first thing to find out about. Their friends told me he was resting, and would be doing so for some time. Unsurprisingly, this appears to be a common situation for a lot of us on passing over.

It was during this short stay I also learnt about three of my past lives through my *guides* (I say more about guides in the next chapter). I hasten to add, in context with what was discussed, that the Grieveson's knew very little about my history back then. Also this was a new experience for me, and I hadn't entirely lost my sceptism for what I was about to hear. The information given varied in detail, from life to life, but in each case what was stressed was that there was something to be resolved, an issue or theme that linked my current life to these previous lives. They made it clear that it was important I understood this – and to work it out for myself. There was, as a result, an emphasis made to hint at what was useful, for me to consider, rather than to convey whole past life story details to me for the sake of curiosity. Let me tell you about them and you'll see what I mean.

The first thing to say is that in all these three lives I was born in the UK and I was also male. In one life, which provided most detail, I was the eldest son of four boys to a wheelwright. I was learning the same trade, and my father had high hopes for my following in his footsteps and eventually carrying on this work as the main bread winner. It turned out that I had other ideas however. I was young and my thoughts were elsewhere. I wanted to travel, to get some excitement, to move away from country life and get around a bit. I left home which, I was told, hurt my father enormously (and hardly surprising). I had no formal education and couldn't read or write. In my travels I arrived at a seaport. With all the hubbub going on there, and, what with my desire for adventure, I very quickly got caught up in it by putting my X on a form, that signed me up for the navy. This was the Merchant Navy. I became a ship's gunner, among other things, and took part in battles over the trade routes in the Dutch East Indies. Researching this later, I probably worked for the English East India Company, which would also suggest the life was set in the 17th-century.

But ever in my young mind I was seeking adventure. I was less concerned with making long-term commitment to a particular skill, trade or organisation. So later when I was well away from home, and getting, what I considered, a raw deal in the navy, I jumped ship, escaped and began a life on a tropical island with, as described to me, as a "dusky young maiden." It seems I had, what followed, to be a good, if comparatively short, life on the island. I met my demise when down on the beach one day I accidently trod on a stonefish and without immediate and proper medical treatment the poison killed me. It was probably a horrible painful death – and any wonder I have very sensitive feet this time around.

Coming forward; in another (this time probably 18th-century) life I was the manager of a large country estate. I had a fair number of people under my charge – possibly around thirty from the sound of it. By all accounts I was a fair but strict person to work for. From the description given I was a responsible, serious and stern person, preoccupied with my work. I wasn't told how I died in that life, but rather the importance of the position, and the responsibilities that went with it, were the main concerns conveyed to me. It sounded like I enjoyed the life and position I had, but was not much fun to be with – quite a contrast to the previous life.

In the third life given I was a young boy. I play a piccolo in a band. I'm in the uniform and military band of Wellington's army. This was to be a very short life for, as I marched into battle, at Waterloo, I was cut down by one of Napoleon's horsemen. I died on the battlefield.

Let me just point out here that this doesn't mean I (meaning my soul) have only ever had three previous lives. No, as suggested above, what was stressed as important for me to understand was that, my current life involves working with the dialogue and themes from these three previous lives – bringing them into balance. I won't labour what these lives mean to me but you may be able to guess they do contain variations on the exercising of one's freewill, or not as the case may be, and the responsibilities that do or don't go with it. I will say that I do identify with all three of the lives, that is their themes (not the memory of them), as something I am working with in this life.

Apart from the themes, the details that were given also have some resonance with my current life. For example (in context with the first life given), in this life I am again the eldest boy of four children – but this time having three sisters instead of brothers. My father in this life was a merchant seaman, and, I might add, I had a strong inclination to follow in his footsteps when I left school but then changed direction more or less at the last minute. One might say I gave a similar response to my father's trade in this life as I did to pursuing my previous father's wheelwright trade – I rejected it; but also came close to working in it. Instead this time around I started out my working life in woodwork, as a cabinet maker – although this covered other aspects such as joinery in practice. And interestingly I did at one point build wooden drum wheels for power cables. In structure, these were getting pretty close to wheelwright work. In this life too I have been a restless person, always looking for the right doorway and never quite finding it – and have mostly created my own pathway in that search. Now in my latter years, I know what I'm here to do but it has taken something of a journey in finding it.

Regarding the country estate manager life I've always felt a strong affinity with large country houses, one in particular that I'll leave from identifying, as it might just be where I was a manager. And finally for what it is worth my favourite musical instruments are in the woodwind section. I took up playing the recorder (borrowed from one of my sisters) and the mouth organ back in my twenties – not in any professional capacity but for the fun of it. All in all, one or two very interesting links between this and these three previous existences.

Soul Implications

Leaving aside all other considerations, the implications of accepting these lives meant that I also had to accept that something or someone had experienced each life. In the manner in which the information was given to me I have no idea what my name was in any of these previous lives, but I think we can say it is a *given* that it's pretty unlikely I had the same name back then as I do now – perhaps a first name might have been the same in one life if that. And further, although I do not have a description of my appearance, in each life, I can be pretty sure that I did not appear, back then, the same as I do now – our appearance of course is informed by our situation, spiritual and physical. Also, I might add, within another life, not given or germane to this current life, I could have been of the opposite gender. And so further, as indeed I mentioned in a the *Fringe Benefits* chapter, this person, that I am now, is not so much my soul per se but a projection, a facet of my soul. I am how my soul appears at this part of its development and learning, this part of its journey. To put this more succinctly, who I am is a direct outcome of my soul's karmic situation. This is combination of my thoughts and actions taken in my soul's past journey, or journeys, and now here coupled with the experience, thoughts and actions taken in this physical life.

There is meaning to life

Some years ago now, I was fortunate enough to be introduced to, and listen to, the Venerable Lama Sogyal Rinpoche talk about life and death. His view is that:

> Each one of us, deep down, cherishes a desire to live and to continue living, which is, in itself, perhaps a strong indication of some basic intuition that there may be a life after death. If life or consciousness failed to survive death, there would be neither meaning to life nor any ultimate justice.[21]

I agree. Of course I agree. It is this notion of there being *meaning to life*, and finding a way towards acknowledging and accepting it, that I identify as being crucial to making sense of the experience of life and death, and in also answering *the soul question*. This is not something we can switch on or off however. This is not playing with ideas and semantics. With my old existentialist hat on I may ask why there needs to be any meaning to life. Ordinary reasons can be found for every decision and step we take on our journeys. One could suggest it is simply what we have been taught by our parents, teachers and peers, it's who we know or perhaps don't know, opportunities we create for ourselves, the law of averages, whether we have *luck* on our side or not. And, we are where we are due to simple natural selection, not because of any divine plan within us. That explanation does on the face of it appear sound, but is it accurate? It is not easy, coming from an alternative viewpoint, to provide such a strong argument, or answer, that the existentialist will be happy with, and the whole debate gets quickly reduced down to belief and faith in the end, on either side.

But we have to consider it is a case of what level the matter is being viewed from. There is, I would suggest, an ordinary level of viewing our situation and there is a more hidden, esoteric, symbolical way of viewing our situation. All the ordinary reasons given are a part of the picture, as things appear, but not the whole picture. Indeed, following a similar observation to that of Sogyal

Rinpoche, we must consider that the mere fact we can pose the question, regarding whether there is meaning to life and death, in itself should provide a big clue that there is a bigger, more meaningful, dimension to life. What I'm suggesting is that our self-awareness has reached this point of self-questioning or questioning our situation, and surely we can all find this just a teeny-weeny bit meaningful.

If we can but notice it there is an undercurrent, a theme, or themes, running through our lives that, if we allow, offer up opportunity for us to begin joining up the dots and to arrive at a deeper understanding of our situation. Once we see this we can't help but also consider there may be some bigger purpose, nay some spiritual purpose to our lives. The way it came together for me, or should I say, that *eureka moment* – as I had been given lots of clues beforehand (including recurring numbers that I write about in *The Other Side* chapter) – was when I began studying natal astrology. Here the idea of there being meaning to life came into play as an unavoidable issue. It became something I had to wrestle with to understand. Here was that *symbolical way of viewing the situation*, and only if there is a meaningful, and ultimately spiritual direction to our lives, does the symbolism of natal astrology start to make any real sense – that is what I believe. I'm not talking Sun signs on the coffee break page here by the way; what one can see in a birthchart are, what I would describe as, karmic themes and opportunities that are playing out in the given life of a person.

Astrology shows we are each born into unique circumstances (based upon time and place of entry), reflecting the uniqueness of our respective natures. We tread our individual pathways. Some pathways can be anticipated to flow more easily towards success in external ventures, in the external world, while others more easily succeed on internal reflective ventures. Some pathways lead towards relative ease in obtaining wealth and abundance let's say, while some are facing more challenging circumstances. To the casual observer this can mean some lives have everything going for them while others are seemingly unfairly treated, and even cut short too. Rather than it being a case of a throw of the dice, as to our lot for just one life – as taught by Christianity – placing this in context with astrological symbolism, a longer spiritual journey starts to unravel and begins to make sense.

The Soul Point

> You don't have a soul. You are a soul. You have a body.
>
> C S Lewis, novelist, poet, academic, lay theologian

At this juncture let us get down to the nub of this discussion and focus on what the soul is. I'm going to do this from an esoteric understanding to provide, what I believe, is an accurate model of what we are and what we are working with. Let's say, to begin with, that your soul, my soul, is invisible to the naked eye. It vibrates at a level that makes it invisible to physical sensors, and yet its existence is arguably self-evident in our being alive. But in another sense our soul is not invisible. When we look in the mirror, or at each other, we are seeing *soul*. But of course we'd say the physical body also gets in the way of seeing what we might objectify as soul. The aura around the body, that some people can see, takes us a little closer. The aura displays in various colours according to the state of health and psyche of the body or person being observed. What is being observed links to the etheric vehicle, that may also include the astral or emotional vehicle, and interpreted by our mind into colours.

Don't worry if some of the terms being used here are not making much sense as yet, I will discuss them, and the aura, in more detail when we look at the vehicles of the soul below.

The soul is the spark of eternal light or life-force. It is permanent, immortal, an indestructible part of the greater good, or God, or, as I prefer, Love transmigrating its way back home.

> The soul is the self, the 'I' that inhabits the body and acts through it. Without the soul, the body is like a light bulb without electricity, a computer without the software, a space suit with no astronaut inside. With the introduction of the soul, the body acquires life,

sight and hearing, thought and speech, intelligence and emotions, will and desire, personality and identity.

Yanki Tauber, Jewish Rabbi and writer[22]

It is my belief that everything in nature is soul first and foremost – that is we, the animals, the plants, the trees, yes and the rocks, rivers and seas – all vibrating at different levels. This belief, often described as *animism*, is very ancient and I'm in good company with some Native American tribes, Hindus, Jains, Theosophists, Rosicrucians, and modern pagans, holding with a similar view. In the last chapter I was describing animals as living in a state of innocence. We could add here that their souls are not, as yet, working at the level of human consciousness but that they can, and no doubt will, one day is a great possibility – but not necessarily as the creatures they currently are.

In our Western thinking the term *soul* is often interchangeable with terms like *spirit, mind* or *higher self* so it can be confusing. If it helps, the overriding view that I have is there is a *traveller* on this (yours or mine) spiritual journey – going from life experience to life experience. Whether I loosely call it a divine spark, soul, spirit or self, is of less importance as long as it fits in with the notion of *traveller* and *spiritual journey*. Like so many other people, and traditions, I prefer to use the word *soul*. It follows, as CS Lewis puts it so elegantly, that each of us is a soul having a body. Indeed, as we will discuss below there is more than one body from an esoteric perspective.

Once we can accept life is meaningful then it is only by incorporating this "traveller" situation being also real and vital does the spiritual journey, and reason for being on the earth, begin to make logical sense. This perspective allows for why one soul may have a short life experience in this life, perhaps only living for a couple of years, and another may have a long life, while displaying great gifts and talents – after having learnt, worked on, and honed these abilities through previous experience and possibly many lives. As Origen viewed it, the soul is going home alright but in doing so is working out towards consciousness, or wakefulness, through experience and learning.

We are souls using, in the vernacular, our brains as the interface with the physical world for the duration of our physical lives. It helps me to use a computer analogy to try to explain this – and in this I'm going to diverge a bit from Tauber's comments above. I understand one's soul to be the power and life in the computer – the computer cannot operate without power, whether sourced from the mains or battery. The soul is also much more than providing the power, as it brings everything into manifestation – nothing can hold together without soul. What is manifest is a projection of soul through energy. The mind is like the software, programmed by previous soul experience, which is also further added to and developed out of one's current life situation. Genetic makeup and life experience will always tend to condition what we can and can't do in application. Soul, mind, genetics, timing and experience combined; give rise to personality and character. One person's mind and fast brain, allows them the capacity to grasp matters quickly and negotiate their world with speed and intellect. Another person's equally healthy mind and brain requires more time to coordinate and negotiate their world. A person whose brain is diseased with Alzheimer's, or has been damaged in some way, will, as we know, probably cause them to be negotiating their way as if in a fog, or in a state of dullness and sluggishness, with only areas and times of possible lucidity – like a computer with some nasty virus. This will clear once the brain/physical body is no longer a part of the equation. And this is where the computer analogy begins to fail me, for the mind, or software, can easily transfer to run, and run better, on the finer etheric body held by the soul. In other words at the end of life when free of the physical, one's personality, memories, judgement and application remain intact, and with any restriction or fog caused by the brain and physical body having cleared.

Vehicles of the Soul

Let us now explore what is a deeper description of how the soul manifests – which might also help us to reconsider the terms we commonly use to describe the soul.

From an esoteric perspective the soul is viewed as having four bodies, or vehicles, during its physical manifestation, or incarnation. With this description I am drawing on Western Theosophical and Rosicrucian traditions. There are other perspectives on this that you might want to explore. I'm going to stress using the word *vehicle* here rather than *body* as, I would suggest, it can be less emotive to look at our physical body particularly as a vehicle or a container first and foremost. We are used, for example, to driving around in vehicles, of one kind or another, and, it is easier therefore for us to grasp how we can get in and out of such vehicles, without harm, and indeed how once broken down we can repair or scrap such a vehicle and/or for that matter, go get another if so required or desired.

The four vehicles of the soul are known as the *physical*, the *etheric*, the *astral* (or emotional) and the *mental* vehicles. These run from lower to finer vibrations and are interwoven with each other, meshed together, though not in any way permanently connected. I might mention there appears an obvious link here with the four elements of Western traditions (and in turn with the cardinal, fixed and mutable signs of astrology) that being the physical with *earth*, the etheric with *fire*, the astral with *water* and the mental with *air*. This, four elements pattern, is considered to repeat in the etheric vehicle itself – as we'll see below.

The Physical vehicle

The physical vehicle is of course the vehicle we are so familiar with. It is the lowest vibration and most dense of the four – made of matter, or energy, as we know. It is a beautiful and fine instrument for existence on the physical plane, with all the limitations and resistance it is likely to experience here. It is our spacesuit for living on this planet, at the physical level or vibration. It helps if we can see it as providing the necessary equipment and opportunity for the adventure, or project, we have chosen to embark upon, for a given period of time.

Given nothing tragic happens to it, it will last for years – its cellular structure being rebuilt many times. Globally life expectancy today is around the *three score years and ten* (as in Psalm 90), while in developed countries an increasing number of us are living up to, and beyond, the hundred years mark. Of course every effort is being made by our medical sciences to find ways of improving health and extending our physical lives for many more years. On proviso we don't look too closely at the pressures this might place on existing services and resources, this has got to be good news for most of us. From a soul perspective such an extension provides greater length of opportunity for spiritual development in a given life – while, who knows, possibly reducing the number of physical returns. Even so, with updated components and adaptions, the physical vehicle will still soon enough wear out – or need to be able to do so. It is not meant to bind the soul for all that long.

The Etheric vehicle

The etheric vehicle looks identical to the physical vehicle and is intermeshed with it as subtle luminous radiation. It operates at a much finer vibration than the physical vehicle. It is described by Horst Helmann[23] (drawing on Rudolf Steiner) as being composed of, "the Four Ethers" – these having (as mentioned above), links with the four elements of fire, earth, air and water. An understanding of how it interacts with the physical vehicle and its function can be found in the extensive writings of the theosophist and esoteric psychologist, Alice Bailey:

> In the etheric body, which is an exact replica of its denser counterpart, we have the organ of active radiatory fire, and ... the vehicle of prana. Its function is to store up the rays of radiatory light and heat which are secured from the Sun, and to transmit them, via the spleen, to all parts of the physical body.
>
> Alice Bailey[24]

The physical vehicle depends upon the etheric vehicle for its life, its health and vitality. The etheric vehicle however must not be taken as a straight carbon-copy of the physical vehicle, rather it is actually the other way around – it provides the template for the physical vehicle. It allows the life-force (life energy or prana) to pervade the physical vehicle for its duration. As the physical vehicle gets older so does the etheric vehicle appear to age and change in its replication. This is relative, however, as once the etheric vehicle is no longer attached (at death) to the physical vehicle, it can be presented as looking younger, even different. This transformation will depend upon the individual mind being awake, and desiring enough to improve or change it. But this change will also eventually happen, by default, when the soul re-enters a new physical situation with the same etheric vehicle.

> The etheric body is really a network of fine channels, which are the component parts of one interlacing fine cord... the silver cord... The etheric web is composed of the intricate weaving of this vitalised cord.
>
> Alice Bailey [25]

We leave in the etheric vehicle when we leave the physical vehicle at the end of its use. Here however there is a marked difference with the analogy, I used above, of leaving a motor vehicle. These vehicles, indeed all vehicles, are connected together by what is often called the *silver cord* or life thread – like an umbilical cord – linking back to the soul. The physical vehicle will terminate only once the cord is broken between it and the etheric vehicle. I suppose, with the motor vehicle scenario, if we stretched it, we could liken it to undoing the seat belt before we get out, but it's a bit more serious than that.

Regarding the etheric vehicle, here's a further thought to consider from Bailey:

> This etheric web... forms a barrier between the physical and astral planes, which can only be transcended when consciousness is sufficiently developed to permit escape... When a man [woman] has, through meditation and concentration, expanded his [her]

consciousness to a certain point, he [she] is enabled to include the subtler planes, and to escape beyond the limits of the dividing web.

Alice Bailey[26]

We can take it from this that the etheric vehicle, as beautiful as it is, actually imprisons the soul until it can ready its escape and move beyond its webbed boundary. This escape is what Buddhists describe as freedom from Samsara – getting off the karmic cycle. It is in the end a prison, of our own continual making, that we are actually undoing.

From a different perspective I might suggest it is the etheric vehicle that has been confused with the physical vehicle in Christian, and the Abrahamic religions generally, regarding the belief in the resurrection of the body. It is the *incorrupt* etheric vehicle that one leaves within at the point of death. One could add that, as it imprisons the soul, it does require a sort of a *Day of Judgement* to move beyond it. But this must needs be an individual moment of decision and release, arising from within the situation the individual soul finds itself in.

The Etheric vehicle and the Chakras

In discussing the etheric vehicle some consideration needs to be given to what many of us will be familiar with, or have heard of; the seven chakras. As has been indicated, the etheric vehicle acts as a conductor for prana – the life-force or life giving principle which energises matter and produces form – hence the physical body. In structure the etheric vehicle is actually a web, a network of fine channels, being composed entirely of lines of force. Where these lines cross each other they produce sensitive points or centres of energy.[27] Where a large number of these lines converge, major centres and streams of energy are produced. There are argued to be seven of these major centres. In the theosophical tradition these are known as the *centres of force*; while in other esoteric and Indian traditions they are better known as the *chakras*. Bailey points out that, "there are seven such, plus twenty nine lesser centres, and forty nine smaller centres [that are] known to esotericists."[28] One could of course take this much further and see how these *centres* also intermesh with the meridians and acupuncture points of the body.

Keeping this simple and to the point, these seven centres of force are aligned with the spine of the human body. They are described as the agents of the soul, the means by which the life-force has direct contact with the physical body. They maintain bodily existence and produce its activity. The centres are as spinning vortices that carry prana to every part of the body, essentially via the nervous system and arteries. Bailey writes, in *The Soul and its Mechanism*:

> They are in close relation with the nervous system in its three divisions, namely: the cerebro-spinal, sympathetic and peripheral. From the force centres the vital or pranic energy is distributed along subtle lines of direction. These lines are called 'nadis' and are closely related to the nerves and at the same time to the arteries; they apparently underlie the corporeal nervous system.[29]

However, to be clear, although there is obvious correspondence between the centres of the etheric vehicle and the physical vehicle they nevertheless belong in different realms – the *nadis* are not to be confounded with the bodily nerves and arteries but rather as their luminous counterparts.

A warning regarding prematurely opening the Chakras

Much information is available via practices, books and videos, regarding techniques to help open these centres of force. This is with the aim of achieving higher experience, awakening and enlightenment, and attempts to raise kundalini energy, or fire, to rise up through the chakras. The various states described can be achieved through the practice of yoga and meditation. But *everything in its own time* is the warning here. One should certainly study the etheric vehicle and its centres of force, but, the warning is to, beware of playing with such fire unless you know how to handle it – it can burn you. Bailey comments:

The whole subject of the centres is dangerous if misunderstood; the centres constitute a menace when prematurely awakened, or unduly energised, and this entire subject can prove most dangerous to the curiosity-impelled man [or woman] and to the ignorant experimenter.

Alice Bailey [30]

And further Bailey says:

I sound here a solemn word of warning. Let a man [or woman] apply himself [herself] to a life of high altruism... When he [she] has done this and both raised and stabilised his [her] vibration, he [she] will find that the development and functioning of the centres has pursued a parallel course, and that (apart from this active participation) the work has proceeded along the desired lines. Much danger and dire calamity attends the man [woman] who arouses these centres by unlawful methods, and who experiments with the fires of his [her] body without the needed technical knowledge.

Alice Bailey [31]

The view here is that without correct practice or intention we can generate real dangers playing around with something we do not fully understand – in the search of experience or enlightenment via technique, rather than spiritual practice per se. Further down Bailey points out that this practice can, "burn bodily or brain tissue" and be a means of opening ourselves up to, "currents and forces undesirable and destructive." All we need to do, however, is to keep it simple: Practice love, compassion and understanding, raise our spiritual game, and such things will follow in their natural order without needing to resort to techniques to help us get there.

The Etheric vehicle and the Aura

A great many of us will have heard of, or have seen the *aura* that manifests around the body of a person. This is considered to mostly emanate from the etheric vehicle. As an aid to understanding this, the etheric vehicle may be divided into two parts: The first of these being called the etheric double – closely resembling the physical vehicle. This extends out around two centimetres beyond the surface of the skin, and provides the framework on which the material body is built. The second part is more appropriately called the aura. The aura is a roughly egg-shaped field of energies surrounding the etheric double. It is claimed it can extend out from a few centimetres up to half a metre or so from the physical body. It, "serves as the interface between the etheric body of the individual and that of the cosmos, and all the forces of the universe are reflected on its surface."[32] We should add here that all life emits this radiation, this aura.[33] The aura is also heavily influenced by the astral or emotional vehicle, and is argued that it is this that actually forms the *second part* of the aura – see Max Heindel's, "ovoid cloud" comment below.

The Astral vehicle

The astral or subtle, or emotional vehicle vibrates at a higher finer level than the etheric and physical vehicles. It does not exist in a spatial sense like that of the physical and etheric vehicles. It is anticipated by its effects. This is a little bit like the way a planet may be discovered by its effects on another planet – for example Neptune was discovered in 1846 and anticipated, using mathematics, by its effect on Uranus. The astral vehicle is the giver of the life-force that sustains the etheric vehicle and more... Meher Baba describes it as, "The vehicle of desires and vital forces."[34] This vehicle is immersed in what is known as the astral plane – the plane of phenomena where what is felt and desired appears immediately or rapidly. This is similar to the Law of Attraction gone mad, or more appropriately without physical resistance to slow it down. Possibly it is of profound significance that now, helped by having the Web in place, we are collectively starting to get to grips with this law and thereby some insight into the workings of the astral plane.

It is, "simply a great reflector. It takes colour and movement from its surroundings. It receives the impress of every passing desire. It contacts every whim and fancy in its environment; every current sets it in motion."[35] Imagine it then as like an ocean responding to every thought and desire. It is in motion with swirls, eddies and tides

LIFE AND DEATH: MAKING SENSE OF IT

as feelings, desires, emerge and fall away again. Carl Jung arguably saw his *collective unconscious* and world of archetypes as like the astral plane – "an "objective psyche", extending in the world at large, bridging mind and matter."[36]

According to Max Heindel's Rosicrucian writings, the emotional vehicle is made of *desire*, from which we human beings form feelings and emotions. He suggests it appears to spiritual sight as an, "ovoid cloud extending from sixteen to twenty inches [fifty centimetres] beyond the physical body."[37]

Where spiritual development is concerned, Bailey points out that one needs to, "so train the emotional body that it will become still and clear as a mirror, so that it may reflect perfectly."[38] There is a clue here as to why we all need to practice meditation. Stilling these waters requires a watchful and discriminating approach to life, so that one is ever seeking to work with higher desires while inhibiting lower desires. This is the route by which the soul can eventually be free of the etheric vehicle too.

The Mental vehicle

The mental vehicle (which, like the astral vehicle, belongs in a different realm and cannot be placed in any spatial dimension), operates within the mental plane and is the container of the mind and all faculties of thinking. It is made up of thoughts, just as the emotional body consists of emotions and the physical body is made up of matter. In esoteric understanding thoughts, once produced, have their own existence as *thought-forms*.

From this level the mind interacts with the other three vehicles. Max Heindel, in *The Rosicrucian Cosmo-Conception*, gives a description on how our soul perceives, from the level of this mental plane, the lower worlds, through the mind and creates thought-forms:

> We ourselves... function directly in the subtle substance of the Region of Abstract Thought, which we have specialised within the periphery of our individual aura. Thence we view the impressions made by the outer world upon the vital [etheric] body through the senses, together with the feelings and emotions generated by them

in the desire [emotional] body, and mirrored in the mind. From these mental images we form our conclusions, in the substance of the Region of Abstract Thought, concerning the subjects with which they deal. Those conclusions are 'ideas.' By the power of [our] will we project an idea through the mind, where it takes concrete shape as a thought-form by drawing mind-stuff around itself from the Region of Concrete Thought.

Max Heindel, Rosicrucian, astrologer, writer[39]

We can deduce from this that how we respond, think and produce ideas, through our mind, is inextricably linked to how developed we are in the other vehicles that make up the lenses of our soul. Our outer world experience, and interactions in particular, help serve or hamper our spiritual growth and objectives. Even so, one's will is all important in directing the mind towards higher thought and spiritually successful outcomes – outcomes that are expressed upon the mental plane and, in turn, filtered down to the lower vibrational vehicles:

The mind creates or formulates those thought-forms (or embodied energies) which express, upon the mental plane, the measure of the disciple's understanding of the Plan, and his [her] ability to convey the embodied mental energy to the etheric body – unimpeded by the emotional nature or by any lower upsurging desire.

Alice Bailey [40]

In simple terms the higher mind, the will, has the ability to create thought-forms that can bypass lower levels of desire and be expressed in love – thus generating transformation and refinement in the etheric and physical vehicles. We have to be careful not to let the mind wander though, but rather to focus it towards right intention.

Let us take this a little further, as it is important to grasp and apply in context with karma. We create thought-forms via the mere act of thinking, and we are doing it all the time of course – the mind is ever busy. Most of us do this in an undisciplined, you could say thoughtless, manner – excuse the pun. We are not truly awake to what we are creating in other words. Much of it we do on autopilot;

we simply copy and reaffirm forms already there. While on one level we create thought-forms ourselves, on another we have a propensity to take on-board thought-forms created by others. We also build onto reaffirmed forms and, without control, it can become a cycle that effectively controls us.

From a psychological perspective thought-forms fill up what we call the subconscious mind. The subconscious holds years of experience and learning, whether this is good or painful, from childhood onwards. Developed from our interaction with the world, our loves, our fears, our desires, and these once reaffirmed become habits or habitual ways of thinking and decision-making – which in turn have consequences. Put simply, what we think and believe about ourself and world, particularly what has become habitual, influences our current thinking, our actions and intentions going forward, and what we then in turn draw towards us – whether that be what we consciously want or don't want to happen in our lives. It works on the basis of what has worked in the past, is tried and tested, and therefore reliable, and best policy is to stick to it now, even though it may actually be holding us back, even doing us harm.

Such a policy of following the *tried and tested* of course is not necessarily unhealthy, but it can be when it is having negative effects or outcomes and where new thought, a new approach, a different perspective is required to bring new light, new understanding and progress – particularly this can be so where spiritual and global matters are a concern and in need of a different approach.

The Light vehicle – the Soul

To complete this description, right at the heart of these vehicles lies the soul, in what is sometimes called the light or causal vehicle. This is the root of consciousness and the innermost essence of the soul. If one is to describe this as a vehicle at all (it is the fifth vehicle on that basis), it is otherwise the divine spark contained, and around which all other vehicles of the soul are built in the process of awakening consciousness. It can be called *pure being* and the interface between the outer physical expression and inner unity in cosmic Love.

Dying is something we do every night

In context with the esoteric understanding of the soul, and its vehicles, it is important to consider that when we sleep, our subtle and mental vehicles can withdraw to leave our etheric and physical vehicles to it, so to speak. This separation actually allows our etheric vehicle to repair and revitalise the physical vehicle. Our subtle and mental vehicles then return to re-engage with our sleeping form as we are waking up. Sleep is therefore arguably akin to death:

> People are apt to forget that every night, in the hours of sleep, we die to the physical plane and are alive and functioning elsewhere. They forget that they have already achieved facility in leaving the physical body; because they cannot as yet bring back into brain consciousness the recollection of that passing out, and of that subsequent interval of active living, they fail to relate death and sleep.
>
> Alice Bailey [41]

Bailey continues on to say that, "Death after all, is only a longer interval in the life of physical plane functioning; one has only 'gone abroad' for a longer period." There is of course one major difference between sleep and death, and this is that in death the, "magnetic thread or current of energy along which the life force streams ... is broken or snapped."[42] We can say therefore that the soul itself is not fixed to the body and can, in such circumstances, be away from the body. Providing the life thread or cord is maintained by the vehicles the soul can keep the body alive. The attendant idea, suggested by Bailey here, is that when we sleep and dream we go through a practice run for death – dying is something we do, or let's say we nearly do, every night.

I wonder, have you ever noticed upon waking from catnapping (if you catnap), how you may experience a sudden body jerk? The experience is like a part of you had shifted out of place and has now snapped back into place. For myself I have experienced this frequently. It can be quite noticeable. I believe this experience is being caused by the realignment of one's vehicles.

Out-of-body experiences, astral travel and lucid dreaming follow a similar pattern to what happens in sleep, but obviously happens in a state where consciousness is maintained. These experiences can also include components of the near-death experience – as noted in the *Fringe Benefits* chapter in context with IANDS.[43]

Does an ant have a Soul?

When the Soul wants to experience something she throws out an image in front of her and then steps into it.
Meister Eckhart, German theologian, philosopher and mystic[44]

Now here's a question for you: Given the above, would an ant have a soul, or is it just a little being that is filling a niche in the greater ecosystem, and completely the product of Nature and evolution?

Over a couple of months or so last summer I had much opportunity to learn a little more about ants, as they proceeded to scout and scurry looking for food sources in our kitchen. The little devils got everywhere for a while. I did my best to avoid killing any of them and spent a lot of time looking at alternative means of preventing them from coming in – and reducing their numbers. Certainly the dustpan and brush were used a lot, to encourage them to leave our house – by emptying them outside in the back garden. And they did eventually get the message... Let's say I have respect for these organised and tenacious creatures that after all have been on the planet for millions of years. Indeed fossil remains are said to go back some 80-million years – and so no one need question their birth-right to go wherever the food, and the success of their nest takes them.

Well anyhow, in answer to the question, the simplest explanation would be to say the ant is the product of nature and evolution and therefore does not have a soul. But to me it has a soul. Indeed, if my belief system is to hold water then I have to say that it most definitely has a soul – but possibly not as so simply stated. The ant operates more on, what I would take to be, a closed collective instinctual intelligence rather than by individual choices and decisions. Probably like most insects, ants go to work with clear inbuilt directives – let's say a blueprint of what they have to do. This is not to say however that ants do not have the capacity to learn, as clearly they do (and need to), and have been observed, for example, showing each other the way to food sources. It's a case of the one who knows the way may have another follow in tandem, and they keep in touch with each other so that the learner is keeping up. The ants are hard-wired to do a range of specific jobs: the females are occupied in finding food for the nest, helping the colony to reproduce and be successful, but also to keep the nest shipshape too – and that means doing the housework. Males do very little, it appears, except to reproduce and die afterwards – and then get recycled, soul-wise, as I see it.

The remarkable thing is that in an ant colony no one is actually in charge (similar to bees) and yet they all work as one unit. The so-called *queen* is just another ant that has taken on the role of manufacturing ants for the colony, but is not in charge of it. They instead know instinctively what they are doing, what role they are playing.[45] So I would say that while each ant is indeed a soul with a body, it is also part of a collective group intelligence that behaves like a group soul, no matter how closed and instinctual we choose to view it.

Each ant is like a cell of its bigger collective. This also reminds me, as I'm writing, that the cells that make up our bodies know where to go when forming a part of our brain or big toe. It is absolutely fantastic that the human body is made up of around 70-trillion cells that in turn start to work from a single egg cell, fertilised by one sperm. Once fertilisation occurs, the egg grows and divides, and then the offspring cells produced by this division grow and divide, over and over again. The miracle continues in that these cells don't just replicate but also organise themselves into lungs, heart, bones, skin, blood, eyes, the brain and much more. No one cell is conducting this operation and yet everybody appears to know where to go, what job they are meant to do. Could there be some kind of hidden yin and yang dialogue taking place that brings about negotiation and direction? It is truly remarkable and should give us cause to think of the magic that surrounds us; a cause to think of who or what is organising this. And so given, how difficult is it for us to consider that maybe the invisible soul is the organiser behind the operation? As a couple are conceiving, the esoteric view is that the soul, through the etheric vehicle, co-ordinates the organisation and development of the new physical vehicle – in keeping with the genetic arrangements of the parents.

Reincarnation and the Soul

My essential argument is that all life does have a purpose, and that purpose is tied in with spiritual development, with consciousness – which naturally ties in with the development of souls.

I'm among a growing number of people who believe that our Earth is a school for souls. I'm largely talking about the human soul level here but it equally applies to all souls. The physical body and the planet provide testing boundaries, limitations that, by comparison with our soul state, means being here and lowering our vibration, is a bit like walking through treacle. It follows too that it is difficult, within the limitations of our five senses, to know anything spiritually with absolute certainty. Instead, if we are enquiring enough, we look for what evidence can be drawn, from our own and each other's circumstances and experience, to structure what we come to believe in as being a close representation of the reality of our situation. By that route we learn to master our conditions in this school of resistance – which in turn helps us to awake and temper our spiritual growth.

We each start out being a soul that is pure but also inexperienced. We would remain so in this immature condition unless we faced challenges and tests to help toughen us and round out our soul experience. That's the theory as to why we are here – or at least part of it, as I plan to explore in a later book.

So let's now move on to looking more closely at how reincarnation fits into this picture. Most religions that believe in our having a soul also accept the notion of reincarnation. Agreed? Well okay let's rephrase that; most religions with – as noted earlier in this chapter – the notable exceptions of the Abrahamic religions accept reincarnation, or tolerate the possibility of it, in one form or another. But then even the more arcane wings of Judaism, Islam and Christianity, "do refer to reincarnation; these groups include the mainstream historical and contemporary followers of the Kabbalah, the Cathars, and the Shia sects such as the Alawi Shias and the Druze, and the Rosicrucians."[46] So arguably most world religions, that believe we have a soul, entertain the notion of reincarnation at an esoteric level, if not – actually there is no *if* about it – at the orthodox level.

Although the basic idea of reincarnation is simple there are a host of differing interpretations, differing perspectives by differing systems of belief, that make the whole matter quite complicated. I'm going to therefore keep this fairly simple. First let's say that the idea of it has been around for a very long time – stretching back probably more than fourteen thousand years in an oral context – and has come down to us via the Hindu Rig Vedic traditions of India, and then via Greek philosophy.

The basic idea, as already described, is that a soul enters into a relationship with what will become a growing physical body from the point of conception. At the end of a given life, depending upon spiritual growth (or a higher *nirvana* state not having been achieved), the soul moves out of the physical into an intermediary invisible state, and eventually returns, with a new physical body. The body can be either gender, or any colour or race type, depending on past experience and current life needs.[47]

That said, there are differences between East and West in these belief systems. In the Eastern view of reincarnation generally, one is trapped in an endless cycle of birth, death and rebirth until one frees oneself from samsara, from the chains of the flesh and desire. A condition of this theory is that as one dies, and leaves the body, one goes through a series of transformations (the Bardos in Tibetan Buddhism) and if one has not prepared for the event, and thereby missed the opportunity for enlightenment, then pretty soon one is incarnating into another body – and so the cycle continues.

In this view, we are in a trapped lonely and dark situation driven by fears of what awaits us on the other side of death. This is, unless, one has of course raised one's game, become more conscious and has led a life of detachment from material things, and from the trappings of desire. The view is that the more we desire and attach ourselves to things, the more we are held, as if by gravity, to the lower vibrations of physical life and matter – and the more we subsequently continue on the cycle, and whatever it brings. It's a good argument for living a simple and humble life with few possessions.

But, if facing death was bad enough, it is no joke making our return. In the Buddhist view (not actually believing in there being a permanent transmigrating *soul* but something ever changing, like a flickering flame that moves from life to life) it is as good as inevitable that we will return to exist in any one of six realms. Which one will depend upon our state at the time of our desiring to return – and what we are then attracted towards. These six realms consist of the *heavenly god realm*, the *human realm*, the *realm of demi-gods*, the *animal realm*, the realm of *hungry ghosts* and the *hell worlds*. Each realm is said to have its own law of attraction. For example, pride draws us towards the god realm; attachment or desire to the human realm; jealousy to the demi-god realm; ignorance to the animal realm; greed to the hungry ghost realm; anger or aversion to the hell realms. On this Sogyal Rinpoche writes:

> As, in the bardo of becoming, the time for rebirth gets closer, you crave more and more for the support of a material body, and you search for any one that might be available in which to be reborn. Different signs will begin to appear, warning you of the realm in which you are likely to take rebirth. Lights of various colour shine from the six realms of existence, and you will feel drawn towards one or the other, depending on the negative emotion that is

predominant in your mind. Once you have been drawn into one of these lights, it is very difficult to turn back.[48]

None of these worlds is spiritually satisfactory because they all link to the same problem of being trapped in samsara – though some are obviously worse than others. Given there are six options, in this Buddhist belief system, it is hardly surprising that one is less likely to be born back into the human realm on consecutive occasions. Tibetan Buddhism tends to bear this out: where it is considered rare to return in human form in the next life.

Unlike the Buddhist view, Hindu belief does incorporate soul (atman), but it does have a similar concern regarding what the soul is likely to return as – whether as a human, as an animal or a plant:

> He is reborn here either as a worm, or as a butterfly, or as a fish, or as a bird, or as a lion, or as a serpent, or as a tiger, or as a person, or as some other being in this or in that condition, according to his works, according to his knowledge.
>
> Kaushitaki Upanishad 1.2

From both Buddhist and Hindu perspectives how one manifests depends very much on one's state of awakening, one's desire and the karma generated during a given previous life. With the Hindu belief, a soul who, say, had a tough life being bullied, a victim in their last life, and not able to register being responsible for what they attracted towards them, might, for example, feel the need to become more headstrong, independent and aggressive in response to others. That powerful need then draws them back into an existence as, say, a tiger or other predatory creature that they may have admired, or wished they could be more like, in their previous existence. Arguably with this belief a person who has committed much wrongdoing during their previous lifetime is just as prone to return in another form, other than human, by the force of the negative karma they have generated.

In the West the concept of reincarnation is viewed less as an endless cycle of birth and rebirth, in search of nirvana, and more as a progressive movement, going from the spirit realm into human form and back to spirit realm at death. This belief is endorsed by, for example, the spiritualist movement and in the number of mediums or psychics operating. In this Western view, which I will expand upon in the next chapter, when one dies one's soul goes to another non-physical level, to what we loosely call the *Other Side*. Time (which doesn't actually exist as we know it) is usually spent there, resting and learning, before one comes back over here. The general view is that, given we have reached a degree of consciousness, we even plan our life, discuss it with advisors, perhaps rehearse it, and plot in certain milestones that we are expected to reach in our next human life. It is also conceivable that some of our sojourns could be spent on other worlds too.

The spiritual goal however is the same in both East and West – that of releasing ourselves from the hold of the lower vibration physical world, from having to return to the earth in a physical body and be instead moving ever onward to higher levels.

By contrast to the East; in the West there is the belief that we are not truly alone in life and death. It may seem that way but we have friends, helpers, loved ones on the Other Side. Even if we have no obvious friends, or known loved ones, we are still loved and cherished. There is also the view that the material world and the body are not intrinsically bad and we should live in abundance and be happy – without, as the Eastern teachers would flag up, getting too close and sucked into it. Between the two, the Eastern viewpoint of reincarnation (or rebirth) appears more pessimistic and fatalistic than the Western view – which by contrast holds a greater degree of optimism that we are on a spiritual journey through a series of steps – and that we will get there eventually if not sooner.

There is, of course, always a danger in generalising on such matters. The reality is that experience will vary from individual to individual. This is reflected in the cases of NDEs where most people, with recall, have reported on having a wonderful experience, while yet others have not had such wonderful experiences. Indeed it appears on the contrary that one or two have been quite frightening.[49] I believe that what we face in moving over to the Other Side will be akin to where we are in our heart of hearts, whether we are generally at peace in our lives or at some discord, fear, dread, particularly at the time of our departure. We attract what comes towards us, but this may not always be so much a reflection of our truer self, rather our current state. What I mean is that this could be similar to how we may experience an inspiring dream on one night and/or a nightmare on another – reflecting our mood and mental state.

Why Reincarnation makes complete sense

If we can accept planet Earth is a place where we souls come to learn, spiritually unfold, then the "threescore and ten," or even one hundred years, lifespan of a human body is unlikely to be long enough for us to complete our growth, our work and to eventually free us from our material situation and desires.

A given life I would suggest is but a chapter in our travel journal. Do we return and return for as long as it takes? Of course we do. There are those of us who believe we have a fixed number of lives on Earth before there is no need to return. I'd argue that this view misses the point of what reincarnation is about. We mostly make small progress in a given life – only speeding up as we awaken to our true situation. For most of us it is going to take many, many lives just to get the gist of the fact that we are on a spiritual quest, and only then the real work begins. It is also quite possible to go backwards too: we have freewill, we make mistakes, we get greedy and selfish, we live in fear and denial of the stuff we are made of, we hurt others, we develop hatred, we commit crimes, and we war with each other. At times the sense of separation can be stronger than the love and compassion we are capable of.

Likewise the notion of our having the one physical life and then being judged on that as to whether we are suitable for heaven, hell or purgatory, also misses the point of why we even bother to have a physical life. It becomes meaningless to believe in such a distorted view of our situation. It is a redundant belief and the sooner we move on from this then frankly all the better. Bear in mind, with the notion of one life, that one person could be around for one hundred years and judged on that, while another person lives for a week or less – and is supposedly judged on that. Could anyone be judged and potentially sent to hell after only a week? I'll leave you to contemplate the likelihood of that scenario.

Karma – the law of balance

In all our interactions we are knowingly or unknowingly creating karma…

> All that we are is the result of what we have thought: it is founded on our thoughts, it is made up of our thoughts. If a man speaks or acts with a pure thought, happiness follows him, like a shadow that never leaves him.
>
> The Dhammapada, sayings of the Buddha[50]

The Wikipedia dictionary[51] describes karma in Hindu and Buddhist beliefs as the, "sum of a person's actions in this and previous states of existence, viewed as deciding their fate..." Or it is, "Destiny or fate, following as effect from cause." But consider also these words of Gautama Buddha:[52]

> What you are, is what you have been, what you will be, is what you do now.

Or note how Padmasambhava[53] said it:

> If you want to know your past life, look into your present condition.
> If you want to know your future life, look at your present actions.

This is so karma in a nutshell. We cannot talk about reincarnation without also talking about karma. Indeed we cannot talk about *life* without talking about karma. Karma is what I would describe first and foremost as a law of balance. Being a Sun in Libra (the scales) you might think I should know about *balance* – well that's part of what I'm learning. Karma is also known by millions today as the Law of Attraction – although possibly few of the millions have made that connection.[54] The first thing to say is that karma is like electricity, it is neither intrinsically good nor bad but rather it is how it is applied that counts. We make it good or bad ourselves in other words. We create it. We can't help but create karma. Karma simply is what we create from moment to moment with our thoughts and actions. Importantly this also makes it dynamic – which means we can change it. We are dealing with cause and effect. We are creating how our future unfolds tomorrow by our thoughts and deeds today. Right now we are creating karma that will either benefit us or, that we will have to deal with, possibly painfully, in the next few moments or at some future time – like a boomerang returning to us. We can take this further and say that we are indeed helping to create our next life, our next chapter, by our thoughts and actions in this life. This is actually a huge statement. It offers opportunity to create the life and future we want or need, than be drawn into something we don't want – the concept is worth mulling over.

We do a good deed for someone, out of kindness, and a good deed is returned (not that we should be doing the good deed with that end in mind). Probably this will not happen immediately as there is usually some delay (in our physical world), but the balance will eventually be redressed. It is the same if we behave badly towards someone; that too will be redressed, probably not immediately, possibly not even in this life.

Much of the way we live and behave will be on a subconscious level – our habits our routines, our constructs, our self-perception – and thus we will be creating karma without our really being awake to what we are creating. Being awake and conscious is the clue to begin working with karma proactively for the better. From there we can begin to change the way we work with it.

Stuff happens

Generally speaking in an emancipated, and educated, culture it is perhaps easier to put an enlightened spin on karma and to consider the concept from, let's say, a comfortable positive perspective. However, as we know, a lot of grubby and nasty things happen in our world and in such, sometimes dreadful circumstances, it may not be so easy to understand or run with a cosy explanation of karma, or indeed a simple linear *action equals reaction* explanation – no matter how true that may be. On a global level much unhappy karma is being generated by ourselves in the way that we live and our attitude to life and each other. As we probably know all too well, in some places on our planet human life is treated as very cheap, easily abused and wasted. People also die from natural causes like famine, floods, disease, earthquakes, tornadoes and tsunamis and we have to consider how that works, in context with karma.

We can ask, in such circumstances, whether for example a person who has met an untimely death or has been abused as a child somehow deserved the experience they received due to their karma. We can ask whether a storm or earthquake that has taken the lives of say fifty people and destroyed the homes of thousands has resulted from their karma. This type of questioning arises a lot and is rarely answered in a way that is understandable or helpful. The problem lies in the misunderstanding of karma and our passing of judgement. If we say this or that person deserved what has happened to them, we are judging them. Of course if a person has committed a crime we may well judge that they deserve to pay for that crime. Or if a person has done good works we may judge they deserve to be acknowledged for that work. In the greater scheme of things however, besides not being our concern, not our business, it is not even really possible to pass judgement on another person's life or their karma.

This is simply because we won't have access to their travel records. We won't know what kind of lives they have lived previously and the resulting karma they generated then – with outcomes that may be manifesting now. So it is mostly not that simple. Indeed let us say we probably won't have access to our own travel records let alone anyone else's. We can of course rightly say that no one deserves to be abused as a child. As a child however we are vulnerable to those in whose trust and care we come under and the karma they are generating. It is also possible that some kind of painful experience is what our soul requires in this life, as part of our learning; a device to help us awaken – perhaps designed to remove a *rose-coloured glasses* take on life that we have carried for lives. For whatever reason, mostly unconscious to us, our karma, our previous actions and decisions brought us into this situation, though not, I prefer to believe, with the intention that we need to experience being abused – and worse become an abuser.

Karma doesn't judge, favour or dislike anyone. It is a law – like gravity. It doesn't matter how good or bad we are, if we jump off a high building, without any means of protecting ourselves from the fall, the chances are we will come to a sticky end. Our actions and decisions will have outcomes. With karma it all depends on who is steering the ship of our lives, how awake we are to what we are creating. In our spiritual development we work *with* karma to steer a steady course towards enlightenment.

To make sense of disasters where many people may die, be injured or lose their possessions, we need to consider that, as well as the karma we generate ourselves, there is also karma created by others – that we may resonate with for good or ill. There is the karma of our family, the karma of our generation, the karma of the village or town where we live, the karma of our country, indeed the karma of our world. As I see it, this can override our personal karma. We may be living a good wholesome and peaceful life but if we are under a dictatorship that subjugates its people, or living in a country that starts a war, we are caught up in the collective karma that can throw our lives into turmoil no matter what.

So karma, that can have an effect upon us, isn't necessarily always initiated by ourselves but can instead emanate via the actions of nature, the actions of other people, by the bigger collectives that we live in. Even so, in order to handle this fully, we need to become awake to accepting responsibility for the karma we attract towards us or we create. Regardless of who initiated it, we can come to resonate with such karma, and it is that resonation that we must change, if it is unhealthy. The old adage, *Know thyself*, is apt here.

As is often said, we have freedom of choice. We have however to be awake to that *freedom* to make an educated choice. Most of us, and I include myself in this, are not yet that awake to be fully functioning in this way. We are though still making that *choosing* whether we are actually conscious or unconscious to our thoughts and actions. So what we create, and how we deal with life experience, determines what we next attract and likewise create – and so it continues.

What Buddhist philosophy will tell us to do is to get our actions right, as a priority – that they should stem from right thinking, from intention to cause no harm to anything or anyone. So we can then have some say in our direction of travel. Outcomes may still be very challenging, we are on the earth after all, and we need to learn from them – indeed learning is a *given*. And learning can very much be new experience, something thrust upon us, not expected. Change can arrive regardless of our composure and intentions. One only has to think of what has happened in Tibet (one of the spiritual centres of our planet), to know that working proactively with karma need be no bed of roses. But, when working with karma two plus two need not necessarily equal four, and it is not always possible to see what positive growth may come out of destructive change. For instance, in being forcefully annexed to China, could Tibet eventually come to be a *Trojan horse*, the unexpected spiritual centre of China? It's a tough question. I'd like to think so, and if so that's karma too.

The twists and turns of Karma

Let us example some of the complications of karma. Let's consider a guy I'm here calling *Jake*. This is a person who, through life's twists and turns, has gotten involved in gun running and drug smuggling. Jake knows the risks he is taking; that there is a likely chance that he may get involved in even more serious criminal activity, and that someone, a rival gang, or the authorities, will endeavour to stop him in his activities. He runs the risk of ending up in jail serving a long sentence, or worse being shot, even killed. Either way, there is a good chance that, at some point, Jake will be stopped in his tracks – and this tendency to head into a cul-de-sac or generate an outcome of being *stopped* is a theme he is continually feeding by his thoughts and actions. Living this way he will be creating unhealthy karma – it stands to reason. This will eventually boomerang back at him. But let's remind ourselves, it may not happen necessarily in this life. We might say of Jake that when it does happen, *he had it coming to him* – or in other words, if he does get stopped it was an expected and justified outcome.

But not everything works out quite so simply. Instead of getting directly hurt or stopped the effects in this scenario are felt by another member of his family. This other person gets killed by a member of an opposing gang. The person shot is his young daughter, *Maria*. Maria will have a theme operating in her life too, that in this case brought her into living with a family involved in criminal activity (or, in this situation, just one family member involved in criminal activity). That doesn't make her a criminal or deserving of what has now happened to her. She did get involved for some purpose, some learning – maybe to help change her father's ways. She simply got caught up in the crossfire of events that drew her into the karma of the whole family – which because of the actions of Jake – lives, in any case, in an atmosphere of fear and mistrust. Let's say, timing-wise, Maria may have been likely to come down with something – but that could have been flu instead of getting hurt.

In the outcome, if Jake loved his daughter then he will, in any case, have been seriously hurt by this tragedy. One could say that if he really loved her he would not have put her life at risk in the first place, and should've known that he was; and the potential consequences. The power to change this scenario was with him.

What might be salvaged from this event is that Jake comes to see the error of his ways and now endeavours to clean up his act – end his criminal activities. The loss is too great. More likely though he will seek revenge for his daughter's death and so the vicious cycle is likely to continue. Of course the person who fired the fatal bullet, that killed Maria, has had his or her card marked, has now generated very unhealthy karma for themselves, that they in turn will have to set right. The sooner they awake to this the better because as things stand they also will continue to generate what amounts to nasty karma, and experience it back through return-fire so to speak.

Another example might be a child, a boy who, only a few years old, has contracted a terminal illness. Again we can say assuredly that he isn't *deserving* of what is happening to him – but as a soul he is *in-learning* of what is happening to him. We could use astrology, or perhaps mediumistic means, to help us gain some insight into the theme/s playing out in his life, but we cannot know for certain why his spiritual journey may have brought him to this juncture at this point – or indeed what the spiritual learning is for his parents as much as he. To us, and to them, it all looks potentially sad and unfair. There may be an intended expression of love, or learning about love, behind the pain. There may also come into the equation an intervention by someone, with specialist knowledge on the illness, that can save the child. And for all we know this is a meeting point, a planned-in milestone for a *rescuer*. The person doing the rescuing may further have been helped by this child's soul during a previous incarnation. There is, therefore, opportunity for a balance to be struck, a kindness to be repaid. But there again, it need be nothing of the sort on the part of the helping hand.

Just like the knot-work of Iron Age Celtic art we are interwoven with each other through the karma we create. Karma can work out in different ways depending upon our spiritual development and adjustments we make. There is also room for forgiveness and the chance to clear unhelpful karmic baggage, through perhaps a life of hardship or of sacrifice, or a change of heart, or changing the way we think, or making some kind of contribution to the world. It may be that for example – in the case above – being a parent and looking after a young terminally ill person allows us to grow in our understanding and human compassion, and help us become more focussed on our true priorities in life.

Where collective karma is concerned, there may be unusual times when we can be caught up in something bigger than ourselves.

We are interwoven at so many levels that, not surprisingly, events can read like simple coincidences when they are not. Regarding major catastrophes I would anticipate that if a person is fully awake, or their current life is urgent, spiritually speaking (i.e. they are trying yet again to get something right to be able to move on), then they will probably set it up to miss the rendezvous, the plane crash, the tornado they were on course for – for reasons they fell ill, arrived too late, lost the tickets, were elsewhere on holiday, something else intervened to stop them, or they suddenly, intuitively, needed to be elsewhere when, whatever it might be, kicked off.

The Soul working with Karma

Karma reminds us that we are here in a dynamic relationship and through it we are able to free ourselves from the cycle of death and rebirth. One could put it this way, without the dynamics of karma our every effort to lift our soul out of the situation we are in, to grow, would amount to nought and our fate would be to literally remain trapped in a never ending cycle of death and rebirth. Karma is like the measure of where we are on our journey, to free ourselves from the cycle. If you add in that souls most probably travel through many incarnations in other forms of life before arriving at human form, then it is also only when we are conscious enough, that is human at this time, that we can start to generate the right kind of karma – by becoming awake and proactive.

On that last note, unlike Eastern views of reincarnation or rebirth, I find it illogical to accept it is possible for a soul, having arrived at a human and therefore potentially self-conscious level, to return down the ladder of *involution*, to go back into the instinctual level of animal or plant form – as a result of karmic debt or by other means. It places the soul in a regressive position inhibiting progress into higher consciousness. No matter to what level of depravity a human being may go to, it is only by returning into human form that mistakes can be rectified, put right. I firmly believe then this reversal is not allowed, is too risky, is a deviation from our spiritual remit. My argument is that no matter what our desire may be (and notwithstanding possible sojourns on other worlds or becoming *earthbound*), once we become a human being we return here as human being until our spiritual work is done and we move on. Further, to my mind, the Eastern view only makes sense should the notion of *spiritual journey* and *learning* be removed from the equation, while at the same time retaining the cycle of birth, death and rebirth. It would, in other words, become simply the process of Samsara, now pointless, and the night terrors that accompany it.

And to complete my thinking here, it is also my understanding that a soul, going past the point of physical death, will not normally be reincarnating into another human life with any immediate effect. There are exceptions of course – as in probably all of those lives investigated by Dr Ian Stevenson and Carol Bowman, discussed in the *Fringe Benefits* chapter – where the emotional pull of human life is so powerful and timely that the soul takes the opportunity to return more or less immediately. The last thing however that most of us would be up to doing is to get back into the physical once we have died. We have to recharge our spiritual batteries and review, make sense of, the life we have just left – and also, we have a lot to talk about with those who love us. And on that note we'll talk more on this matter in the next chapter.

Notes & references

[1] Sample, I. (2011, 15 May) Stephen Hawking: There is no heaven; it's a fairy story. The Guardian.
[2] Monty Python's *Life of Brian*, also known as *Life of Brian*, is a 1979 British comedy film starring and written by the comedy group Monty Python (Graham Chapman, John Cleese, Terry Gilliam, Eric Idle, Terry Jones and Michael Palin), and directed by Jones.
[3] We have to keep in mind that the gospels, which are the main source for the life and times of Jesus (along with the Pauline epistles, and Josephus), were not only written a long time ago, they were also arguably written a fair time after Jesus lived. Mark's gospel is considered to have been written around 40 years after Jesus lived, Matthew's around 60 years after, Luke 60 years after, and John possibly 70 years after. These are estimates. Other estimates (e.g. the New

International Bible) place the writings closer to Jesus' death. It is argued that Mark's is the oldest account, written around the time that St Paul was spreading the Christian word, followed by Matthew and Luke who possibly both drew on Mark's writings for their take. John's account draws from a different source and is therefore most probably later than the other three accounts. These gospels are also believed to have been written in different locations, which give credence to the notion that the story had already spread, was probably common knowledge, when they were writing it down. Forty to seventy years after an event is long time for accounts to remain factual, without a hint of embellishment. No doubt Christian converts, writers included, were the main oral source for these writings. We have to also bear in mind that, as the Church grew, it developed its promotional message as much for political advantage as for spreading the word of Jesus, and these writings might well have served such an intention.

4 The Holy Bible (1957) King James version. Collins.

5 Note that later in John's account, Jesus does give Thomas permission to touch him - see John 20:26, 27. Jesus has by then broken all ties with his physical body. Thomas comes to see and believe but, I argue, seeing and believing in the etheric version of Jesus. What should also be considered here is that John (20:26) writes: "The doors were locked, but Jesus came and stood among them..." No locked door could stop him from appearing – that's a big clue to John's understanding of the situation.

6 Article 11 of the Catechism of the Catholic Church. http://www.vatican.va/archive/ENG0015/__P2G.HTM [Accessed 27/05/2014].

7 Catechism of the Roman Catholic Church 364. http://www.vatican.va/archive/ccc_css/archive/catechism/p1s2c1p6.htm#364 [Accessed 27/05/2014].

8 Catechism of the Roman Catholic Church 365. http://www.vatican.va/archive/ccc_css/archive/catechism/p1s2c1p6.htm#365

9 Catechism of the Roman Catholic Church 990. http://www.vatican.va/archive/ccc_css/archive/catechism/p123a11.htm#990 [Accessed 27/05/2014].

10 Christian mortalism. See http://en.wikipedia.org/wiki/Soul_sleep [Accessed 27/05/2014].

11 This was a rescue excavation (1970s) in advance of a vestry extension being built onto a village church in Cambridgeshire.

12 Monothelitism ('doctrine of one will') is a particular teaching about how the divine and human relate in the person of Jesus - whether Jesus had one divine and one human will (the Christology argument) or two natures and one will (the Monothelitism argument). Political arguments raged for years over this. Find out more http://en.wikipedia.org/wiki/Monothelitism [Accessed 25/05/2014].

13 David, W. and Gibson, M. (1980) *Reincarnation and the Soul in the Parables of Jesus.* DeVorss & Company.

[14] Origen – see Wikipedia http://en.wikipedia.org/wiki/Origen [Accessed 27/05/2014].

[15] MacGregor, G. (1978). *Reincarnation in Christianity: a new vision of the role of rebirth in Christian thought.* Quest Books. MacGregor argues for Origen believing in reincarnation and teaching it.

[16] Schaff, P. ed. (1994)[1885] *The Anathemas Against Origen. Nicene and Post-Nicene Fathers: Series II, Volume XIV (The Seven Ecumenical Councils).* Peabody, Massachusetts: Hendrickson Publishers.

[17] Origen op. cit., see under sub-heading 'Character.'

[18] Synod of Constantinople (543) was convened to condemn Origen - http://en.wikipedia.org/wiki/Synod_of_Constantinople_(543) [Accessed 25/05/2014].

[19] Grieveson, A. (2011) *A Series of Past Lives.* Kindle Edition.

[20] At this funeral I took a pair of wellingtons and shovel with me. After the burial I changed into my "wellies" and helped the caretaker to backfill the hole. It felt good to be there, just the caretaker (who knew my father) and myself. To be participating in the burial, rather than a detached mourner, as I have been at other funerals, was special.

[21] Rinpoche, S. (1988) *The Survival of Consciousness: A Tibetan Buddhist Perspective.* Article in Self & Society.

[22] Yanki Tauber. *What is Soul?* http://www.chabad.org/library/article_cdo/aid/3194/jewish/What-is-a-Soul.htm [Accessed 27/05/2014]

[23] In The Four Ethers, Horst Helmann, drawing on Rudolf Steiner, clarifies these with the forces that act on the four seasons of the year – in the cycle of activity and rest. He goes on to further the association with the four elements as such: The warmth ether - fire; the life ether - earth; the light ether - air; the sound ether - water. Visit http://anthrophils.wordpress.com/2013/04/02/the-four-ethers-a-summary/ [Accessed 27/05/2014].

[24] Bailey, A. and Khul, D. (1971) *Ponder on This* [Compilation] The Lucis Press Ltd. P114.

[25] Ibid. P115.

[26] Ibid. P115.

[27] This is similar to the lines of force (ley lines) that are said to run around the Earth, and where these cross are considered important and sensitive centres of energy - often associated with paranormal experience.

[28] Bailey and Khul (1971) op. cit., P37.

[29] Bailey, A (1930) *The Soul and its Mechanism.* Lucis Trust Press Ltd.

[30] Bailey and Khul (1971) op. cit., P37.

[31] Bailey and Khul (1971) op. cit., P38.

[32] Drawn from The Different Bodies of Man http://www.plotinus.com/subtle_bodies_copy.htm [Accessed 21/06/2014].

[33] Take a look at the page about the aura on Wikipedia - http://en.wikipedia.org/wiki/Aura_(paranormal). [Accessed 27/05/2014]. Carries various beliefs and interpretations.

[34] Baba, M. (1967) *Discourses 2 San Francisco: Sufism reoriented* P145. ISBN 978-1880619094

[35] Bailey and Khul (1971) op. cit., P23.

[36] CG Jung comment – see http://en.wikipedia.org/wiki/Astral_body [Accessed 27/05/2014].

[37] Heindel, M. (1953) *The Desire Body*. The Rosicrucian Fellowship.

[38] Bailey and Khul (1971) op. cit., P24.

[39] Heindel, M. (1909) *The Rosicrucian Cosmo-Conception* (Chapt 3: Man and the Method of Evolution). The Rosicrucian Fellowship.

[40] Bailey and Khul (1971) op. cit., P271.

[41] Bailey and Khul (1971) op. cit., P271.

[42] Bailey and Khul (1971) op. cit., P271.

[43] International Association for Near Death Studies (IANDS) website - http://iands.org/home.html [Accessed 27/05/2014].

[44] ARAS (2010) *The Book Of Symbols: Reflections On Archetypal Images*. ARAS - The Archive for Research in Archetypal Symbolism.

[45] For more information on ants check out: http://en.wikipedia.org/wiki/Ant [Accessed 27/05/2014].

[46] Reincarnation on Wikipedia http://en.wikipedia.org/wiki/Reincarnation [Accessed 27/05/2014].

[47] It occurs to me that the incidence of people being, in their view, born into the wrong body (sensing they are female in a male body or vice versa), could possibly be due to their soul having spent many lives in one gender, and now finding difficulty accepting being born into the opposite gender – when their soul needs to experience that gender.

[48] Rinpoche, S. (1992) *The Tibetan Book of Living and Dying*. P295. Rider.

[49] Holden, J. (2003) *Distressing Near-Death Experiences*. IANDS. This document is available in PDF format off the IANDS website.

[50] Müller, F. M. (2004) *Sacred Books of the East, Vol. 10 - The Dhammapada*. Motilal Banarsidass.

[51] Check out http://en.wikipedia.org/wiki/Karma [Accessed 27/05/2014].

[52] Rinpoche, S. (1992) op. cit., P93.

[53] Rinpoche, S. (1992) op. cit., P93.

[54] Grabhorn, L. (2005) *Excuse Me, Your Life is Waiting*. Hodder Mobius. This book is about the Law of Attraction. Grabhorn writes in context, "There is no karma from past lives. That's all victim stuff. And there is not a victim amongst us only co-creators..."(p24) She misses the point that if fully explored and understood she would see the Law of Attraction is a western rehash of the Law of Karma. This is otherwise an excellent book for exploring the Law of Attraction.

CHAPTER 6

THE OTHER SIDE

Is there an *Other Side*, a place we go to after death? If there is such a place what is it like? What will we do there? For that matter, where is it?

> Our ideas about death have been erroneous; we have looked upon it as the great and ultimate terror, whereas in reality it is the great escape, the entrance into a fuller measure of activity, and the release of the life from the crystallised vehicle and an inadequate form.
>
> Alice A Bailey, esoteric writer, theosophist[1]

Am I entirely right to say (as I did in the *Are You Ready For This?* chapter, using a bit of logic) that for the most part we can really, bottom line, only talk about *belief* or *faith* in the afterlife than to know it as something real? Well, that is going to be true for the greater majority of us at this time, particularly those of us who need some kind of undeniable proof. It reflects our human condition where it can be a challenge to step outside of the limiting senses we live in, and rely on, to guide us in our world. I hasten to add though that evidence for the afterlife is mounting, and besides it is not how everyone is seeing this matter. Experience can change how we view things. I trust that reading through the content of the *Fringe Benefits* chapter you will have been given some cause to consider that the afterlife is based upon more than belief or faith. Rather it is based upon a premise, from which, when you pull all the strands together, a picture emerges of a situation that can be predicted, with some confidence, to exist. Indeed one might propose it is more real than the illusion of solidity that we live in here. There are also those amongst us who would go a lot further and say they have actually been to the Other Side (we'll hear from one or two of them below), whilst others would claim they receive direct communications from the Other Side, and that therefore, based upon such evidence, for all of them, the afterlife does most definitely exist – having less to do with belief or faith, but rather a *knowing*.

While working through this chapter I'm going to take it as read that our soul life is a continuum; that we are more, much more than the limits of our physical circumstances. If this is not what you believe to be the case at this stage let me ask you to suspend your disbelief for a while, through this chapter, and see how you view it at the end. I'll also be drawing on some of my own experience in this chapter to underline points of discussion, or to give example.

Starting from This Side

Shortly we're going to take a trip over to the Other Side. Well okay not literally at this point but based upon what we can garnish from those who have been up close to it and those, who I trust, have spoken to one or two of its residents. Before doing so however I want to take a moment to consider our situation on what we may as well call *This Side*, or from our point of arrival to the place we are in now. From where I am coming from the two inevitably go hand in hand – two transition points of a cycle, and equally important.

So let me start here by saying it is my understanding that all, or most of us will have already experienced being on the Other Side – it won't be new to us when we go back there. In our incarnations we will have spent probably many lives over here and each time have returned back over there. It may appear strange when we go there, after the impressions of living within physical conditions for so long (or what appears to be a long time), but it will have a ring of familiarity about it, and well, of course, it may take a while to recall and adjust. If you have ever been into a cinema during a matinee session; watched a movie, with the lights out of course, and then emerged back out into daylight at the end, you'll know how strange and disorienting the otherwise familiar world outside, with all its continuity, noise and busyness, can suddenly feel – after one has been away on an adventure. Similarly coming out of a deep sleep can leave us disoriented for a while as we adjust. But of course what I am talking of here represents a bigger change. It is a return to our true home. Well I should qualify that as *home* is relative; a better description is to say it is our truer state, a step in the right direction, from where we are now; where we are no longer driving around in, and hampered by, the human vehicle and physical world.

Through the tunnel

There are hands, trying to pull me. Strange hands, pulling, it's too tight... Oh God, I'm out. Out of the tunnel. There's a harsh, glaring light everywhere. I can't open my eyes, I don't want to open my eyes. There are hands, more hands on me, and too much noise, too loud. I'm cold. I'm so cold. Who are these people? I don't want to be here. Please, just let me go back...

Sylvia Browne, writer, medium[2]

This comment was made by a client under regressive hypnosis with psychic medium Sylvia Browne – and written about in *Life on The Other Side*. You might be thinking, "Well if this is what going over to the Other Side is like I want none of it," and who would blame you. And if that were the case, Browne might also agree with you. Further on she says, "That settles it... I will never take a hypnosis subject through the nightmare of their birth again." Yes, you probably guessed it; this wasn't, in other words, commentary on hands pulling anyone through a tunnel to the Other Side. The description was about someone arriving here, to our physical world.

While we may talk a lot about NDEs, and going through a tunnel following death, it is sometimes overlooked that we arrive here in the physical world through the birth canal – another tunnel. By all accounts, seeing it in the round, this is not such a nice place to come into from the spiritual side of life, indeed with hindsight we may choose to describe it as a kind of hellish backward step, a place of linear time, of beginnings and endings, of past and future, of restrictions and limitations, of happiness and sadness, of boundaries, of life and death, of duality. There are however darker states, outside the physical world, that we can put ourselves into, and so if we think things are bad here they can get a whole lot worse – and we'll look at this soon enough.

Forgetting who we are – and why we came here

Most of us forget our spiritual identity as we return to the physical world. This stands to reason as coming here we are slowed down in our energies, our vibration. We become limited by the physicality of the body, which we also come to identify with as we grow into it. Slowly but surely we become the name we are now given as a child, perhaps Samantha, Adebayo, Yasmin, Josh, Akihiko, Thomas, or Josephine, and we develop into the person that we associate with our name. We get filled with the experience of our family, our peers, our culture and the gender we have moved into, and, over a fairly brief amount of time, any memories we have, of where we came from, begin to fade, get put on the back burner, and are eventually subsumed by our dealing with the world on this side.

It is possibly also the case that our brains are not wired to support remembering our bigger life. Consider Dr Eben Alexander's view on this, in *Proof of Heaven*:

> To understand how the brain might actually block our access to knowledge of the higher worlds, we need to accept ... that the brain itself doesn't actually produce consciousness. That it is, instead, a kind of reducing valve or filter, shifting the larger, nonphysical consciousness that we possess in the nonphysical worlds down into a more limited capacity for the duration of our mortal lives.

And he considers there is a very definite advantage to not remembering our bigger life:

> ... it is that forgetting our trans-earthly identities also allows us to be 'here and now' far more effectively ... ordinary life holds too much information for us to take in at once and still get anything done, being excessively conscious of the worlds beyond the here and now would slow down our progress even more.
>
> Dr Eben Alexander, neurosurgeon, NDE experiencer and author [3]

We could however consider one person's brain being more receptive, more supportive than another, for recalling past life memories and being able to retain them. We know there are the accounts of children – such as James Leininger[4] discussed in the *Fringe Benefits* chapter – remembering past lives, so it is most certainly possible to remember something of a previous existence. Given one has the propensity and openness it is also a skill that can possibly be learned and developed, as a person learning to round out their psychic abilities, or who is in the process of becoming a medium, may testify to.

As suggested in the *Fringe Benefits* chapter – in relation to Carol Bowman's comments on the young age by which we may remember a past life, or begin to forget it – I'm inclined to think that as children the tendency will be there for us to remember something of a previous existence. However, unless this remembering is acknowledged and supported by someone, usually our parent/s or siblings, it is probably soon gone – like a dream we have awoken from and now can't recall.

Getting in touch with our spiritual agenda

Of course the reason we have arrived here at all, in the physical world, put in simple terms is two-fold. It is to awaken to our spiritual situation and move on from being here – and the continuing treadmill of returning here. It is also to be of some kind of service to other souls where we can – who are likewise seeking to move on. The whole is encapsulated in love, love for oneself, love for others, and love for the opportunity, the situation, we are in. Given that, it is important to consider that in other respects our forgetfulness of our past suggests it is all the more of a challenge to recover, to become awake to, our own spiritual agenda and plan of action, that we have decided upon for this trip. That we do have an agenda, a plan is an esoteric *given* and boils down to arriving with the karma of our past and an intention to redress that karma – or at least some of it. This plan may be quite simple or complex, having been designed for us by advisors or by ourselves with the help of advisors. Or, possibly, if we are well along our journey, it may have been designed entirely by ourselves – with, let's say, a thumbs up from the right sources.

It may be that the narrative of our life rolls out naturally in a manner that doesn't require us to be that aware of our past, or need to be too concerned with there being any kind of agenda involved with our current life. I mean by this that other people, our parents, the friendships we build, our work, may help provide the structure that makes sure we are given opportunity to find our spiritual feet for this life journey. Following in one's father or mother's footsteps, where vocation is concerned, might be just what is needed for one person to make headway, and yet for another the very obvious of what not to do – something to push against. For another person, following an orthodox religion provides just what they need at this point on their journey, to give a firm routine and ethical structure to their life. For yet another person it is joining a movement that challenges convention that sparks their fire. It could be that we have come with the sole purpose to develop a particular skill or express a particular talent. It could of course be we have come to live a quiet life this time, to make some necessary adjustment in context with the exhaustion of a previous life. There are obviously going to be as many variations on this theme as there are souls.

We may spend many lives having our existences being played out in relatively unchallenging circumstances, spiritually speaking that is. As we become awake to the need to progress however then by some device we will probably seek to make sense of life and remind ourselves of what it is we came to do in our *here and now*. As we are awakening there will come the need to explore and nourish ourselves through experience, through study, through our attraction to topics of interest, directly holistic and spiritual in nature or what could, at first, be more borderline, such as humanitarian concerns, perhaps concern for the environment, interest in holistic medicines, becoming a vegetarian. It may involve a radical change of lifestyle, joining a group with similar interests, working for a charity or charitable cause, perhaps living in a type of commune with a wholesome cause or agenda.

With regard to there being an agenda, or plan of action, awaiting us: A number of us, it is fair to say, will at some point become aware of that possibility and go looking for a plan either under our own volition, or by seeking help to find one. Probably some of us do find what we believe or accept to be our spiritual agenda. Others of us become disillusioned when we don't find one, or one that fails to meet our expectations. This can all become a bit like looking for the *Holy Grail* out there.

> Daiju visited the master Baso in China.
> Baso asked: "What do you seek?"
> "Enlightenment," replied Daiju.
> "You have your own treasure house. Why do you search outside?" Baso asked.
> Daiju inquired: "Where is my treasure house?"
> Baso answered: "What you are asking is your treasure house."
> Daiju was enlightened! Ever after he urged his friends: "Open your own treasure house and use those treasures."
>
> Extract from The Gospel According to Zen[5]

For those of us struggling with this, I'd suggest that we drop being overly concerned with the search and get on with our life. Put it this way, if it is urgent enough our spiritual agenda will find us – or we will trip over it when we least expect it. We need to be receptive to the possibility of finding it, of course. Another way to say this is that the planning was important before we arrived but now it is what we are experiencing, thinking and doing here that is important – which in any case will affect our recovering our plan, or not, as the case may be. Besides, we have our *own treasure house* and all we really need to do is follow our heart, our inner voice, and definitely follow a spiritual practice that provides the foundation for our agenda to emerge. The pieces of our plan will then come together by themselves if they need to – or, and this is important, we can create a new plan – make it one that incorporates compassion, love and understanding as aimed-for goals.

Actually if you want a starter plan of action to help you establish, or re-establish, your own spiritual plan and agenda, you'll find one under, *Six months to live* in the Appendix. I would encourage you to follow any such plan of action under your own steam as much as possible – at least until what you are growing is becoming well rooted, watered, and you are committed to it. Note, you will probably find anyhow you are often alone on this journey and at times it will be challenging. If I can offer advice, try to remain tenacious, enjoy the scenery and always try to appreciate and be grateful for what your life is bringing to you – the trick, or more likely the hard bit, is to take *responsibility for it*, however which way it is manifesting.

Of signs and guides

Taking this, life plan, matter from another perspective: in terms of, *being receptive to the possibility*, of bumping into one's life plan, I would suggest to anyone tenaciously pursuing this outcome that you keep an eye out for the signs around you. These might indeed entail hints, markers or milestones that you have prearranged, or have been prearranged for you, to rendezvous with. They could of course be creations stemming out of your own, current, activities and thoughts. I believe we all have signs that help to light our way. It is easier to get to grips with this if we can also accept – as I have flagged up before – we live in a dynamic, symbolical and meaningful world. Yes I know I keep using this word *meaningful*, but I do want to get it across. So much hinges on grasping this, as I see it, reality. We resonate with what is around us. We'll get little hints, sometimes big hints that we are on the right or wrong track – but of course we need to recognise these when they arrive.

These hints may be in the form of an invitation to an open door, or open road. They may come in the form of resistance, a symbolical brick wall in a direction we are attempting to go in – implying our route may be either blocked or requiring more effort to succeed in. They may come as a helping hand perhaps from a stranger, or possibly by, what Carl Jung described as, an outcome of synchronicity, where events have no obvious causal connection but can in themselves be meaningful. For example, I lived in a flat at an archaeological field centre for a number of years. At the time I was given opportunity to move to the centre I was already happily living in a town house (the same town house where one of my ghost stories took place) where I had stayed for some time with work colleagues, and where everything was familiar, friendly and to hand. The opportunity to move to the new centre also meant living by myself, relatively *out in the sticks* (near gravel quarry pits – later to become part of a new country park, now called *Ferry Meadows*), and therefore somewhat disconnected from the team, with potentially a much reduced social life as a result. It was with some trepidation that I decided to move there. The point to this story is that the key to this flat was then sent to me, through the post, by my employer. It came sandwiched in what looked like two old library index cards, to make it less obvious and stiffen the envelope. On one of these cards was written the words, "Action of a Tiger" and on the other, "The Future Looks Promising." The cards had served their purpose in getting the key to me, and none of what was written on them was actually intended for my benefit, by the person who sent the letter. However I was by then more accepting of there being symbolism and meaning to life, most of which admittedly can be difficult to read, but this wasn't. I took what was written on the cards as good news, as an endorsement that I had made the right decision to go it alone – and indeed it was. Looking back this move to live by myself, for some time, transpired to be one of the more important milestones on my journey.

Thinking on, this idea of symbolism operating in our lives shouldn't really be so odd for us to contemplate. We are part-way there with our feelings. I mean, talking of flats; how often, when looking to buy or rent a house or a flat, do we decide by what we feel is right – and probably in the first few seconds of our visit? Even when all the obvious boxes are ticked it will come down to how we feel about this house or that location. Sometimes everything fits and we go with it. Sometimes everything fits but we can't go with it –

there being something not quite right. And, when someone asks for an explanation on our decision we may find it difficult to explain – and we probably say, "I can't quite put my finger on it but that's the way I feel." The reason we feel this way is there symbolically, and probably in spades around us if we could but read the signs.

In context, and drawing on some personal experience again, I'm reminded of one of the forms of hints or *nudges* I've regularly experienced – that one might call *numerological hints* or omens. I know others have had similar experience, and indeed it was even the main feature of a movie, *The Number 23*, that starred Jim Carrey. This is to do with recurring numbers. In my case it is the number *41*, and also *14* that have cropped up in all kinds of odd places during my life. It started with 41, a number a friend, Eddie Black, and I used for our motorcycle sidecar outfit that we raced on grasstrack, in the UK, during the Sixties – Eddie owned the outfit and chose the number. Sometime after I stopped racing I began noticing the number cropping up again. At first irregularly in places, such as on car number plates, on buses, on tickets, on telephone numbers, on houses I would be visiting, on tables I would be given in restaurants and a host of odd places too.

Initially I put it all down to association with the past, and my, subconsciously, picking up on the number as a result, but the occurrence got so noticeable during the Seventies[6] that I began to keep a record of its occurrence. I also sought to make sense of it by consulting the Chinese oracle, the I Ching, which I was starting to use at the time. The I Ching consultation provided hexagrams, *36* and *5* to help explain it – and I'll let you do the maths. The insight provided was very helpful. A year or so later I found this number could reverse to 14, and I then went through a spate of seeing 14 in all sorts of odd places, and also becoming associated with 41. In numerology both these numbers reduce to number 5 (as does the number 23 in the movie) which is a number of *change* and *movement*. I came eventually to understand that the number 14 cropping up was corresponding with a green light on my journey and activities, or my being on-track, being in the right place at the right time. The number

41, on the other hand, is a red light, a warning, indicating likely difficulty, tests or some kind of danger ahead and to be alert – just like, for that matter, racing on grasstrack with the same number. The discovery might also suggest I was attracting this number, perhaps both numbers, before that period of my life but just hadn't noticed it happening.

Probably the most important aspect of these recurring numbers has been that they provoked me into exploring life on a deeper level. Not all such clues will necessarily be that meaningful or easy to interpret – especially if we go out looking for them. But if it is happening often, and being repeated, particularly in circumstances where it takes you unawares, or off-guard, where it may be a little spooky in its occurrence, it most probably is a clue that you need to consider a little more seriously, and the meaning behind the symbolism explored and understood.

Meanwhile, if you are embroiled in the search for your own Holy Grail, and have reliable means, try getting in touch with your guide. We all have a guide (or sometimes more than one guide) and/or helper or both. The helper could be a family member who has passed on and who has our best interests at heart. I've had a discussion with one of my guides (see my past life readings, in the previous chapter). I can say with some confidence that a guide is a soul who, like any of us, will have been on Earth, no doubt a number of times – and who has progressed in their spiritual development. Our guides may have spent many adventures with us. It is even possible that we have been their guide in other lifetimes, but this seriously depends on our experience and development.[7] Guides or helpers are not allowed to directly interfere with our lives but they can drop hints that we might pick up on to encourage us on our path – this is sometimes with the emphasis on *subtle*. The guide I spoke to told me that I would be meeting, "someone special and moving to an area with a sea in it." When I said I'd always liked the idea of living by the sea, he told me not to take him quite so literally. Well a good number of years on from that discussion I met my beautiful life companion, Annie. She was in the process of moving out of London when I met her, and invited me to join her – it was on a business footing at the time. I was up for it and we moved to an area not with a "sea" in it, but with a "C" in it – that is, we moved to the Cotswolds. I bet, if my guide was listening in back then, he smiled when the penny finally dropped.

Of course there are equally big clues, to our spiritual intentions and direction, in considering the country we are born into, where we are now living in this, that or other country; and especially in our relationships. Family, friends, partners will provide meaningful insight into where we are at and heading on our current journey. It is again a case of whether we pick up on them, or not, in symbolical context as much as anything. We may love our parents, friends, partners, brothers and sisters, grandparents, aunts and uncles, etc., very dearly but we also need to try to see what they symbolise or represent for us, what they are the *bringers of* into our lives (likewise we for them) – or alternatively what they take away from our lives or challenge us on. What is it they have to teach us? Does the relationship and learning help or hinder our quest? Also what does it say when we don't have such relatives or indeed friends around us?

On the point of families: it is important to comment that some souls tend to stick together and form group incarnations – meaning they may spend time with each other over a number of lives, and probably swap places or roles in their group situations. To me this is a bit like holding each other's hand through life experiences, giving each other support. In some way the learning is being repeated or is something of a shared learning. Sounds wonderfully secure, even a bit like a time-travelling drama group, but it is still important to grasp whether one is growing as a result or being held back. Eventually one does have to do it under one's own steam. Of course these are often young souls needing additional support in early incarnations. Souls also incarnate in generation groupings too and share generation intentions and learning needs.

Whatever way we arrive it needs to be said that all the people we meet, and especially those with whom we form important relationships, are holding up a mirror to us, they mirror something within us that is wholesome and good, or some part of us that is challenged, where growth and adjustment is being required. As we know, some people we meet will be passing ships, while yet others will become fellow travellers, for all or a part of our journey. Others will test our metal for all the wrong reasons, and others for all the right reasons. As I know, from looking back, one or two of the so-called *passing ships*, may be surprisingly instrumental in providing a needed link to the next milestone in our journey – certainly this is true in my life. We can learn something from all of them – and indeed are meant to learn from them – and they from us, of course.

Systems to help find your spiritual agenda

If you really want to get insight into the karmic theme/s operating behind your life, I'd suggest you get hold of, and make a thorough study of your astrological birthchart. It will give you a snapshot of the situation you have entered into. It is your *plan of action* written in symbolical form. Indeed you really need look no further than to study and act on it. Looking at things even through basic astrology can also flag up interesting group patterns that can provide further insight into links with the people you are with. For example, simply looking at Sun-signs in my core family group, consisting of my parents, sisters and myself (six people), the pattern involved my father (a Leo) and my mother (an Aquarian), a further Leo sister and also an Aquarian sister – therefore four people born on the same opposite signs – the Leo/Aquarius axis. One other sister is a Gemini and myself a Libra – which in turn means there were two Fire signs and four Air signs in the original grouping. On a broad, positive, sweep, a group theme of friendliness, being sunny, witty and communicative, while encouraging optimism, detachment and independence, was prominent in my childhood home. This core pattern can also be seen to have developed out later around a Leo direction, with all four sibling relationships having a Leo involved. My Leo sister married a Scorpio. My Aquarian and Gemini sisters each married Leos, and my partner is also a Leo (with, by the way, Aquarius rising – that Leo/Aquarius axis again). Talk about being with a pride of lions, or in the lions' den – dangerous methinks. All of this is meaningful and a resource to be understood. You might see what you can find by checking out your own family birthdates just on Sun-signs alone. If you have access to an ephemeris and wish to go deeper look for other themes – definitely check out the Moon, Saturn and Venus signs too, as these will help to provide insight into the nature of your relationship/s.

One can of course gain much nourishment and insight regarding one's *meaningful* journey by other systems that provide such facility – I'm thinking of for example the I Ching (already mentioned), the tarot, and numerology. On the latter, I hasten to add that much symbolical knowledge can be gleaned about one's circumstances from studying numbers, and their meaning, in context with one's name, date of birth, places one links with, street names, house numbers, telephone numbers, and the pin numbers we have also chosen. This is especially so where we have chosen numbers without giving much thought to it – or where, alternatively, numbers have been chosen for us. All can aid our understanding of who we are and the kind of choices we are making. Finally let us not underestimate getting spiritual insight through active choice as in applying the Law of Attraction, through prayer, and through contemplation and meditation. Remember our larger goal is always to become more loving human beings – to follow our heart, as easy or difficult as that may be.

Hell, Fire and Damnation – avoiding the dark side

We have freedom to choose our pathway on the earth. No one forces direction upon us – or shouldn't. We know that for a great number of people this is not how it is playing out at this time – with the rise in human slavery and trafficking often in the news. We learn eventually to take responsibility in that too. I have been arguing that operating at an instinctive level, an animal may take action that might to us be thoughtless, even vicious and savage, and yet it is natural behaviour

---

and the animal remains in a state of innocence and blameless. We human beings don't have that luxury – if you can call it that – any longer. We operate at a higher level of awareness and are therefore responsible and culpable for our actions. There may be the exception of where a person is imbalanced, psychologically unwell and not therefore orchestrating their actions with the capacity of clear reason. In this state it is fair to assume that while such a person carries responsibility for their actions, as the next human being – they are not awake to that responsibility and so it may be lost on them. Sick or not, all our actions generate karma that will affect ourselves, as well as possibly affecting others, and, although this can be positive in some circumstances, it can just as easily be negative in nature; and all the more reason why a sick unstable person needs to be supported, healed and helped to be get back on the right path to wakefulness.

Going against the current, against the light, with intention, is always an option but not one to be recommended as it has obvious consequences, repercussions – I mean (paraphrasing Mark 8:36) what does it profit anyone to gain the whole world and by doing so compromise their own soul, their own spiritual health? There's nothing intrinsically wrong with having power, wealth and abundance, rather the issue may lie in how we came by it, what route we took to get to that position – and what we then do with it. That's where the good or damage can occur. It's often a case of, *it ain't what you do, it's the way that you do it.*

Crime doesn't pay

Of course most of us would agree with this heading. From the spiritual perspective crime against another on the physical level may be of less concern than how it affects their soul, or for that matter the perpetrator's soul. Let's say for example I stole something from a person and they didn't notice I had taken it. They are unaffected by it, and probably think, when discovering it is missing, that somehow they lost it. I might think I have gotten away with it. In a worldly sense I have, but regardless of what they know, I know I took something that wasn't mine to take. I have generated some negative karma by my actions. This will need to be taken stock of by my soul and need to be brought back into balance – in this life or another life. I have to set the records straight, give the item, or it's equal, back somehow. It could mean that I have something of value taken from me, that I maybe haven't noticed – but that's not really setting right a wrong under my own volition. It might more favourably work out that I meet the same soul, in a different life, and wholeheartedly give them something, at least to the value of what I took from them. I could likewise see the error of my ways now and, let's say, give it back to the person I originally took it from, and redress the balance immediately. We have choices and we make choices that determine outcomes.

In the story of Robin Hood, he and his merry men steal from the rich and greedy to give back to the poor, the abused and downtrodden, the underdog. Robin and his men committed crimes yet with good intention in a worldly sense. They were only giving back, and balancing the books of what had been taken in unfair taxes and extortion. This would suggest a levelling out of karma. It also of course links in with the British sense of fair play. What Robin did was considered noble and right, but this assessment is based upon human justice and not necessarily spiritual justice. The story is based on a skewered eye-for-an-eye mentality. Not everyone who is rich deserves to be robbed (well does anyone deserve to be robbed?) of what they have, no matter how they came by it. Not everyone who is poor is deserving of receiving, what is in effect, stolen property (well does anyone?). Two wrongs don't make a right. Robin and his men could not have known the karmic situation of the people they robbed or the people they gave to, so spiritually they were wrong in their actions. It makes for a great story, but let me tell you that had the Sheriff of Nottingham gone through a change of heart and given back taxes to those he had taken from unfairly, by his own volition – as indeed in the *awakening* story of Scrooge – then that would've been a very different saga. It probably wouldn't be so well remembered as Robin's story but the bells would have been ringing in heaven – on the day the Sheriff gave it away, by his choosing.

Talking of heaven

One has to form one's own opinion but I don't buy into heaven or hell in the orthodox portrayal of these as *places* – or to include purgatory for that matter. This story goes that depending upon how one has behaved on the earth, one is sent to heaven or hell, and then that's it; you're in heaven or hell for keepers – or possibly in purgatory, at the crossroads of the two. It's partly the, *for keepers* bit that I have an issue with, and also their representation as fixed places in the orthodox sense. There will always be room for our making amends and for forgiveness or, alternatively, becoming the fallen, through our thoughts and deeds. I do however firmly believe in a state of mind, or what might be more appropriately called a *state of soul*, whereby heaven and hell do exist, can appear very real and long term. Love exists in abundance and finds its own level, and by contrast hatred, ignorance, arrogance and darkness can and does also exist on the Other Side of physical life, and it too finds its own level.

Talking of hell

Rightly or wrongly I believe that all souls, who have entered into the human form, are essentially wonderful, full of hope – or at least we start out that way as children. Yes, we have propensities and capacities to lean in certain directions, that are not always necessarily healthy, but providing we are taught well, and develop a healthy conscience and moral code, then if we do something wrong, our awareness of a wrongdoing means we have a choice, most often, to put things right in this life or, if not, well we'll probably have to do it in the next life. There is however the possibility that one or two of us bring forward a darker character and we don't seek to put things right. Rather we seek to deliberately hurt others, for a host of reasons: for money, for revenge, to frighten people, for our own satisfaction, out of our own fear, or we draw pleasure from the power or control we have over others. Spiritually, if we live by this sword and fail to redress the matter, we most certainly will <u>not</u> die by it – because the soul can't die. Death in the spiritual does not exist, but we may as well be dead as we can take ourselves into a very dark spiritual state.

> Between the Earth realm and the heavenly realms, there exist two hellish realms known as the earthbound realm and the void. Both of these realms can be considered hell because they are the two darker levels.
>
> Kevin R Williams, founder of NDE Research Foundation [8]

A view, among psychics and mediums, possibly not all, that makes for a lot of common sense, is that there are dark levels or *planes* on the Other Side. These are there because souls, in simple terms, have created them – no God, nor Devil, need be involved in this. First off it is important to say that souls who are in a fixed denial of their own death, or who have been damaged, or have fallen into an abyss of their own making, by their deeds when in the physical, who have fallen so low, who do not also seek to redeem themselves, can become *earthbound*. They become grounded, remaining trapped in their own situation through ignorance, desires and fears rather than go towards the light – which is within their capability – or they fail to allow themselves to be helped towards the light by others sent to help them. Some in this regard continue to identify with a physical life they have led, continuing on with their thoughts, activities and routines, even though now over, and could have been for tens even hundreds of earth years. They can become, and then remain, trapped in their habitual mindset. They can be oblivious to help offered, or they reject help for fear of what will happen to them if they accept it – if they let go of what they are trying to get back to. For others their intentions may be more perverse. They may know they are dead physically and seek to take full advantage of their hidden state. They may believe (similar to the Bill Wilkins' personality in the Enfield Poltergeist story) they could be killed off if they let go – so engrained is their fear and separation. It may be because of what they got up to in life – if they have had a human life, as some may not – and, in context, what they are getting up to now, that they fear going out of the frying pan into the fire, of a greater darkness, what some call the *Void*. Williams writes in his article, *Hell and the Near-Death Experience*:

> The ... void is totally devoid of love, light, and everything. It is a realm of complete and profound darkness where nothing exists but the thought patterns of those in it. It is [however] a perfect place for souls to examine their own mind, contemplate their recent Earth experience, and decide where they want to go next.[9]

If normal physical life can sometimes be described as a kind of hell, then it can be taken with a pinch of salt when compared to the states we are looking at here. They really are closer to the hell of orthodox religion but with the difference being this is a state of mind, not a place per se, but real nonetheless. The void is not necessarily all bad. It depends upon one's spiritual health and intentions. From Williams' perspective, the void can be, "a beautiful and heavenly experience because, in the absence of all else, they [souls] are able to perfectly see the love and light they have cultivated within themselves." But for others it is a, "terrifying and horrible hell because, in the absence of everything, they are able to perfectly see ... the lack of love and light they have cultivated within themselves."[10] The void is a state for reflection, for cleansing and healing wounds, a state for purification. A soul can get trapped there until, to coin a phrase, *one has seen the light* and a different course of action can be chosen, and help arrives.

To comment further on the earthbound state: This is a fixation, a chronic state, and not to be confused with the state of the soul who is temporarily finding it difficult to accept they have died, and who resides within their familiar life pattern following death. Either by disorientation or their sense of urgency to complete something, or their needing to stay close to grieving loved ones. It goes without saying, death is a huge change for most of us, having enormous implications regarding what we can and can't now do. Finding oneself outside of the physical body, now unhampered by its restrictions, can be like getting out of a prison. But coming out of prison, after a long stay, need be no walk in the park. Rather leaving behind what we were familiar with, the regular routine, the *normality*, can be as equally scary as prison itself. On proviso one eventually moves in the right direction, and/or accepts help, all is fine. Meanwhile being earthbound is a *no-man's land* state, is a prison one puts oneself into, and those lost souls imprisoned in it can also be willing inmates with a preference to hanging around the earth. As indicated, some souls, it is believed, actually thrive in this state.

Such perpetrators most probably desire to get back into the physical world, to inhabit a physical body, rather than go to the spiritual realm where they belong. Because of their situation however they cannot be reborn in human form. This is similar to the Hungry Ghost state of Buddhist belief. The Buddhists believe that this realm holds those who have committed excessive amounts of terrible deeds and who are obsessed with desires they cannot fulfil – and who are consequently tortured by the experience. Psychic medium, Rachel Keene (RachelKeene.co.uk) writes of such souls:

> There are … some truly dark souls who just want to snuff out any glimmer of light they see – especially in children as their light burns brightest. These low entities tend to remain earthbound by choice eventually because they know from a past life or lives that the dark place awaits, so instead they choose to deliberately linger here and cause havoc.
>
> Rachel Keene, psychic medium [11]

Keene also describes a "dark plane" similar to the void described by Williams:

> When a person who has willingly chosen to harm others with their deeds dies, there is a dark plane of existence waiting. Those who go there have a potential eternity of darkness, wandering about aimlessly, absorbed in reliving their mistakes and wrongdoings, even enjoying it – and therefore staying stuck – not learning.
>
> Rachel Keene [12]

It does need to be reiterated that even in this apparently hopeless state, help is always readily available. All it requires is that help is requested *from the heart* so to speak, that there is remorse and a desire to move into the light – and leave behind unhealthy habits. It is perhaps important to flag up here that all of us, souls, are individuals but also, in this awakening, we are bound together and therefore all of us are affected by souls living in dire straits and in need of being healed – whatever their motive.

These souls may live in dark fear and shun the light, but it is love, their soul is made of the stuff, that cannot be destroyed, that keeps them from disappearing altogether. Eventually they have to return from whence they came – as all beings do. I like Keene's further comment of hope for these souls – and I'm sure she is right about some spirit guides too. She writes:

> It is often those who learned the most painful lessons that become great spirit guides, knowing both the light and dark sides of life and spirit existence. If they have truly atoned and progressed so far as the lightest planes with the darkness far behind them, then there is no chance they can become dark again because the desire to be so is just not there anymore.
>
> Rachel Keene [13]

Let us keep in mind that the greater majority of us will never be sucked into such unwholesome conditions, when we die, as we have successfully avoided creating such states in the way we have lived – whether consciously or unconsciously. Most of us may not live the lives of saints but we are well intentioned, we will have loved, have been loved in return, have given to others and received from others, have done our best, from what we know and believe to be true, at any given time. There is no need for us to fear death in this way; we will be simply returning homeward, back towards our original state. It cannot be stressed enough however how accepting there is life after death, before we die, helps us better to cope and more quickly adjust to the eventuality of physical death – and even better if we can also grasp, and act on, the spiritual implications operating behind this transformation.

Moving to the Other Side

However which way we cut it, physical life is short – with much of it being a reminder that well, yes *physical life is short*. As suggested before, it's better than a fair bet that in the noise and dust of life few of us give much time to thinking about our death, even less preparing for it spiritually. For a great many of us we will meet the event unprepared for what will happen next. So let's consider what will happen next...

I would say we are moving towards getting a more accurate picture of what happens at death as we learn more about the process. The esoteric understanding of death has long been known, and this has been added to by professional and dedicated psychics and mediums. But the other exciting aspect to this is the discoveries of our medical sciences exploring near-death experiences. As more people are resuscitated and brought back from death, possibly in the future many hours after they have died, the picture is set to become even clearer. At this time the picture of the Other Side may not yet be in high definition but nevertheless the form and some definition is coming into view. We certainly live in exciting times.

We need to consider that in the process of passing over to the Other Side, how we die will have a bearing on what happens next or what we do next; whether we are happy to move on, or possibly in a state of being distraught and confused. There are, of course, going to be as many stories of the experience of dying as there are people going through it. And, judging by NDEs, we might add that getting to the Other Side will often be a happy experience with helping hands to get us there, but not always. Let's example three types of death to see how they may possibly play out:

A sudden death in a motor accident

Imagine you have just had a very serious motor accident – indeed a terminal event. You may for a split second have seen it coming and braced yourself, but then after the event, well there you are. One moment you were driving down the motorway to a very important meeting – that could have had encouraging implications and outcomes for your business, your life and family situation – and the next moment, BANG. Right now you are beside your car – and doubtless confused. You are in a state of shock, you are alive and somehow you got out of the car. Yes you have all your faculties and yet...

At this point there is too much going on to worry about making any sense of it. You are in travel mode, and now this sudden and dramatic change has occurred. This complete interruption to your journey is self-evidently disorienting. Unable to accept what is going on, there is every likelihood that you will be soon endeavouring to carry on to your meeting – you may indeed be more focused on the damage to your car, how it can be fixed, to continue your journey, than any damage to yourself. Within minutes the emergency services arrive and begin to deal with the situation. They begin to unzip your car – no way can it be saved now – to free what you can now plainly see is a body. Shockingly, you recognise it as your own body, but how can that be? An air ambulance has now arrived and your body is now being worked on by medics. They are trying to resuscitate it to bring you back. You hear clearly what is going on. Let's say they don't succeed onsite and urgently need to get your body to the hospital. So now your body is placed inside the ambulance, and it is on its way. Still in shock, with a degree of panic now setting in, you are also inside the ambulance, as a passenger, staying with your body, but as much as you try to draw attention to yourself you don't succeed. No one seemingly can see you. This doesn't help you to cope with what is happening. They are working on and talking to your body, endeavouring to get some recording of life in it. None of this is making any sense; none of it can be real.

You continue to puzzle out what is going on. Next you begin to regroup and your thoughts turn yet again to the meeting you were on your way to attending – and suddenly you're there. You are now at the venue for the meeting. There is no one around. The meeting is not until later in the morning and people have still to arrive. Now you think of home and your family, how are they going to take this –

and in a flash you're there, outside your house. Just how you got to either of these places doesn't make much sense right now, but no time for that. You go to use your key in the front door but in all the confusion you can't find it. Desperate to get in you go to knock on the door but in your panic you put your hand through it. And now oddly you are inside your home. It is as if your whole being had simply passed through the closed door. Inside you hear the phone ringing and, now see your partner picking it up and receiving news of your accident. They don't yet know for sure how serious it is. He or she is distraught, in shock, and in no time has dropped everything. They are now getting into their car. And now they are heading to the same hospital, as the air ambulance. You also got into the car with them, and are trying to communicate to let them know you are okay – but you're getting no reaction. It is just like the situation in the ambulance, like you are not there or can't be seen. The whole thing is bizarre. At that moment your thoughts turn to an old friend who you haven't seen for some time. It is someone linking to your childhood past. Why they popped into your mind you are not clear about but they might have the means to ending this nightmare. Suddenly you find yourself on a street. You recognise it as the street where they live – but it's miles from where you were a moment ago. You look for their house but can't recall what it really looks like or what number it is. You try knocking on a door or two but there is no knock, just your hand going through; and your search becomes all in vain.

You think back to the ambulance, and next thing you are there back in it again – it has just landed at the hospital. The medics have done everything they can to bring you back but it hasn't worked and you are pronounced dead on arrival at the hospital. Meanwhile you think of your partner and are now back with them driving to the hospital. You so want to let them know you are okay. You stay with them for the rest of the journey. Being with your partner provides some comfort in this stressful time. Oddly though you now take a moment to notice, in all the confusion, there is also a peace and a sense of lightness about you. You are still you but it is like you have lost all sense of bodily feeling and restriction.

Your partner eventually arrives at the hospital, and now you are with them as they are being told of your death. Your partner is visibly heartbroken and distraught. You try in vain to comfort and console them. You comfort yourself in the knowledge that this is just some kind of amazingly vivid dream and you'll wake up shortly.

And so as this drama continues to unfold, you will probably be going along with it all the way but unable to do anything about it. Your body ends up in the morgue. You have no desire to stay in such a spooky place with it. Maybe you hang around the hospital until the undertakers take your body away, but more likely you will have gone back to your home, with your partner. The atmosphere at home is dreadful, very sad and mournful. Other relatives have turned up to help – but you meanwhile can't do anything to help at this point. You will probably be in a yo-yo state, one minute feeling at peace with your new found freedom, and the next stressed at what has happened, and the odd disconnect you are feeling. You could be like this for days – although it won't necessarily seem like days to you. You stay around for your funeral and possibly, if you were uncertain before, you now get the message: you are dead. This is no dream. You died in a road accident. But could it all still be a dream, a drama being played out in your mind? You have always believed that death is final. "How could it be anything else?" you muse. "None of this is making any sense" becomes like a mantra playing away in your mind.

What one believes and/or accepts about death will have a bearing on the position one moves into at the point of death. If, in our story, you don't believe you survive death, and therefore certainly don't believe you can be dead (of course you are not dead, probably never felt more alive), then you may surmise you are experiencing some weird dream that will be shortly over, with normality resumed again. And with that in mind you may spend a lot of time trying to get back into the physical world, trying to wake up, going back home, visiting your friends, your place of work, even attempting to pursue a normal routine, as if you were still in it. The really weird thing about this is that no one can see you or hear your requests for help. Well okay sensitive people might pick up on your presence. But probably not many people will sense your presence as the human body, with all its limitations, its busyness, cultural input and wiring, is not that great an instrument for picking up such vibrations. Certainly less so as we have become more disconnected from Nature.

But, anyhow to cut a long story short. At some point, either in the very early stages, or it could be one day much further on, help will appear. It may be while you are busying yourself in your old routine, and frustrated with how pointless all of this activity is becoming – indeed when you are contemplating there has to be an end to this, something more, and you are ready to move on... This *help* is someone who can see you and can converse with you. This being is going to be the helping hand you need to help you find your way home. Although this person probably tried to communicate with you immediately after your accident, and has possibly been around you ever since, you were only focused on the situation you were in, and in no state to take in the reality you had moved into. But now you are receptive, now you can see them, and the joy, that they can see you and acknowledge your needs, is overwhelming.

At some point, in other words, someone – it could be a person we recognise, a family member or friend who has already passed over, perhaps someone whose job it is, or it could be a group, or it may even be, what we describe as, an angel – will come to collect the person who has just died – and especially if they are up for going but can't find their way. Of course another person suffering the same fate may not hang around and instead find themselves being drawn through the tunnel reported in NDEs. Much of this hinges on how easy it is for us to let go and move on. For some of us, possibly many, it is not that easy – particularly if, as mentioned, there is urgent unfinished business, loved ones to care for, that leaves us in a restless state. Where a soul has spent an inordinate amount of earth time in this limbo state, greater efforts to help them home will be made. This may indeed come from human efforts too – through an unravelling of a person's story, setting a wrong to right, bringing some sense of completion, through communications, prayers and blessings.

A suicide attempt

Let's now look at another death, or near-death experience. Imagine that, for whatever reason, you have had enough of life and have decided to do something about it – that being to take your own life. You are in a deep emotionally dark state that either no one has really picked up on, or they have been unable to help you out of. This is possibly because you have not felt able to really confide in, or discuss what is going on for you, with anyone. And now you wish the hopelessness of it all would end. You are planning therefore to make your escape through this final act. Actually there is probably very little rational planning in this, more a case of being driven by despair to end it all. There may be more than a dollop of self-pity or sentimentality in your mixed-up mind, huge feelings of disappointment with how life has been treating you, feelings of abandonment, and anger in there too. All of this is going to be conveyed in a desire to get out, or possibly show the world what it is losing, perhaps to make someone sorry for not giving you more attention, or the love you needed.

Anyhow, against any rational judgement, you have taken your life. We'll spare the details of how you did it – it's all going to be sordid anyhow. But hang on… you think you have taken your life but now what is going on? You were meant to end it, caput, and yet you're still here. You find yourself outside of your body and still very much alive. You are also still connected to it. There must be some kind of mistake. Confusion reigns over expectations. The link between you and your body may not be entirely severed at this point but it would need urgent medical help to get you back into it. The dark depression hasn't really left you; indeed it is now possibly worse as it is getting mixed in with a sense of having done something that hasn't worked. It didn't all go away and you are now in the same place but it's all so different too.

One scenario: At this point there may be a rushing sound as you are dragged into a dark place with no light – except there is a pinpoint of light ahead of you which is now growing larger. You are travelling towards this light and emerge through it into a grey, misty, serene if barren landscape. You see a river ahead of you and you make your way to it. There is someone on the other side. They are now talking to you, even yelling, telling you that it is not your time and how you must go back while you still can. You recognise this person as a family member. It is your grandfather who died a couple of years back. You never quite got over his death. It lifts your spirits to see him. Even though it has a fast current, you want to cross the river, and you are feeling strangely happier, and a bit more positive about going forward. Suddenly you feel a pressure on your chest and a jerk – and with that you are back in your body, and in a hospital being resuscitated. Someone found you just in time.

Another scenario: Similar to the car crash victim you may have become stuck in your circumstances, the place where you took or attempted to take your life. And now, having been found, you are seeing relatives and friends reacting to what you have done – which we can assume, will be devastating. Yet you are not now in a position to ease anyone's pain, to redress the matter, to put things right. It will most probably be different to the car crash in that the atmosphere may all look and feel like the mood you are in – dark and unhappy – but yet possibly at the same time you may be feeling a sense of peace. There is of course one very important difference to the car crash situation. This event was intended, even though you were not thinking rationally, and you probably had no idea of what you were going to meet with. Very probably you expected there would be nothing on the other side of death – and now you are left wondering if your suicide attempt worked. You are still here. In all likelihood someone else is already ahead of you, there to help you across if that is the outcome. Again this could be a family member who has passed over. They will however be wanting you to go back to your body if there is but a glimmer of hope.

If the emergency services have caught you in time you will be brought back and then describe a near-death experience, which probably wasn't as encouraging as the experiences other people have. If they didn't get to you in time, then well, you are dead and the being with you will, if you let them, help you homeward. You must bear in mind though that you are probably going to feel a strong sense of remorse, failure and loss for a long time – by spiritual standards. You'll probably remind yourself that a human body is an expensive and holy piece of kit – it is not meant to be thrown away, and certainly not in this manner before time. There's a huge lesson to learn in this, and you may well apply this learning in your next life – by perhaps by becoming involved with medicine or counselling, perhaps directly helping others to avoid taking their own lives.

Studies in near death experience and attempted suicide have indicated that a small number of people do experience similar events to non-suicide NDEs. However when Dr Kenneth Ring analysed the NDEs of twenty four people who attempted suicide, he found that:

> Among them, no one reported the tunnel phenomenon, or saw a brilliant but comforting light, or encountered a presence, or was temporarily reunited with loved ones who had died, or entered into a transcendent world of heavenly beauty. Instead, the suicide-related NDE tended to be truncated, aborted, and damped down. It began with a feeling of relief or peace and continued with a sense of bodily detachment to the same degree as non-suicide-related NDEs. But it tended to end, if it got this far at all, with a feeling of confused drifting in a dark or murky void – a sort of twilight zone.
>
> Dr Kenneth Ring, Co-founder of IANDs, NDE writer and researcher[14]

Ring goes on to say in his book, *Life at Death*, "the research strongly suggests" that the person undergoing a suicide-related NDE is less likely to reach any kind of completion. Instead he says their experience, "will tend simply to fade out before the transcendent elements, characteristic of non-suicide related NDEs, make their appearance." All in all his description suggests the suicide-related

NDE is likely to be a very unfulfilling grey and limbo-like experience.

Assisted suicide comment

Whether it is right or wrong, this is a topical issue that will probably remain controversial, for some time to come, across countries. In the ideal, there is argument, from a spiritual perspective, for saying that where a soul's physical body no longer serves any purpose, that it is worn out or no longer working (or, to liken to a car, a *write-off*), that if the person so wishes to die they should be helped to do so with sensitivity and respect – with no one being criminalised for helping. The person may need to be able to move on and continue with their journey rather than being hampered further by connection with the body. In certain extreme circumstances such as where a person has a severely paralysed body, or is in a coma, with a body that has no chance of ever recovering normal functions again, the likelihood is that the soul of that person already spends more time away from their physical body than ever in it.

Of course, an alternative view would be to say that a person in this difficult position may still have something to learn from their situation, or to offer to others, particularly loved ones who may value the experience of caring, and so should continue on. It is a difficult decision-making situation, but one most probably without blame whichever decision is chosen.

From the viewpoint of preparation for death however so much will depend upon proper advice in terms of what is to come on the Other Side, so that the person may best prepare for the next part of their journey. As this type of death can be planned it can also be treated like an expected death with all the attendant circumstances. I might suggest the person contemplating this action take a look at, *Six months to live*, in the *Appendix*.

An expected death

Those who have the strength and the love to sit with a dying patient in the silence, that goes beyond words, will know that this moment is neither frightening nor painful, but a peaceful cessation of the functioning of the body.

Elizabeth Kubler-Ross, psychiatrist, pioneer of near-death studies[15]

Here you are a person who is about to die. You are at home, or perhaps in a hospice, and in very loving circumstances. You and your family know you are going to die shortly. Of course no one wants this to happen. You are well aware of what is happening. You are apprehensive of what is about to happen but a part of you also accepts it, even embraces it. It is like you have arrived at a railway station and are now waiting for your train to arrive. In this situation the Other Side will be well aware and prepared too. Loved ones, friends or contacts will have made preparations in advance to take you homeward. As you go through this transition you may well experience what people share in the NDE stages, indeed, as you get close to it, you should not be surprised if you are seeing and talking to visitors, relatives or friends, from the Other Side, who are there at your bedside ready to transport you. All of this helps to give you confidence that you will be having a safe journey, in good company – and a beautiful arrival.

Facing such a major change, possibly leaving loved ones behind is likely to be an emotive, upsetting and frightening time. Yet when the moment does arrive you may be surprised how easy, serene and wonderful your departure is, and how yet you are not really leaving anyone that you won't be able to see again. How wondrous and joyful life might seem to you from this point, of letting go.

Comment on these scenarios

These three scenarios of death I hope help to give you a flavour of how the transition from physical life to the Other Side may occur – and possible reactions and outcomes depending upon how one has reached that point of transition. They also serve to reflect how most of us can be ill-informed and ill-prepared for our death. Once in it the very process itself however may help awaken us to the fact we have gone through this before – it is not entirely new to us. It may suddenly seem all so familiar, even beautiful and joyful, and for that reason we are more likely to find our way forward towards the light, or be open and happier to receive help than not. It is however our ties with the physical life we are leaving that will be pulling us in the opposite direction. Depending upon our circumstances, letting go may not be so straightforward or easy therefore, indeed for most of us this will surely also be the case. A phase of adjustment and rest will therefore be required for most of us; that will also vary from individual to individual. We will however still be able to keep an eye on our loved ones – even if direct communications with them is now less likely.

Time out

Once we are outside of the physical body, time, as we know it, doesn't exist. One can move from A to B instantaneously by thought or desire. We are no longer restricted to the linear, left or right direction of travel, the past or the future, the young or the old. Consider Williams take on this in his, *Nothing Better than Death: Insights from 62 Profound Near-Death Experiences*:

> When you die, the fixed measurement of Earth time becomes soft and flexible. It stretches and shrinks like a rubber band. Entering the spirit realm feels like you were there just a few moments ago. Your time on Earth seems like only a brief instance. You can examine the events of your past with great clarity and detail than you ever could in life. You can linger in your past for what seems like hours. When you are done, it seems like no time at all went by. ... You feel eternal once again. There is no way to tell whether minutes, hours or years go by. Existence is the only reality and it is inseparable from the eternal now.
>
> Kevin R Williams, founder of NDE Research Foundation[16]

This description of our being outside of time, when we die, might sound like sci-fi and be hard to swallow. Williams is not alone in describing our relationship to time in this manner. You will find it is a common understanding among psychics, mediums and those who study metaphysics. Although, obviously, it is not something that can be easily demonstrated, dreams can aid our experiencing of this phenomenon even if we cannot make sense of it. I've exampled *catnapping* before and it serves a useful purpose here again. When catnapping you might more easily be aware that a whole mini dream story, with a beginning and an ending, can play out, in this hypnogogic state, that in earth time amounts to a few moments or minutes. For instance, I've experienced nodding off in a relatively short piece of music, had an involved dream, and awoken with the music still playing. I can therefore accept, just as easily, that over there, the same and the reverse may be true, that three of our earth years may amount to a moment or two. Mind you, three earth years over here seems like a moment or two to me, as I've gotten older.

A more serious point I'd make here though is that by earth time measure a lost soul can hang around for aeons and yet from their perspective it is only a moment or two after whatever may have caused their demise. So indeed in our motor accident story above, notwithstanding help offered, it is conceivable that this particular lost soul might still be there looking to unravel things long after the event, indeed long after the other actors in that sorry drama, relatives etc., have moved on with their lives – or have even peacefully passed over and now, even possibly, coming back to help this soul.

Arriving at the Other Side

Well now let's take this to the next step and visit the Other Side to see what we can pull together about it.

Quite a number of people who have gone through a near-death experience say that they have had a first-hand glimpse of what it is like on the Other Side, even though for only a short while. Indeed enough of an intense experience for a number of them to say that they are no longer afraid of death, which is a very big statement against how most of us view death.

It is shaping to look like a lot of us may experience the *tunnel*, in its varying forms, as the means to transport us through the dark to our spirit realm. Revisit the *Fringe Benefits* chapter if you want to recap on the common stages identified in NDEs. Personally I keep an open mind on this "tunnel" being the case.

In a number of NDE accounts there is frequently the journey towards the Other Side that is then met with some kind of barrier, a wall, a stream, a fence in place, and often a relative to tell the soul to go back to the body. So although the person may have an amazing and vivid experience, a real taste of the freedom one can expect, they don't necessarily see this Other Side, or not much of it. Not in a manner that would satisfy our curiosity of what is it like over there. You know what I mean, like we might ask someone what it is like to be in some place around the world, such as say Australia, if we have never been there, and in that scenario the person replies by telling us that they got as far as Sydney Airport, and were then told to go back, at the gates. It sort of doesn't cut it.

That's not true of all near death experiences however. Some people have stayed over a while. Consider writer and counsellor, Diane Goble's NDE experience, drawn from her, *A Near-Death Experience – Beyond the Veil*:

> Suddenly, we burst into the white light and a whole new reality was revealed to me, similar in appearance to the physical world, but, in this higher vibration, more colourful, more beautiful, more amazing. I saw plants, trees, mountains, lakes, animals, and shimmering crystal-like buildings, some very large and ornate. There was no sun but light was everywhere; no shadows, no darkness. Also nothing seemed solid, rather always changing; borders weren't well-defined.[17]

She saw beings that, "didn't have physical bodies, but were distinct fields of energy," and yet some did, "appear human-like" but they didn't walk, "they floated." Goble also comments that she didn't see any vehicles or means of transport, "I was told they travelled by thought." And added that, "Here, there is only love, peace and joy…"

Or consider Dr Alexander's experience, taken from *Proof of Heaven*. He did see what he described as "people" and nature in abundance:

I was flying, passing over trees and fields, streams and waterfalls, and here and there, people. There were children, too, laughing and playing. The people sang and danced around in circles, and sometimes I'd see a dog, running and jumping among them, as full of joy as the people were. They wore simple yet beautiful clothes, and it seemed to me that the colours of these clothes had the same kind of living warmth as the trees and the flowers that bloomed and blossomed in the countryside around them.

Dr Eben Alexander, neurosurgeon, NDE experiencer and author[18]

Note how both commentaries paint a scenario involving a beautiful, verdant and pleasant landscape – a welcoming place to be.

Music on the Other Side

There's music too. Music doesn't get a lot of mention in NDE reports, or communications through mediums. But I have more than a suspicion it will be everywhere – beautiful music – that you can tune in or out of, if and when you wish. I believe we will discover that sound and music play an important part in holding it all (soul and manifestation) together. Consider the following extracts...

Alexander writes:

Then I heard a new sound: a living sound, like the richest most complex, most beautiful piece of music you've ever heard. Growing in volume as a pure white light descended, it obliterated the monotonous mechanical pounding that, seemingly for eons, had been my only company up until then...[19]

And Goble writes:

There are musicians and choirs, and beautiful music can always be heard. They are also artists, dancers, singers, inventors, builders, healers, creators of magical things... things they will manifest in their next lifetime in a physical world.[20]

Resting after the journey

Once we arrive on the Other Side it is common to need to rest. What happens for a lot of us, it appears, that by whatever means we get to the gates (okay if you believe you are going to see gates, and St. Peter, you probably will), either by helping hands or via the tunnel, we next mostly go into a long sleep on our arrival. This sleep essentially allows for mental adjustment to be made. Harking back to the *prison* comments I made earlier, it is hardly surprising we need it. It crops up a lot in comments through mediums/psychics. I mentioned in an earlier chapter that just after my father died I visited Andrea and Alan Grieveson and, when I asked after him, I was told from their contacts that he was sleeping.

The Other Side not like the physical world

Let us keep in mind in all of this that the Other Side is not like here because we are obviously not in a physical body, or physical world, anymore when we are there – rather we arrive in our 'etheric' or spirit body. As suggested before, all our mental faculties will be there with us. In appearance, if we lived to be a ripe old age, we will continue to look our age but we can now also choose to look at our best (whatever age we prefer), it's our choice. It needs be said though that like anything seemingly new to us, we will need to relearn how to change our appearance. We are relatively translucent now; with all signs of disability and illness gone, all signs of dementia, any physical condition we may have suffered from, now gone. There's a lot more vividness of colour in this other world – and we are also more radiant. I would also say that our moods and what we are thinking are more easily read by others too – we are transparent in more ways than one – hidden agendas are not so easy to maintain.

More importantly it is not like over here because over there we can individually create the world we inhabit and how we wish it to appear. We will soon find out that it is what we *think*, what we *imagine* and *feel* that has power to change things rapidly over there. Our thoughts are the way we create what we want, and communicate with each other – telepathically – and the way we move around.

But I'm overlooking the most important difference to what we have been used to on the earth. This spirit world is driven by love. You'll find it everywhere. It is probably hard for us to imagine, or remember what this is really like. That feeling of giving and receiving love in the way that it is continually nourishing – and with it all stress, fears and anxieties are just no longer present – you just know you are *at home* in yourself, with a capital H. It takes a while to adjust and get into the routine however – and for most of us it will probably be a case of getting back into a routine, as we will have spent more time in our etheric condition than ever over here in the physical.

The Life Review

> Another beautiful structure is the Hall of Justice where people go before a Council of Elders who are highly advanced spokespersons of God who help us decide how we are to progress further into the spirit realm.
>
> Sylvia Browne, writer, medium[21]

Depending on our ability to comprehend where we are at, sometime after our arrival and adjustment, we will need to go through a review of the life we have now left. People who have gone through a NDE sometimes report having a life review – like watching a video of their life – taking place within the short time they are away from their body. My guess is that, where the cord, linking to the physical, is broken, and death being final, most of us would take a while before we are ready to review our lives – but also not too long. This is absolutely crucial for our soul development, that we recap on where we have got to. We are only as good as our last outing and performance but, in the fullness of things, and if need be for the sake of progress, we may view the recent life in context with other lives we have experienced too. This life review is no different to, over here, going on say a business trip abroad, to test our new products or a market, then reporting back on one's return. The desire would be to place the new findings and experience in context with what has been done in the past, in order to progress the business forward.

Whether this review is carried out by a "Council of Elders," as Browne describes or not, I can imagine that at this spiritual level one's guide/s and possibly other advisor/s or teacher/s may certainly be involved in the review – particularly if we are not exactly developed enough spiritually to deal with this review just by ourselves.

The Other Side as seen through mediums

At this point I want to turn to one or two mediums[22] to add clarity to the Other Side, and begin filling in the gaps. While we are over here, and cannot remember having been over there, our best information and evidence of what it is like on the Other Side comes from what those who have passed over tell us. Apart from NDEs, this is most often achieved through communications, from the Other Side, with those of us who have developed mediumship abilities on this side. The following exploration therefore relies on what can be deduced, from such communications, and the people who have written about them.

Let's begin by drawing on comments from the popular UK psychic medium, Derek Acorah (FreeSpirit-tv.com). Here is his take on our situation regarding moving to the Other Side, and what happens next:

> It is … my belief that at the end of our lives here on earth we undertake our journey on to the world beyond … where we are reunited once more with all the people who we have known and loved … here on earth. After this brief reunion we are taken to a place of rest and recuperation where we recharge our spiritual batteries. I refer to this time as 'the sleep state.' It is dependent upon the manner of our passing as to how long this period of recuperation will last.

We next face our life review:

> Once we have been renewed we are then given the opportunity to review our time here on earth. Have we achieved the goals we set out to achieve before incarnating into our earthly lives? Do we wish to return quickly to a physical life or do we wish to remain in the spirit world for a time? The choices are ours but ultimately we all work towards our own soul growth.[23]

Probably most mediums and spiritualists would agree with these comments – particular the final comment regarding "soul growth."

Earlier in the process of writing this book I wanted to get answers to what it might be like on the Other Side by entertaining the kind of curiosity FAQs (frequently asked questions) we might commonly be asking if, let's say, we met someone returning from a trip over there, and we were planning on taking a trip over there ourselves – he said, tongue in cheek – and needed some idea of what we were letting ourselves in for. So I devised a list of questions with the intention of getting input from an old contact, the medium Andrea Grieveson. I sent the list to her and she obligingly wrote back with her answers. Apart from the curiosity questions, what was also at the back of my mind was that we can be a fearful lot, fearing change, almost as much as death, and, one of the things we might want to know therefore is, how much is, over there, like here? Arguably we might feel more comfortable in facing death if the world we are moving into has a ring of familiarity to it. I should add, not wishing to confuse the situation, that, as we have been over there more than here, even if we can't remember, the question should more properly be reversed to, how similar is over here to the world we know better, over there? Anyhow, in context with this concern I also wanted to know Andrea's take on what happens concerning other creatures, other lifeforms over there too. So, not to delay further, here are the set questions, and Andrea's answers to them.

I began by asking her if, when on the Other Side, will we visually look like we do here – that is until we return for another life when we will, of course, be a different person?

[Andrea] *It seems that people do look just as they did when in the physical world – while any injuries, illness or impairments disappear. However one's appearance may also change as one becomes more aware.*

[Q] Likewise will people, who knew us here on the earth, recognise us on the Other Side – when they eventually come over?

[A] *People do not all graduate to the same level when they die, but those who do appear on the same level will recognise each other.*

[Q] Given that we had just died, would we also look the same age over there as we do here?

[A] *At first we have to become aware that we have just died, which is not always an easy thing to realise, but to anyone meeting us we will look the same as we did here when it happened. At some stage we will know that we can choose to appear younger if we wish to.*

[Q] If we pass over as a child do we continue as a child there, or change and grow up as we would here?

[A] *I gather that children who die young are brought up until they can understand about death, but it seems there are many variations to suit each particular child.*

[Q] Do we eat and sleep there as we do here? Would there be any point to eating and sleeping?

[A] *People can do as they want in the next life. If they want to continue almost the same as when in the physical, then they can. It is not a question of there being any point, but a question of their awareness of what habits they need or need not continue with.*

[Q] What would we do with ourselves all day on the Other Side – if day even exists?

[A] *'Day' does not exist, as time does not exist. It seems we do exactly what we want to do. Just imagine going out into a very large garden where you can see lots of jobs you want to do there. Unlike here in the physical world, you won't feel hungry, or tired, or in need of a loo break. You won't have to stop until you are ready to do so. You just get on with whatever pleases you. You might like to go to listen to music, and, as soon as you think about it, someone will appear to take you where such things are going on. There you will meet many others with similar tastes, so you will have very pleasant conversations and discussions. Whatever you are drawn to will go on for as long as you wish.*

[Q] From being on the Other Side, how easy or difficult do you think it will be for us to see, and communicate with, the physical world?

[A] *Initially we will focus on people we knew in our lives and become aware of some of their thoughts, providing they are not shrouded in grief. However I do not think we would be able to communicate with anyone at all until we have trained ourselves to project our own thoughts very strongly indeed. Many would give up because most people, in the physical world, have very busy and noisy minds and rarely relax enough to receive thoughts from the Other Side. We physical people do not readily give up our time to 'step out' into the quietness necessary. So I think it will be very difficult indeed.*

[Q] In a number of ways I gather it is similar over there to here. Is that because we, individually, have desired it to be like that, and have created it, or because the Other Side is intrinsically similar to here?

[A] *I think the Other Side is intrinsically similar to here because many people desire it that way. It will be so for us until we want change. Gradually as our awareness of ourselves grows, so we withdraw from situations that once attracted us, into different ones that attract us now.*

[Q] To pursue similarity further: do we live in houses over there?

[A] *If people wish to live in houses over there, then they do so.*

[Q] What about public structures: do we have civic buildings, places of learning as here?

[A] *People have created such 'buildings' because it is what they wanted, so such must exist for those who want them.*

[Q] Would we find vehicles on roads there, as here?

[A] *There is no need whatsoever for vehicles or roads as we have here. Thought is the mode of travel.*

[Q] Taking it further still, would we find anything over there resembling our towns or cities?

[A] *There will be clusters of 'buildings' because people do like to be near others, and because people want to have things similar to what they have always known, then, for them, there will be towns of varying sizes.*

[Q] What about pets: do they live with us over there?

[A] *People who want pets will have them, and those who don't want pets, won't.*

[Q] What about other animals, would we for instance find cows in fields there?

[A] *I do not think we would find cows in fields unless that is the only way you can imagine a field.*

[Q] What about elephants, tigers, whales; are they over there?

[A] *Not for me but there may be some people who need them in their world.*

[Q] What about smaller creatures, do insects live over there when they die?

[A] *All animals belong to a different energy group we know as 'Nature.' People who like butterflies on their flowers will, of course, see them.*

[Q] Would there be seas, trees, rivers and mountains there?

[A] *I understand that there are bodies of what appears to be 'water' but it is not wet, rather some kind of invigorating energy. As there are flowers and gardens for those who like them, then there are also trees and mountains for the same reason.*

[Q] If we put it on a scale of 1 to 10 (with 10 being extremely similar), how similar would you say the physical world and the world on the Other Side really are?

[A] *I do not think you can rate the two states at all because it depends entirely on the awareness of each individual. Whatever people need to find, they will find. If they expect nothing because they do not believe in life after death, then that is what they will be inclined to find. They will not be conscious of anything and will no doubt have a very long sleep.*

Andrea Grieveson's[24] answers are based on what she *knows* from the communications with those who are over there. Her answers certainly help endorse much of my own understanding of what it is like on the Other Side. I hope the information provided will have helped to satisfy some of your curiosity too. Her comment on people who, "expect nothing because they do not believe...," is interesting and reflects comments I made under *Shades of Pascal's Wager* (in the *Are You Ready For This?* chapter). I have already discussed a potential danger, for those of us who don't believe in life after death, of becoming earthbound in our non-acceptance that we have actually died. What Andrea flags up here is another potential aspect of this, and this is, a person unable to accept their survival of death could, "have a very long sleep" – possibly even to sleep between physical lives I wonder? This appears quite reasonable to my understanding. This might also be another reason for our not remembering a previous existence, when we are over here.

Her comment on animals, belonging to a different energy group, and her comment on people, that they do not necessarily, "graduate to the same level when they die," are important as they conjure the notion of there being groupings of souls, and then levels within groupings – which agrees with observations from other mediums. In consequence one might surmise that domesticated animals – because of their interaction with humans – have a better chance of graduating to a higher level within their energy group, and then possibly to even move on out of their current group into a higher energy group, and so on to consciousness.

The really big message that comes through Andrea's comments though is that we move to a level that reflects where we are at spiritually, and also we create what we want to see, where we want to be, and be involved with. I'm also reminded of Jesus' comment to his disciples, "In my Father's house are many mansions; if it were not so, I would have told you." (John 14.2). It implies also that people visiting the Other Side, through NDE, are less likely to experience the same vision as each other but indeed could be drawn to quite different Other Side perspectives, depending upon their own natural propensity and level of spiritual development. This should not be that difficult to envision either as, look around you; our physical world is made up of different locations and landscapes, different weather patterns, and different human traditions, different races and cultures. Depending upon when and where we arrive over here, we can have a very different experience from each other.

Drawing on Rachel Keene again: she describes how from her perspective, "there are many different planes of existence. So for example, Hitler won't be in the same place as Gandhi."[25] Hitler will have taken himself to a lower level – that dark place also talked about above – through his actions, and will have a lot of undoing to deal with, to heal the wounding he has caused. But there is hope in this that he can eventually make it right – and help to heal the souls he has injured. Keene's view of the Other Side corresponds with Grieveson's view where she says, "I believe that we can and do create our own reality when we cross over, as time, physicality and space are no constraint." And she continues:

> As for what Home looks like, well, there are beautiful open spaces with the typical imagery we have come to know as 'Heaven', endless fields and skies, amazing colour, beautiful huge building structures such as Halls of Records and Halls of Learning ... but on the whole space and time does not apply there as we know it here, so we can and do, create our own version of reality over there.

And she adds...

> For example; if we wanted to recreate a favourite place from this life, we can, although this tends to be temporary as we learn to visit those places if they still exist here in the physical world. Even if we want to build ourselves a palace, we can, but equally we don't need to *be* anywhere at all, we can just exist in a pure light form.[26]

Following on from Keene's comment that, "we learn to visit those places if they still exist here in the physical world," we can say that one thing evidenced with regularity, through psychic medium events, is that from the Other Side we can still visit loved ones and places back here. However to take on-board Grieveson's, "very busy and noisy minds" concerns; to get our messages across to loved ones, from that other state, we are probably going to have to do it through

---

LIFE AND DEATH: MAKING SENSE OF IT

the support of a medium. This interaction is clearly an art to be relearned once back over on the Other Side – and there are doubtless ground rules to abide by, for spiritual health and safety, in doing it – yes and you thought you would be done with health and safety once leaving here. The visitations, it appears, can be regular once we have the hang of it. I imagine that we might liken this to *remote viewing*[27] or projection. We think it and we are there.

With the matter of *communications*; you will often hear mediums talk of helpers on the Other Side. Colin Fry calls them *enablers*, or souls who make the link in order to help another soul, who is not yet able to do it by themselves, to come through in communications. Also Fry often mentions how a communicator is endeavouring to build himself (or herself) up to improve on the link for getting across the impressions on the medium for what they want to say. All serve to evidence active involvement and participation from the Other Side.

So where is the Other Side?

I have purposely left this question until this point as I trust that, from the descriptions already given regarding the Other Side, this question may have, in part at least, answered itself already. It is the kind of obvious question that anyone, and especially children, might ask and should be addressed. The simple and best answer is to say it is right here, right now. But that is also dependent upon one's vision. It is either close by and next to us, as if through a glass divide, or as distant and opaque as division by a brick wall. As it is in a very different dimension to the physical dimension, the lower vibration we exist in, it cannot be pinpointed in the same way that one might give the coordinates of a physical place such as Venice, and say it is 45.44° North, 12.33° East. It is arguably as near or far as we wish to make it.

However this doesn't necessarily satisfy everyone's curiosity or understanding, or indeed what mediums may believe... Sylvia Browne, for example, claims (in *Life on The Other Side*), that the Other

Side is only, "a mere three feet above our ground level" and importantly is a replica of Earth, only more perfect. She says,

> Our seven continents, our mountain ranges, plains, and deserts; our oceans, seas and rivers; our forests, jungles, islands, foothills, and every other work of nature on earth, all exist in their original perfection on the Other Side ... That includes earth's two lost continents. Atlantis thrives in the ocean on the Other Side, that corresponds to our Atlantic, and in their Pacific lies the huge flourishing continent of LeMuria.[28]

The similarity with the Other Side doesn't end there. She continues:

> The familiarity of Home isn't limited to natural wonders. Many of the human-made wonders on earth actually existed on the Other Side first and were subconsciously remembered and re-created here.[29]

She cites the Pyramids, the Sphinx, the Hanging Gardens of Babylon, the Great Wall of China and the Taj Mahal, as gracing the landscape of the Other Side, "as uncompromised as if they were just completed this morning."[30] She includes the weather – being gentle, with no rain and a constant temperature of 78° Fahrenheit (26 degrees Celsius), similar to air conditioner settings here.

Her view also adds a bit of a *spanner in the works* on what has already been described above regarding how we create what we want. She believes in a world that is already there and created for us. There's much less emphasis on creating our own *slice of heaven* as it were. Admittedly she does make allowance in her vision for people to create their own home, if they so choose to, and some choose not to have a house or fixed abode, which is what Grieveson and Keene are also saying, or implying.

Browne's view definitely offers comfort to anyone fearing the unfamiliar when we go over. Indeed it sounds a very beautiful Earth-like world that, for those of us used to modern living and conveniences, would soon have us feeling at-home and good as back to normal once we've settled in. From an esoteric perspective, it is not difficult to see where her viewpoint is coming from – in part at least. It runs something like this: If all forms in physical existence also have an etheric form, then Earth is no different, and the etheric form of the earth will be the template, the more perfect version – and it will interact with what is going on, on the physical earth. This concept is however a little hard for most of us to contemplate, or buy into, as she paints it for we also know that Earth has been changing over millions of years and that the world we see today is the result of those changes, which are of course continuing to occur – tectonic plate movement, volcanos, earthquakes, polar axis shift, the effects of ice over millions of years, extreme weather conditions and the work of the oceans, you name it, all contributing to a physical world today that is very different from comparatively, a short time ago, by geological timescales. To make it more acceptable or possible, one has to consider this, in the same way as our own etheric vehicle remains a perfect mirror of our physical vehicle, even after years of wear and tear.

As an alternative to this worldview, Theosophists hold that the Other Side begins further out. The reason being, they argue, the Other Side is more appropriately in the *Astral Plane* – or in this case the astral vehicle of planet Earth – perhaps three to four miles from the earth's surface. It is another consideration.

Browne may indeed be right, or right in part, regarding buildings over there being replicated over here. Alternatively this could possibly be a perspective that souls in need of the comfort of the *familiar* generate – that being creating a world there, the same as here, as Grieveson was suggesting. Or there could be another possibility: It could be the perspective as is being presented to her by Francine, her spirit guide. In other words this is what Francine relays because this is what she lives in, what she sees and experiences at her level, and so for her it is quite real.

That said, Browne's description of the Hall of Records (that I would anticipate as holding the fabled, Akashic Records of every event taking place on the earth) sounds a truly beautiful building and place of learning – as indeed do the other halls existing there, and the spiritual growth they offer. Great civic buildings are also a feature of a number of NDE visits to the Other Side.

Returning to Earth for another life

Regardless of how accurate or inaccurate the Other Side is presented to us, all psychics, mediums and spiritualists tend to agree that the point of all this is the concern for growth in consciousness, and moving to higher levels in our understanding, in our soul growth, in our ability to love. Here, on planet Earth, we face resistance, tests and challenges. By comparison to our life, on the Other Side, over here, we are, as it were, driving with the brakes on. There we can learn quickly, if we are of a mind to; everything flows and it can feel so wonderfully easy. But even over there we will not be yet done with our learning and will still need first-hand experience in order to grow. The point will come when we will need, once again, to put ourselves into more testing circumstances – hence we are bound for another incarnation. Here are comments from two mediums on that step:

> Before we incarnate into our earthly life, before we are even physically conceived, when our spirits are still resident in the world beyond, we are given choices. Those choices concern our lives here on the earthly plain... What we want to achieve, the experiences we wish to undergo and what we want to make of our spirit selves. The ultimate aim for any spirit is to ascend to the higher spiritual realms – to gain soul growth. To achieve this we have to ensure that we have had as many experiences as we possibly can ... in our earthly incarnations.
>
> Derek Acorah, psychic medium, author[31]

> At some point, people recognize the need for even further advancement and therefore choose to return to Earth to gain this spiritual advancement. With the help of a spirit guide, they decide on an incarnation which will meet their goals. They then proceed to the Hall of Justice where they meet once again with the Council of Elders. Here, the Council prepares people for their next incarnation.
>
> Sylvia Browne, medium[32]

Now we are coming full circle. When we are returning to a physical life, depending upon how spiritually awake we are, very probably we will have a meeting/s with our advisors, whoever these may be, and with our guide/s for this coming life. The plan for the move will be discussed. Clarifying what we want to achieve is crucial for the experience. It will contain adventures and dangers to help or distract us. Just like in any project development, targets, milestones, deadlines, dependencies and constraints, may well be anticipated and pencilled in. None of this can be earmarked for certain. A reminder here that there is no fate operating other than the fate we create for ourselves consciously or subconsciously. As mentioned earlier, I suspect that if one's life is absolutely critical to get right then we may get a big dollop of nudges to point us in the right direction – so that it might appear fatalistic to us, or to an outsider observing our situation. This is not to rule out attraction however, and the odd circumstances that can sometimes bring.

And so we come to return for another physical life and another part of our soul journey – and are drawn towards suitable parents for the experience. Timing will be crucial for our entry into the physical world, as this sets the initiation point of the journey that is, simultaneously, symbolical and meaningful. Given it all goes to plan, we are here for a new life with a new name, possibly we are a different gender from the last life (or last few lives, which is not necessarily going to be easy to come to terms with), and possibly on a very different part of the planet from our last visit.

But in describing our return, we cannot rule out that it may not be Earth that we are bound for in this new life. It might be elsewhere, a very different kind of temporary and conscious existence, on a different world.

The Other Side in summary

In summary let us look at what we may deduce from our visit to the Other Side: Firstly it may not be that far away from us. If Sylvia Browne is right, it is three feet away, making it a little larger than

Earth in circumference – or it could be three miles out according to Theosophists. Either way the Other Side is anticipated to occupy the same location in space, as Earth – as it travels around the Sun and through the Milky Way. Should we then reside on the astral plane, when we pass over, or visit, this plane will not interfere with our physical plane, as it vibrates on a higher frequency – just like radio stations can co-exist side by side without interfering with each other's wavelength and reception. In any case, as most of us do not see this plane it might as well be light years away from where we currently are.

Next, the Other Side is what we make of it – what we attract and what we create. You want it to look familiar, look like the home and environment you currently live in, or lived in, you can. You want to move more up-market you can. It literally is all in the mind, but no less real – indeed it appears to be a lot more vivid and real than anything physical.

We can note a very big difference for life over there, in that we live in a greater atmosphere of Love, and we move and have our being through thought, emotion, feeling and desire. We get around through thought and desire – so no need to take our chariot or our Mercedes with us. We also communicate by thought, by telepathy.

In moving there, our current soul evolutionary status will, like water, find its own level, and draw us to where we best belong. There is greater focus on the individual and soul growth. Yet our living in Love together will ensure we have what one could call a collective landscape so that we do also see and experience what others see around us. Those beautiful buildings talked of will exist through collective desire – as indeed will more natural landscapes that we enjoy.

The flora and fauna of life, we know as Nature, may not be there under its own steam, other than in representation, if we have thus desired it to be there – and pets most certainly can be there on that basis. It is my understanding that souls operating at the level of Nature – the plants, the animals, insects you name it – will not be able to fully experience an Other Side yet but rather they will rest and very quickly re-emerge, recycle into their physical form again.

Summerland

From an esoteric viewpoint – as held by Theosophists, Spiritualists and Wiccans – the Other Side, so-called, that we've been discussing here, that most of us are also likely to experience in the afterlife, has a more appropriate name. It is called *Summerland*. Summerland, the very name conjures comfort, serenity, a place of warmth, beauty and peace, a place for recollection and reunion with loved ones; a place of rolling hills and verdant fields, similar to the earth at its best – indeed Blake's *green and pleasant land* comes to mind.

Summerland is seen as a place of rest for souls after, or between, incarnations on its opposite number, the physical earth. Now what corresponding name could we possibly give to the earth from this perspective? How about *Winterland*? Yes sounds appropriate.

Starting from the physical plane, Summerland is seen to be located within the astral plane and the second of seven planes – made up of the *physical, astral, mental, Buddhic* (or *unity*), *spiritual, divine* and *monadic* planes.[33] This might give you a clue that, although some believe it is our final resting place, it is clearly not the summit of our journey. No doubt it is a great place to be but not for long stays, unless one is happy and content taking it easy as a couch potato – not wishing to progress that fast in one's spiritual growth. We come eventually to see Summerland as another plane of illusion, a kind of false heaven, where we see what we want to see and be what we want to be, but that leads us nowhere except up the garden path – and granted, in every way, it is a very beautiful garden path.

As much as this Other Side, this Summerland, will feel like *home* and that we have *arrived* when we get there, we will sooner or later come to realise it is only a resting point on our journey, where we may bathe in Love and self-remembering, to restore ourselves. But being *in Love* is not yet being *of Love*. There is much more work to be done on our spiritual unfoldment, to become closer to Love, to be more awake. When we are ready we will once again test our metal, our resolve, to continue homeward – and this time, who knows, we will reach beyond the Other Side... as we know it, or think we know it to be.

Notes & references

[1] Bailey, A. and Khul, D. (1985) *Death: The Great Adventure*. Lucis Press Ltd

[2] Browne, S. (2000) *Life on The Other Side*. Piatkus

[3] Alexander, Dr E. (2012) *Proof of Heaven*. Piatkus

[4] Leininger, B., Leininger, A., and Gross, K. (2009) *Soul Survivor: The Reincarnation of a World War II Fighter Pilot*. Hay House.

[5] Sohl, R. & Carr, A (1970) *The Gospel According to Zen*. The New English Library Ltd, London.

[6] One in particular occurrence comes to mind. This was on an archaeological site, on farmland outside Peterborough (UK). Just the other side of the fence to the field we were working in, the London Brick Company was busy extracting clay to produce bricks. There was a rail-track running by the fence. On the track the company had railway trucks taking clay from their excavations to the ovens. These ran independently, one at a time, presumably on some kind of pulley system, and each was numbered. They would go up to the factory and eventually return. Now the times I happened to look across and spot the number 41 carriage going past was uncanny – and it wasn't as though there was a routine time for that particular carriage to go past our location.

[7] Just to add here. A guide is not the same as an angel. An angel is seen as a messenger who will never have been incarnated in human form but remains a pure lifeform of their own. They are considered different to us souls but can manifest similar to us in their appearance – although claims suggest they can be very much larger than us, with or without wings. Unlike a guide, an angel is said to be able to act in or on our lives if they are told to from a higher source. This might be, for instance, if we are in danger of terminating our life before we are allowed to, or it might be we have a special task or mission to perform and the lives of others may be in danger if we don't perform it. I often think of angels as being a bit like the Vulcans of Startrek – operating at a high intelligence, pure reason without signs of emotion. However, as I indicated in the Introduction, I believe the guardian angel, which each of us is said to have, is not necessarily an angel at all but actually our higher self or soul making its presence felt (as if separate from us) when we are in need.

[8] Williams, K. Article: *Hell and the Near-Death Experience*. http://www.near-death.com/experiences/research14.html [Accessed 02/06/2014]

[9] Ibid.

[10] Ibid.

[11] Rachel Keene. Quote drawn from her website http://rachelkeene.co.uk/faq-life-on-the-other-side/ [Accessed 02/06/2014]

[12] Ibid.

[13] Ibid.

[14] Ring, Dr K. (1980) *Life at Death*. Coward, McCann & Geoghegan.

[15] Quote from Elizabeth Kubler-Ross Foundation - http://www.ekrfoundation.org/quotes/ [Accessed 02/06/2014]

[16] Williams, K. R. (2002) *Nothing Better Than Death: Insights From 62 Profound Near-Death Experiences*. Xlibris Corporation.

[17] Goble, D. Article: A Near Death Experience - Beyond the Veil. *http://www.beyondtheveil.net/nde.html* [Accessed 02/06/2014]

[18] Alexander, Dr E. op. cit.

[19] Ibid.

[20] Goble op. cit.

[21] Browne, S. (2000) *The Other Side and Back*. Signet

[22] I could also use the term 'psychic' here as in many people's minds mediums and psychics mean the same. Derek Acorah for example calls himself a psychic medium (and sometimes a spiritualist medium). My understanding is that a psychic will make a mental connection and pick up on atmospheres - around a person or around an environment they are in. He or she will be able to read energy fields - who is there or coming in - and be able to view the past, present and possibly the future. A medium on the other hand, more or less 'does what it says on the tin' i.e. they are a go between, they talk to dead people - and the dead people through the medium get messages across to others - or possibly talk directly through them to others. I consider the word 'medium' as most appropriate here.

[23] Derek Acorah. Drawn from his website http://freespirit-tv.com/2011/09/derek-acorah/ [Accessed 02/06/2014].

[24] Andrea Grieveson has also written two books. Check out: 1. Read How We Died. 2. A Series of Past Lives. Both can be found on Amazon.

[25] Keene, op. cit.

[26] Keene, op. cit.

[27] Remote viewing – some of us can do this over here. Check out: http://en.wikipedia.org/wiki/Remote_viewing [Accessed 02/06/2014]

[28] Browne, op. cit.

[29] Browne, op. cit.

[30] Browne, op. cit.

[31] Derek Acorah. Drawn from his website http://freespirit-tv.com/2011/09/derek-acorah/ [Accessed 02/06/2014].

[32] Browne, op. cit.

[33] For the seven planes, see https://en.wikipedia.org/wiki/Plane_%28esotericism%29 [Accessed 01/03/2016]

CHAPTER 7

LIFE AND DEATH: MAKING SENSE OF IT

A question: After all that has been covered in the previous chapters, on matters of soul, life and death, is this going some way towards helping you to make sense of it?

In this chapter I'm going to revisit some of the main points of what this book has been driving at – including picking up on my *where to next* comments, that I made much earlier in *The Good Life* chapter, and to offer some suggestions on this.

Let me start by saying I think it is a fair assumption that, for a lot of us, we live in an increasingly sophisticated, complex, restless and impatient world. There are estimated to be over seven billion of us living on our planet, and, of course, while not all of us live within what we might describe as modern capitalist, industrial, or democratically driven economies, a lot of us do – and judging by our needs for material things, happiness and security, this number is set to grow. For the most part this book assumes some familiarity with this situation and the challenges it brings to our spiritual health, to being open, or remaining open to, as I see it, the spiritual reality we are in.

Where and when we allow them to, or encourage them to, the plants and animals are getting on with life, as they have done for a very long time, but for us, well, as Jesus said, "the son of man has no place to lay his head and to rest." This is so true at this time and, in this situation. We are encouraged to look after our own needs and less the needs of others – although I don't underestimate there are amazing acts of kindness and self-sacrifice mixed in with this. We are also becoming more divided by the extremes we are creating, by those of us who *have* (often much more than we actually need or will ever use) and those of us that *don't have*, and fair to say often a deal less than required for a tolerable level of living with dignity. One could say we certainly need our wits about us, and a healthy moral compass, to steer our ships across the open seas to safe shores in this climate.

In the last fifty years or so, beliefs we might have once held dear as unquestionable truths about life, death and afterlife have been explored, tested, reasoned and often judged as no more than myth. In context a lot of what we have been taught to believe has arguably been shown to be biased, skewered for political purpose, for hidden agendas, or to be patently less than the truth. One outcome being that our orthodox religions have, in a number of countries, come under increasing scrutiny with many of us questioning our faith and walking away from believing in what they offer. From my perspective, where religion and belief is concerned, I think there is a strong theme of change going on, that is global and will gather apace. It is my perception that we are going through major and collective growing pains and are on the verge of a breakthrough in our understanding. I have every faith it will work out well in the end if we keep our wits and reason about us.

The rise of the Internet, and especially the Web, has most certainly been instrumental in helping to speed up this change. It is beginning to influence a global level of organisation and, for that matter, a global awareness. We are, through this and our media generally, becoming more aware of our similarities and differences, how we live, in other parts of the world, and under differing circumstances and regimes, and with more immediacy. As we link up with each other, borders, political or otherwise, are being overridden or broken down. Even though this networking and social media can be on a very superficial, and sometimes suspicious, level of interaction at this time – as we bring our baggage, and not always healthy desires, with us online – this will surely change as our networks grow and mature, and we likewise grow and mature.

It is probably fair to say that more of us are now acquiring our knowledge, ideas and beliefs, nay for some our very identity, through our online activity and networking. I for one don't underestimate the inherent dangers in this. It is risky, but overall I tend to trust that the goodness of it outweighs the dangers.

Quenching our spiritual thirst

Arguably with the plethora of information, viewpoints and beliefs available online there is a tendency for a growing number of us to become much more savvy, and rightly so, about our world, but also more selective, more questioning and secular in our world view too. At this time this secular view largely ties in with humanistic thinking, and the *mechanistic reductionist paradigm* for life and our world, as presented to us by our more orthodox sciences and those of us who happily call ourselves, *sceptics*. It would seem some of us are almost, dare I say, religiously driven by our scepticism for anything not fitting into this mechanistic worldview of life. Our sciences have fought hard to explore and dispel superstition (rightly so) but also, likewise, anything pertaining to an *holistic-spiritual paradigm* has tended to be tarred with the same brush. All holistic spiritual views, beliefs and arguments have tended to get lumped together and cast out there on the *fringes*, where such perspectives can be held at arm's length and labelled *pseudosciences, superstition* or similar. Make no mistake though; our subscribing to a mechanistic worldview does not mean we are dealing with an all-encompassing truth or understanding of reality. It provides a truth based upon, albeit, sound reasoning when placed in context with physical or measurable evidence that our world provides. On the other hand, it is thereby also limited; being, at this time, unable to acknowledge a wider spectrum involving the less obvious, the less visible, the paranormal, the meaningful and spiritual.

It is from this mechanistic perspective on things that we arrive at what I describe as the *brain-centric* view, or belief, about life. In other words, we believe, and accept, that our wonderful human brain is the cause of consciousness, mind, personality, character, you name it, rather than it being an instrument used by the soul – through the mind – to interface with the physical world.[1] And the assumption with this, of course, being that when the brain dies, we die – period. In terms of appearances it does offer the most obvious and sensible conclusion based upon the physical evidence. But appearances can be deceptive, and in a big way…

> All truths are easy to understand once they are discovered; the point is to discover them.
>> Galileo Galilei, astronomer, philosopher, and mathematician

Take for example the story of our *heliocentric system* as proposed by the astronomer, Nicolaus Copernicus. For thousands of years our planet Earth was theologically, scientifically and politically reasoned, by probably most of us (apart from the earlier Greeks who knew better), to be unmoving at the centre of our universe – with the Sun orbiting us and not the other way around. This was the *no questions asked* accepted worldview. Now we know the truth, but we've only known it since 1543 – a lot less than five-hundred years. And once it was proposed do you think such common sense and logic was easily accepted by everyone? Copernicus died on the same day as he received an advanced copy of his treatise; *The Book of the Revolutions of The Heavenly Spheres* – which gave his argument for his heliocentric system. There are some grounds to believe that he planned it that way – to allow the truth to come out only as he was departing. The greater majority of us then took a long time to come to accept it. I mean, come on, we are supposed to believe we are all on a globe (instead of something flat, that some people, no doubt, still believed), that is at the same time turning and moving around the Sun. What weird magic and superstition is this? It's got to be rubbish. We don't see or feel any of this happening. Wouldn't we all fall off as the Earth turned over? Wouldn't the wind generated by the movement be knocking us and our buildings over? Wouldn't the seas be constantly tidal? I mean, talk about pseudoscience and believing in the paranormal... The idea was ridiculous at best. We all knew the Earth was unmoving, solid as a rock, and at the centre of the cosmos.

At the time it was indeed argued to be pseudoscience or, at very least, poor science by those powerful enough to oppose it – in this case the Church, who regarded it as *heresy*, with obvious political motive behind the opposition – as Galileo was to find out some seventy years later, being on the receiving end of the Inquisition for supporting the heliocentric theory of Copernicus. But to stick with the point: if something, as big as the way the Sun and Earth relationship works, could be so easily missed and/or misinterpreted for thousands of years, may it not be possible that we could be wrong in our current denial of the fringe, holistic and less visible? Will the brain eventually be established as an instrument of the soul? I have no doubt it will.

Spiritual malnutrition

One symptom of our having a non-spiritual view, or lack of any spiritual intent and direction, is, like it or not, we create a vacuum in our lives, and one that in the normal run of things, being preoccupied with our daily affairs, we can be unaware of. This becomes a hunger that we then attempt to ignore, sublimate, reinterpret, or quench with our day to day living, with our work, our family, friends, activities, hobbies, escapes, pleasures and with things, with our possessions. Living by *all things in moderation* is of course fine and to be recommended but in this vacuum we can more easily overdo it and end up becoming overfull of experience and things. While we pursue our *bucket list* in our search of fun, adventure, and our identity, I'd suggest more realistically we are pursuing the antidote for our misunderstood dis-ease. We buy the latest movie, the latest gadget, the latest holiday package, the kitchen update, the new car, house move, the latest this, that and the other. The hunger goes away for a while when we succeed, or make the change, until the novelty of the *new* wears off, as it always will, and then the hunger starts to return. Investing in the transitory for the answer frankly gets us nowhere. We are not actually tackling the cause of our problem that is simmering away inside, and we can remain starved, unfulfilled, disconnected – even with a huge network of social media friends, stimulation and things around us. Further if left under-nourished we can more easily get ill, out of balance, out of harmony and carry a crock of fears that we keep under wraps – that eats away at us. The biggest, as we know, we probably don't even admit to ourselves, and I won't admit it into the discussion again here, well not at this point.

We can become so ensconced in our secular non-spiritual beliefs that we only add to our malnutrition by our being sceptical of any viewpoint that offers us a spiritual lifeline, or let's say challenges what we already believe. At best the whole can become a circular internal debate with seemingly little resolution. If we are only ever looking for evidence that meets and/or challenges our criteria of disbelief, that at the same time must/needs satisfy the expectations and constructs of that disbelief, we may never find it or find enough of it. We may have to step outside of our *doubting-Thomas* position, suspend disbelief, at least briefly in other words, before we can really start looking.

It might seem too, from our viewpoint, that it also requires a very big leap of faith to believe there is anything spiritual beyond our well-reasoned position. But I would ask in return, does it really require such a big leap of faith? Okay, as I have said elsewhere, without the kind of concrete evidence our sceptism may require we can at best really only talk of *belief* and *faith* in the spiritual. You might say it then does come down to how much of this concrete evidence we need in order to reconsider our situation. What I have endeavoured to do in this book is demonstrate that there is evidence, and growing evidence, from different perspectives, to challenge our sceptism on the matter of life and death – or more appropriately, regarding the existence or non-existence of the *afterlife*. I believe these perspectives do provide directly, or circumstantially, the evidence we need – that the afterlife does indeed exist. Also that in turn they can help to open doors and give us direction to quench our spiritual thirst and heal the vacuum in our hearts. At very least the intention is to cause us to question whether our assumption regarding a *big leap of faith* is entirely accurate. I'd suggest that, if we leave aside the array of paranormal experiences – that a large number of people claim to have witnessed[2] – and only focus on the reported NDEs and past life memories (particularly those reported by children), we have enough of a question mark, against the apparent fact that when the brain stops everything else stops. There is great hope in the mounting evidence.

And so, where to next

As we are all involved in this birth to death journey, there is obviously good reason why we should be interested in what happens next, at the end of life, and it beholds us to endeavour to get a clear and accurate handle on it as we can. So, let me say that if, after working through this book, with its questions (particularly in the *Are you ready for this?* chapter), explorations and explanations, we still view life as essentially meaningless – the outcome of natural forces that will eventually finish us – then this is the sense we have made or are making of it. This is where we are at. It will, I'm sure, be found to be inaccurate but nevertheless it is the conclusion we have arrived at. We have at least given ourselves the opportunity to consider this perspective on things. And indeed we can always revisit the spiritual argument again, if we so wish. It is, anyhow, my humble view that (providing we have given things a fair shot), whatever we believe in this context is alright and is still a part of our spiritual unfoldment and journey – on the important proviso; we also allow others the same freedom to discover and decide by their own volition. Adjustment will eventually come, perhaps in another life. If it is going to take us a little longer than our fellow man to get to an acceptance of the spiritual life so be it. I believe, we will get there, and, for that matter, we will come to realise that actually we have little choice in the end but to go with the flow – and find our way homeward.[3]

Now, if instead we have been sparked into considering, there is something bigger to unravel here, then wholeheartedly we must get on with the unravelling, and not be put off by anyone telling us not to dabble in such morbid matters as *death*, or that what we are getting into is for the gullible and superstitious, and beneath our intellect or capability. Remember our flat-world experience of life (as projected through things like our job, our car, our home, our family, our wealth, our towns and cities) begins to become a little skewered when one starts to view it from outside of our norming twenty four/seven constructs of it. It very quickly takes us to the realisation that our lives, for all their apparent permanence, are remarkably short, transitory, lived on a big ball hurtling through space at a fair rate of knots. What we are involved with behoves us to look up at the stars and attempt to grasp our direction of travel.

The Soul on another physical journey

Our situation on this earth seems strange. Every one of us appears here involuntarily and uninvited for a short stay, without knowing the whys and the wherefore. In our daily lives we only feel that man is here for the sake of others, for those whom we love and for many other beings whose fate is connected with our own.

Albert Einstein, physicist, philosopher [4]

Let's remind ourselves of the nub of *how it works* coming to Earth, from the spiritual perspective I have been presenting. The beginning point of our lives, our re-entry into the physical world, is the result of our past actions, our karma, now coupling with an agenda for growth in this particular life. What is also the case is that we rendezvous with a given point in time, a given place and the necessary physical body – all set going by an attraction to circumstances that are suited to our karmic state. Importantly this links in with the genetic form, and gender, our body will take and the way we are likely to be raised.

The moment we arrive in the physical world is like a pebble being dropped into a calm lake and the ripples flowing outward are as the rhythm and pattern our life will tend to take. As I suggested earlier in the book, we are of course no tabula-rasa as we arrive. We are a dynamic soul, with potential and propensities intact, but what we then begin to experience informs the development of our personality, our character for this life, and we come eventually to resonate with, and identify with, our physical situation.

There is no blackboard in the sky, on which God has written our purpose, our mission in life... And that all I have to do is to find that blackboard and find out what God really has in mind for me... the blackboard doesn't exist, so your purpose is what you say it is. The mission is the mission you give yourself.

Neale Donald Walsch, actor, author, spiritual philosopher [5]

At this juncture, of identification with our developing physical life, we can be a long way off from remembering any spiritual mission we planned, or had planned for us. In context with Walsch's quote here, we might actually look a lot closer to home for the "blackboard" and the "purpose" he talks of. We needn't trouble God in other words. Rather the blackboard and subsequent mission, I'm thinking of here, can be catered for by the expectations of our upbringing, by our parents, or whoever is raising us, by our peer group, by our religious, educational, cultural and national circumstances and experiences. We become imbued with whatever fills us to a large part. The Jesuits (attributed to St Francis Xavier) are alleged to have said, "Give me the child, until he is seven, and I'll give you the man." No matter whether they, or St Francis, ever did say that or not, the theory, as any psychologist will tell you, holds true. What happens to us in our early years tends to give shape to our lives and form our outlook on life. And by this process our perceived mission for good or ill will be written and indeed, for some of us at least, sealed in the habits, in the patterns of behaviour, our taught needs, our work ethic, becoming our hopes and expectations. These that have now been ascribed to our subconscious, that in turn drive our lives – that is if we let them.

Of course operating from this remit we may make excellent headway in the world as loving human beings who have also been taught to be emancipated free thinkers – aligned with best heartfelt intentions. But likewise, following what has become our subconscious mission, or creating our lives from this standpoint, does not have to imply we will turn out good or successful people, that we take responsibility for our actions, that we make commitments, that we live by a healthy moral code or that we have consideration and respect for others. Where I am especially with

Walsch is in his suggesting that we free ourselves to create our own mission. I am reminded that, as is my belief, we created our intended mission before we arrived here in physical form, and so, when we come to be the creator of our own mission in life, it may well be we will tap into the one we had planned anyhow. Regardless, it is *far better we live by our own truth than attempt to fit into the pigeon-hole someone else has placed us in.*

To get to such a point however we may have to draw a line in the sand on our fears, and the baggage of our past, step outside of the norm, deal with the narrative we have imbued, the play, the act, the scene, that career we went into for the sake of our parents, the family and contacts we have made that now appear to hold us back. And all of that may not be so easy to change unless we really awaken, establish clarity of purpose and want it to happen. There are doubtless growing pains experienced by most of us seeking to move on – certainly I can vouch for this in my own journey.

Life on Earth is spiritual opportunity

Coming to the realisation that we are creative beings, with our own mission, is a hugely important step forward in our emancipation and in taking responsibility and control over our lives. This step, taken wisely, can enhance our spiritual life and open doors to wisdom and understanding that was previously invisible to us. Here I would mention what one person, who calls herself *Kimberlee*, experienced through a NDE (via iands.org). She met with what she describes as *angels* and said she was told by one what our purpose on the earth is:

> Our purpose here is to discover unconditional love within ourselves and then offer it to others.

> We are all on the path. What differs between us is the road we take, the experience we choose, and how much we have learned about love... No one road is better or more important than another. It is all a matter of what speaks to your heart and feels like home within. We are here to explore, experience and find joy in the process of living an earthly existence...

Our evolution and ascension as a spiritual being happens organically at a time when we are ready to receive it. We are all constantly growing, evolving and changing. But, this is not anything we have to force or for which we need a certain skill set.[6]

We are encouraged to find love and happiness here on the earth, indeed to, "explore, experience and find joy in the process of living an earthly existence," and we are allowed to take our time to grow spiritually.

We do need however to be growing spiritually in a given life though if we are to become more emancipated, more "unconditional" in our love for others. There will come a point too where we will need to speed up this process of spiritual evolution and rely less on an organic evolution to get us there. There will come a point indeed where we realise we do have a mission, a spiritual purpose to get on with. In some way we come to accept the need to be in service to humanity.

With regard to getting an alternative viewpoint on this, and one that does indeed seek to speed up our spiritual development, take into consideration the following passages. These are taken from *The Betty Book*.[7] This book, first published in 1937, is considered to be a classic with psychics, mediums, and in parapsychology.[8] In this passage, from the *Do It Now* chapter, the author raises the issue of, "Why the hurry?" over our spiritual development. He poses the question with the spirit entities that the medium, Betty, is linked with, and the question provokes a strong reaction:

Why the hurry? We are supposed to have all eternity before us... It takes considerable of a sustained effort, if it [spiritual growth] is to amount to anything. It involves a radical change in point of view ... for the average man [or woman] of sufficient maturity to take this in, [when] routine and habit are pretty well established... He [she] is fairly well content with things as they are. That is his [her] natural life on earth. On the other hand the spiritual life is the natural life after he [she] dies. Why not postpone all this development to what would seem its natural season and environment?[9]

He then explains how this question brought up more than he expected. He had hit upon a *vital question* that opened up a whole new debate with the gist of it being that: "this spiritual quickening, this conscious contact, must take place at some point in our evolution. The sooner we attain it the better. It can never be entirely postponed to 'its natural season and environment.'" And at this point they also emphasise the urgency and the approach in order to achieve progress:

> 'Arouse yourself.' they insisted, 'It is worth your greatest effort ... Fix firmly in your mind the things to cling to... The first is grim determination to succeed; and the second is a great heart hunger which is the call of love... [For] when you come here it is more difficult to make the voluntary choice than you can imagine. It seems that you would unhesitatingly choose the side of truth, but it will be almost impossible for you to do so unless you have made yourself an agent or disciple while on earth...'[10]

I'd suggest we might take full note of this. This is crucial. The angel's message to Kimberlee holds that there is no rush to our learning and unfolding. It is further down to us as to what direction we decide to go. No one will be pushing us along. However that is not to say we won't get the occasional nudge/s. We are all on the path towards enlightenment even when we are taking two steps back to go one forward. We just take different paths to our getting there. If we can accept we are here to become more loving and conscious beings, regardless of what we have been taught to believe, or understand to be the purpose to our life, then we truly are making headway anyway.

However, and there is the *however* in this scenario. We can spend many lives returning to the physical and hopefully enjoying those lives. Although let's face it all or most lives involve some suffering between birth and death – we age, we experience illness, loss of loved ones, unexpected setbacks. For that matter a huge number of us do indeed live miserable lives on our planet in poverty, with malnutrition, in slavery or under dictatorships, often without the basic education that would emancipate us. The *however* is that at some point we will need to start making our way homeward with more conscious intention, more gusto, more urgency. There will come the calling from within to get on with it. When that spark of awakening occurs in us we must go with it to expand our understanding – regardless of resistance. There, right there, is the work to be done. If you can hear that sound from within, then *don't dilly-dally* is the request made by those souls speaking through Betty in *The Betty Book*.

Urgency from a Buddhist perspective

We needn't necessarily turn to spirit entities to learn about spiritual urgency. We can find this closer to home, and notably in Tibetan Buddhism.[11] One could say the passage from physical life to death and beyond is an intrinsic part of Tibetan culture, and their knowledge on life and death has become popular in the West through *The Tibetan Book of the Dead*.[12] This knowledge is best understood through the bardos – also mentioned in *The Soul Question* chapter. The Tibetan word *bardo* means transition or a gap between one situation and another – and these gaps contain opportunity.

Depending upon which are included, there are up to six bardos[13] with each forming an important transition in the birth-death-birth cycle. The transition at death is seen as the most important opportunity for change, through readiness and wakefulness. To draw on Sogyal Rinpoche again (whose book, *The Tibetan Book of Living and Dying*,[14] is now considered an essential companion for Western understanding of the Book of the Dead); he leaves out two of the bardos – dreams and meditation – to describe the four bardos concerned, more directly, with the life and death experience. These are: 1. The natural bardo of this life; 2. The painful bardo of dying; 3. The luminous bardo of dharmata; and 4. The karmic bardo of becoming. He describes the bardo of dharmata, beyond our having just died, as the point where everything becomes absolutely clear to us, where we have opportunity to grasp unconditioned truth, the nature of reality, the true nature of existence. He writes:

> The luminous bardo of dharmata encompasses the after-death experience of the radiance of the nature of mind, the luminosity or 'Clear Light,' which manifests as sound, colour, and light.[15]

The opportunity in this, is that, if we can fully recognise and embrace this moment then, according to Tibetan wisdom, we can achieve a state of *nirvana*. His Holiness, the Dalai Lama,[16] defines nirvana as a, "state beyond sorrows" or "freedom from cyclic existence."

This moment of opportunity is comparatively fleeting however. For the Buddhist it involves years, and possibly many lifetimes, of spiritual practice to be in readiness for when it arrives. Miss the opportunity – and, it has to be said that without that preparation and discipline we most probably will – we end up experiencing the next bardo, the "karmic bardo of becoming." In my understanding that means we arrive on the Other Side in our etheric body, but with the condition that our work is unfinished. Rinpoche writes:

> The karmic bardo of becoming is what we generally call the Bardo or intermediate state, which lasts right up until the moment we take on a new birth.[17]

So what we would call our experience on the Other Side resonates with Rinpoche's fourth bardo. And it follows, with the Tibetan view, that being there means we are then stuck in a cycle of becoming, and further means there is an *inevitability* about our coming *new birth* as eggs are eggs. In other words, at some point we will need to visit being born again – until we can get our spiritual growth right and move on.

Getting the bigger picture

For those of us who would seek to unravel a bigger picture, operating behind our lives, so much hangs on our getting this knowledge of ourselves, and our place in the bigger scheme of things, into order and structure. It will, if we allow it to, seep through us, change the way we think and live. It will free us to live within a spiritual framework. We will come to understand life and death do go hand in hand, are in harmony when viewed from a wider perspective. In a meaningful view of the world we came here to live and be happy but also to do something for our soul before moving out of this situation and towards home. One has to cut through all the noise of modern life, all the glamour and distractions to get to the root reason for being here – and then get on with our mission. If we don't do it we can rest assured we will be here again, with a similar remit – that we have set for ourselves – and so the wheel continues to turn.

Everything that appears solid is ultimately energy and therefore, in my view, ultimately soul and a part of Love. I believe we will, further down the road – after we fully acknowledge our role as custodians of our planet – get involved in the collective mission that is concerned with service and lifting consciousness on the planet for ourselves and all lifeforms. This is way off in the distance at this time, although each little step we take to awaken individually can only help the process along and bring forward, what I see as, the desired outcome.

It's coming...

And let me just throw in another aspect of this for you to consider: Judging by the observations and anecdotal accounts of individuals (so often put down to over-active imagination) and the amount of aerial activity that we are collectively observing, photographing and filming these days, I suspect that it is not going to be all that far off before we will publicly be meeting our brothers and sisters from elsewhere in the cosmos, from another part, or parts, of our Milky Way galaxy. If, as Fred Hoyle rightly anticipated, seeing a picture of our planet from space for the first time was a, "new idea as powerful as any in history," then imagine what a huge wakeup-call, and game-changer, meeting conscious life from elsewhere will be by comparison. When this happens we will be thrust a lot closer to the truth of our reality. Our coming *normality* will be paranormal by any comparison to where we are now.

Mark this...

So here we are, alive and living on planet Earth. Let me state our circumstances as I know it to be true. Whatever you believe right now, mark this: **Your physical body will eventually die** – and you knew this would happen when you signed up for the experience. **You will also survive this experience** – as no doubt you have done many times before. You need have no fear of this happening and that you will come through it.

When this situation arrives, at its most natural moment – which is not really death so much as a withdrawal, discarding of a vehicle – you (your soul) will move out of your physical body, through one of its exits,[18] and the cord that links you with your physical body will, at that point, be disconnected. You will no longer feel any physical pain. You will have all your faculties. You will still be you, but now your mind will become as clear as a bell. When this moment arrives you will need to retain your wakefulness and trust, so as to go with the flow of what happens next. This involves acceptance: Accepting you are dead, accepting help will be around, will be available. Accepting you will not lose your links with loved ones. At this point be ready to move on into the light.

After you have rested and adjusted, to what appears as a new situation to you, but actually may not be that new, you will come to find that how you have lived your recent physical life will come into sharper focus. Very probably you will notice how much you have given and how much you have taken, in your relations with others – how much love you invested into your life. It will have consequences for how you are, how you view yourself, how you now live with yourself – whether you have made the progress forward that you wanted or not will be the measure – and all will serve to help you decide what you plan to do in the next round, when that eventually arrives.

What if...

> As far as we can discern, the sole purpose of human existence is to kindle a light in the darkness of mere being.
>
> C G Jung, psychiatrist and writer[19]

What if all of us came to believe in (or better than that, *accept*) life after death, and accept the reality of the spiritual journey, and what if we then applied this understanding in our lives now? I anticipate this would have a huge effect on the way we view the world and each other. We would consider our lives here very differently. We would look at life in the long term and treat our planet with a lot more regard and respect. We would treat each other and all plants and creatures around us with a lot more love and respect.

We would live within the natural law of karma (or by whatever name we give it), knowing that we reap what we sow, what we do unto others we do unto ourselves – for good or ill – and that the balance of our thoughts and actions will be redressed naturally. We'd have the promise of eternal life under our belts and in our hearts, and we would want to awaken and fully participate in this bigger adventure.

> You shall know the truth and the truth shall set you free.
>
> Jesus (John 8:32)

At this point most of us are not yet ready to accept such a paradigm. We have yet to begin to explore the spiritual reality more thoroughly and awaken in our own time. But much can be done to support our exploration and in context I believe our children's education needs to include a more rounded perspective and understanding of the issues and beliefs about life and death – particularly the afterlife – so that they can be better informed and freer to choose the route they take.

My desire is to see a range of viewpoints being put into the learning curriculum on this matter; to possibly include:

* The views and beliefs, on life and death, of world religions.
* The views and beliefs on this matter of our sciences.
* The views and beliefs of psychology.
* The views and beliefs of practitioners in holistic subjects, arts and crafts, and those that explore such areas.
* The views and beliefs of paranormal investigators, psychics, mediums and spiritualists.

That each child, at some stage in their education, be encouraged and allowed to form their own judgement as to what they believe. And what they come to believe being based upon open and fair representation of knowledge available from each perspective. If the focus is especially to explore various views on the *afterlife*, this need not be a huge undertaking – and yet it is so important this matter be included in the learning curriculum.

In the same way as a child is expected to know about the world, the environment, their language, mathematics, geography, history, demographics, economics, choosing a career, their government, and his or her place in it all – particularly in context with work and social life – so, I believe, it should be that every effort be made to help each child understand about life and death across the spectrum, from existential to spiritual viewpoints. To be given the opportunity to learn about and explore various beliefs. It is in my opinion patently wrong to avoid covering this important area in our education, or to do it on a token basis, by offering religious education based upon one world religion or alternatively none at all. It is patently also wrong to treat perspectives on life and death as somehow less important than being a success in the worldly sense. Indeed what better than a human being encouraged to, *kindle a light in the darkness of [their] mere being,* and live life in the full roundness of human experience.

And with that final comment, it just leaves me to wish you all good speed, wonderment, love and success on your soul journey homeward – and if you get there before me; put the kettle on would you...

Notes & references

[1] An argument I have heard against this is that when people suffer brain damage their personality can alter too – thus suggesting personality emanates from the brain. My answer is that if a problem arose with the car you drive that meant its performance dropped off or it was less reliable to get from A to B, you would probably alter your behaviour driving it until it was fixed. In negotiating the world the soul is only as good as the condition of the brain it works through or drives.

[2] In an online poll by About.com, 71 percent of respondents believed they had had a paranormal experience. Unfortunately the poll doesn't say how many people actually responded other than a "terrific response" but nevertheless a useful *straw poll*. http://paranormal.about.com/library/weekly/aa083099.htm [Accessed 07/06/2014].

[3] I might add, as an aside, that from a much broader perspective, I see the current secular, humanist position as indeed a potentially healthy one for it is in direction either ignoring or challenging the status quo of orthodox religion. To my mind this could be like clearing away the deadwood of the past and creating a vacuum for something else to emerge – that I trust will be spiritual, not religious, in nature.

[4] Albert Einstein quote taken from Wikiquote http://en.wikiquote.org/wiki/Albert_Einstein [Accessed 07/06/2014].

[5] Neale Donald Walsch is author of the series, *Conversations With God*. This quote from Byrne, R (2006) *The Secret*. TS Production LLC (DVD)

[6] Kimberlee's story from International Association for Near Death Studies. Full story at http://iands.org/experiences/nde-accounts/922-my-awakening-with-the-angels.html [Accessed 07/06/2014].

[7] White, S. E. (1965) *The Betty Book*. Dutton.

[8] The book is described as, "the story of the amazing spiritual revelations received through the medium, 'Betty'" – taken from the 1965 jacket. The work is drawn from messages given by a group of discarnate entities (that the author called the "Invisibles" in the book) to Betty. The interactions began in 1919. These communications were given in an out-of-order fashion, amounting to four

hundred type written pages over a period of a year and a half – from which the book was written. Fifteen years further on there was a further fifteen hundred pages of text. The author claims that the pages used for the book covered a range of topics but they only made sense when, like a jigsaw puzzle, they were later reorganised into their intended order.

[9] White (1965) op. cit.

[10] White (1965) op. cit.

[11] Tibetan Buddhism makes a valuable contribution to the matter of spiritual urgency. It also offers a different perspective on the after-life that you may wish to explore further. It does not believe in the *soul* per se, rather Buddhist belief is in our current life being akin to a stream of consciousness that is linked to the immediate past life experience, and the karma generated behind this. By similar argument, they suppose we live in a world of phenomena, of impermanence, where only change itself can be considered permanent, and thereby there is not necessarily the same belief in life being *meaningful*.

[12] Fremantle, F. and Trungpa, C. (1975) *The Tibetan Book of the Dead – The Great Liberation Through Hearing in the Bardo*. Shambhala.

[13] See Wikipedia http://en.wikipedia.org/wiki/Bardo#cite_ref-2 [Accessed 07/06/2014] where it cites six bardo: The first bardo begins when we take birth and endures as long as we live. The second is the bardo of dreams. The third is the bardo of concentration or meditation. The fourth occurs at the moment of death. The fifth is known as the bardo of the luminosity of the true nature. The sixth is called the bardo of transmigration or karmic becoming.

[14] Rinpoche, S. (1992) *The Tibetan Book of Living and Dying* (p103). Rider.

[15] Ibid., p104

[16] Dalai Lama XIV (2005) *Essence of the Heart Sutra: The Dalai Lama's Heart of Wisdom Teachings*. Wisdom Publications

[17] Rinpoche (1992) op. cit., p104

[18] The soul is believed to exit the body via the solar plexus or the head – depending upon one's level of consciousness. Check out Bailey, A. (1985) Death: *The Great Adventure*. Lucis Press.

[19] Quote from Jung, C. G. (1972) *Memories, Dreams and Reflections*. Collins Fontana Library.

SIX MONTHS TO LIVE

> While I thought that I was learning how to live, I have been learning how to die.
>
> Leonardo da Vinci, painter, sculptor, architect, inventor, writer[1]

It is a *given* that most of us really don't know when our death is going to arrive and whether we prepare, or how we prepare, for the event is of course entirely up to ourselves. What follows here are some constructive thoughts and ideas to encourage you to think about the matter. These are not intended to be upsetting or depressing. Given we are in wholesome circumstances, we all want a good and long physical life. But we know every beginning will have an ending and it is a sign of human maturity to consider and make preparation for that eventuality, to make it as comfortable and successful as we can.

What I want to get across here is the importance of being mindful of your eventual death, and to consider what you can do now, no matter what age, to prepare for it emotionally and spiritually.

Better still why not use the time you have left to rediscover and reacquaint yourself with your spiritual agenda. Oh, did I hear you say you have no idea what that might be? No matter. Imagine you have been given six months to live. Things are urgent, but it is also a useful chunk of time. What might you do to get your act together and be able to say, on the Other Side, you made some headway in the time that was left? If you have a clear idea then great but if not then consider applying the following stepping stones to prepare yourself for the change. And if you think about it, this is not such a bad frame of mind to develop with regard to maintaining that sense of urgency and moment of opportunity. Check out the following agenda:

1. Meditate. Make meditation a lifestyle choice. Get into the habit. This is crucial practice to any routine living, and importantly to open the heart

and head to other possibilities. Practice meditation to help quieten the mind and help you to be centred, in getting in touch with your soul, to help you return to *beginners mind*, as Zen Buddhists describe it. If you need to make peace with your god, higher self, soul, then now, not tomorrow, is the time to begin to do it – and you may find it of great benefit to your life anyway.

2. Practice compassion, being giving and loving to all people, creatures and plants. No matter whether you are a Buddhist or not, follow and practice the Eightfold Path of the Buddha for the way to live on this planet. See link below for more on this.

3. Eat healthily and take regular exercise. Keep as fit and as healthy as you can. Don't bring on the move sooner than you need to – you want to go at the right moment.

4. Get inspired and get some laughter into your life. Spend time with others. Music, nature and comedy can be great life-invigorating, life-enhancing and life-giving devices.

5. Regardless of your work and other interests, get studying philosophy and spiritual texts – dig into any philosophical, religious or esoteric knowledge that appeals to you. You'll doubtless find clues to your own *agenda* in your search. Try viewing yourself as a citizen of the cosmos, of which Earth is a part, and where that might take you in your learning. Learn as much as you can about life and death in a manner that means something to you. Find and follow a path you are at peace with.

6. If you are of a mind to, get hold of – and get some professional help to understand – your astrological birthchart. Discover the numerology surrounding your life, and explore the I Ching to answer profound questions and help uncover your path. You might also check out the Ten Bulls of Zen to help you identify your goals and where you may be now. See relevant articles on astrology and the I Ching, below.

7. Why wait until you have passed over: Take time out to pursue a review of your life, from a spiritual perspective. Consider what has worked, what hasn't, where you have *given* and where you have *taken*.

Consider how much love you have or haven't spread around – but also be kind to yourself. Find some means, in your *here and now*, of redressing the balance if that is needed. Be of service to others – for the giving and joy of it. You might try *random acts of kindness* if at a loss as to what to do.

8. Always let those you love know how much you love them. And seek to resolve any disagreements and disharmony in your relationships. Make sure you try to heal or bring closure on any family or friend wounding or rift before your departure. You will find it really reassuring to get such matters resolved anyway.

9. Consider anything urgent, or what you would really like to do, before you depart. Is there anything important outside of this plan that you need to complete, to finish, or need to get on with right now? Is there any place or person you need to visit? What would help you to complete on your stay here before you go there?

10. If you can, turn the situation on its head and imagine that you are currently on holiday in a foreign country. You are learning all you can about it, and your place in it – and shortly you will be returning homeward.

At the point of your death, stay awake, trust your instincts to know where you are, and which way to go. Look for the light and be brave. Alternatively after six months, if you're still around in the physical, give yourself a pat on the back, perhaps celebrate in some way, and then continue with your journey, for the next 6 months – there'll be plenty to do in the short time you have left.

📖 **BONUS ONLINE CONTENT**: Need some further help with some of the pointers above? Download the following articles from the book's website: 1. Get Healthy Get Meditation; 2. The Eightfold Path of Buddha; 3. Tips for Staying Healthy; 4. Twelve Life Enhancing Books; 5. Get Real About Astrology (parts 1 & 2); 6. Wise Up on The I Ching (parts 1 & 2); 7. How to Find Your Self. Visit the **Free Article Resource** on the book's website, **LifeandDeaththeBook.com**

Now for some of the more mundane but equally serious considerations

Now let's deal with some of the more mundane considerations. In context, with your eventual death, think about the following, particularly relating to your loved one/s:

1. Get a *will* drawn up: A will is essential to legally divide up your estate. This is something that can be done at any time (so you don't have to be mid-life or later to be thinking of it) and, to be on top of things, the sooner the better. You can do this yourself – check out the Web – or go through suitable solicitors or specialist will-writers. Once written, a will can be changed by you if, as or when, your circumstances alter.

2. Think on, it is really important to sort out any loose ends in your life. Make sure you let loved ones know of anything that may benefit them after your passing. Equally make sure you are not going to burden them with any bills, no hidden unfinished business that may hurt them. If you have keys to, say, a safe or other important lockup, bank account/s, or if you have logins and passwords to important online accounts, that they should know about, then do now make sure they know about these. Let them know how or where to access such personal and private information should they need to. There will, of course, be formal channels that any next of kin will need to follow, in order to be able to access such as a bank account, but they will benefit by knowing in advance who you have an account with, and what it is.

3. This is not a time to keep skeletons in the cupboard that might damage others, or cause others to think badly of you if discovered. Confide with whom you need to, make amends, and clear out any garbage. Aim to get closure, or make a clean and wholesome break with any darkness in your past – and particularly forgive yourself of wrongdoings. This is good advice at any time. You can't take *things* with you but you can take regrets and resentments with you. Don't wait, do it now.

---

4. Discuss how you may keep in touch with loved ones after your departure – and lodge a note to this effect with your nearest and dearest. How will they know you, if contacting them from the Other Side? In the physical, if you moved to the other side of the world, you might well use a mobile, landline, letter, email or internet phonecall, but in the spiritual you will probably use a human exchange, a medium, and it will help loved ones to identify you if you have pre-arranged some kind of ID or message that the receiver will know you by. Alternatively, it could be you agree on something, in the home, that you affect – move a picture, turn lights on and off. Electrical items are the most easy to manipulate. But nothing too spooky, the aim is to let people know you are still around and taking interest, not to scare them.

5. Organise how your funeral is to be conducted – whether burial or cremation, whether you want a wake or not. This is not something any of us want to necessarily be dealing with, but do think about it. You could write out a simple plan of action to make it clear – and leave it with a loved one. Such information is best lodged with next of kin, alternatively friends, or whoever you may have selected to act as trustee or executor of your estate. If you feel it necessary you can also lodge such information with the organisation you have planned to undertake your funeral. Also you might consider paying in advance for your funeral so that costs are covered – and covered against inflation.

6. From a financial aspect you may already have, or want to consider taking out, life insurance to help cope with costs and also support for loved ones. Make sure they also know if you do take one out.

7. If you follow a particular faith or religion and would like a representative to see you, at or near the time of your passing, make sure this request is known to whoever is looking after your interests.

So just think how you might apply some or all of these steps in your life right now. Don't wait until you've passed over to the Other Side, and thereby less able to resolve unfinished business back here. It's not so easy to administer from there…

Notes & references

[1] Bortolon, L. (1967) *The Life and Times of Leonardo*. London, Paul Hamlyn.

BIBLIOGRAPHY

Books

Alexander, Dr E. (2012) *Proof of Heaven*. Piatkus

American Bible Society (1976) *Good News New Testament*. William Collins/Fount.

ARAS (2010) *The Book Of Symbols: Reflections On Archetypal Images*. ARAS - The Archive for Research in Archetypal Symbolism.

Atwater, P. M. H. (2007) *The Big Book of Near-Death Experiences: The Ultimate Guide to What Happens When We Die*. Hampton Roads Publishing Company.

Baba, M. (1967) *Discourses 2* San Francisco: Sufism reoriented. ISBN 978-1880619094

Bailey, A (1930) *The Soul and its Mechanism*. Lucis Trust Press Ltd.

Bailey, A. and Khul, D. (1971) *Ponder on This* [Compilation] The Lucis Press Ltd.

Bailey, A. and Khul, D. (1985) *Death: The Great Adventure*. Lucis Press Ltd

Bibby, G. (1956) *The Testimony of The Spade*. Alfred A. Knopf.

Bible (1957) *Holy Bible Illustrated*. King James version. Collins Clear Type Press.

Bortolon, L. (1967) *The Life and Times of Leonardo*. London, Paul Hamlyn.

Bowman, C. (1998) *Children's Past Lives: How Past Life Memories Affect Your Child*. Bantam.

Brown, R. (1989) *The Reincarnation of James the Submarine Man*. Rick Brown publisher.

Browne, S. (2000) *Life on The Other Side*. Piatkus

Browne, S. (2000) *The Other Side and Back*. Signet

Byrne, R. (2006) *The Secret* (book), Atria Books – also a movie of the same name.

Clark, E. M. (2012) *The Experience* (Near to Death), Friesen Press.

Dalai Lama XIV (2005) *Essence of the Heart Sutra: The Dalai Lama's Heart of Wisdom Teachings*. Wisdom Publications.

David, W. and Gibson, M. (1980) *Reincarnation and the Soul in the Parables of Jesus*. DeVorss & Company.

Dawkins, R. (2000) *Unweaving the Rainbow: Science, Delusion and the Appetite for Wonder*. Mariner Books

Einstein, A. (2006) *The World as I See It*. Citadel Press Books.

Evans, E. P. (1906)(1987) *The Criminal Prosecution and Capital Punishment of Animals*. London: Faber & Faber.

Fort, C. (1973) *The Book of the Damned*. Sphere Books Ltd (Abacus paperback series).

Fremantle, F. and Trungpa, C. (1975) *The Tibetan Book of the Dead – The Great Liberation Through Hearing in the Bardo*. Shambhala.

Gardner, H. (1993) Frames Of Mind: The Theory Of Multiple Intelligences. Basic Books (first published 1983).

Grabhorn, L. (2005) *Excuse Me, Your Life is Waiting*. Hodder Mobius.

Grieveson, A. (2011) *A Series of Past Lives*. Kindle Edition.

Heindel, M. (1909) *The Rosicrucian Cosmo-Conception (Chapt 3: Man and the Method of Evolution)*. The Rosicrucian Fellowship.

Heindel, M. (1953) *The Desire Body*. The Rosicrucian Fellowship.

Henderson, J. A. (Scottish Award Winning Author) (2010) *Edinburgh: City of the Dead*. Black and White Publishing.

Holden, J. (2003) *Distressing Near-Death Experiences*. IANDS.

Hunter, M. (2005) *New light on the 'Drummer of Tedworth': conflicting narratives of witchcraft in Restoration England*. Birkbeck University of London.

Hynek, J.A. (1972) The UFO Experience: A Scientific Inquiry. Henry Regnery Company. ISBN 0-8094-8054-9.

Iverson, J. (1976) *More Lives Than One? The evidence of the remarkable Bloxham Tapes*. Souvenir Press, London.

Jung, C. G. (1972) *Memories, Dreams and Reflections*. Collins Fontana Library.

Kubler-Ross, E. (1975) *Death: the Final Stage of Growth*. Spectrum Books.

Kuhn, H. (1958) *On the Track of Prehistoric Man*. Arrow Books.

Lazar, R. (2010) *UFOs & Area 51 - The Official Bob Lazar Video - Alien Technology Revealed*. UFOTV® The Disclosure Movie Network

Leakey, L. S. B. (1960) *Adam's Ancestors: The Evolution of Man and His Culture*. Harper & Row.

Leininger, B., Leininger, A., and Gross, K. (2009) *Soul Survivor: The Reincarnation of a World War II Fighter Pilot*. Hay House.

MacGregor, G. (1978). *Reincarnation in Christianity: a new vision of the role of rebirth in Christian thought*. Quest Books.

Moody JR, Dr R. (1977) *Life After Life*. Bantam Books.

Moody, R. A. (1990). *Coming back: A psychiatrist explores past-life journeys*. Bantam Books.

Morris, S. C. (1996) *The History in Our Bones*. BBC Education.

Müller, F. M. (2004) *Sacred Books of the East*, Vol. 10 - The Dhammapada. Motilal Banarsidass.

Playfair, G. L. (2007) *This House is Haunted*. The History Press.

Richie, G. R. and Sherrill, E. (1978) *Return from Tomorrow*. Revell books.

Ring, Dr K. (1980) *Life at Death*. Coward, McCann & Geoghegan.

Rinpoche, S. (1992) *The Tibetan Book of Living and Dying*. Rider.

Rogo, D. S. (2005) *On the Track of the Poltergeist*. Anomalist Books.

Sagan, C. (1997) *Contact*. Mass Market Paperback. First published 1985.

Sagan, C. (2002) *Cosmos*. Random House. First published 1980.

Schaff, P. ed. (1994)[1885] *The Anathemas Against Origen. Nicene and Post-Nicene Fathers*: Series II, Volume XIV (The Seven Ecumenical Councils). Peabody, Massachusetts: Hendrickson Publishers.

Snow, R. (1999) *Looking for Carroll Beckwith*. St Martin's Press.

Sohl, R. & Carr, A (1970) *The Gospel According to Zen*. The New English Library Ltd, London.

Stevenson Dr I. *Hypnotic Regression to Previous Lives*. University of Virginia, School of Medicine.

Stevenson, Dr I. (1977) *Cases of the Reincarnation Type*, Volume II, Sri Lanka. University Press of Virginia.

Stevenson, Dr I. (2000) *Children Who Remember Previous Lives: A Question of Reincarnation*. McFarland & Company.

Stevenson, R. L. (2011) *Edinburgh Picturesque Notes*. Kindle Edition.

Watson, L. (1973) *Supernature*. Hodder & Stoughton.

Weiss, J. E. (1972) *The Vestibule*. Ashley Books Inc.

Wendt, H. (1972) *From Ape to Adam*. Omega.

White, F. (1998) *The Overview Effect: Space Exploration and Human Evolution*. American Institute of Aeronautics & Astronautics.

White, S. E. (1965) *The Betty Book*. Dutton.

Wilde, O. (1892) *Lady Windermere's Fan*. Act III Lord Darlington

Williams, K. R. (2002) *Nothing Better Than Death: Insights From 62 Profound Near-Death Experiences*. Xlibris Corporation.

Articles/Journals

Beirne, P. (1994) *The Law is an Ass: Reading E P Evans, The Mediaeval Prosecution and Capital Punishment of Animals*. Society and Animals, Vol 2., No1. The White Horse Press, Cambridge UK.

Dart, R. A. (1925, February 7) *Australopithecus Africanus: The Man-Ape of South Africa.* Nature journal.

Geller, U. (2001, 31 December) *When Uri met David.* The Telegraph.

Holt, J. (2004, 1 December) *The Man Behind the Meme: An Interview with Richard Dawkins.* Source: A Good Atheist Secularist Skeptical Book Collection.

Parnia, Dr S. (2013, July 29) *Back from the Dead: Resuscitation Expert Says End is Reversible.* Der Spiegel Online. Interviewer Marco Evers.

Parnia, S. et al. (2014) *AWARE – AWAreness during Resuscitation – A prospective study.* Resuscitation journal.

Rinpoche, S. (1988) *The Survival of Consciousness: A Tibetan Buddhist Perspective.* Article in Self & Society.

Sample, I. (2011, 15 May) Stephen Hawking: *There is no heaven; it's a fairy story.* The Guardian.

Shushan, G (2009) *Conceptions of the Afterlife in Early Civilizations: Universalism, Constructivism and Near-Death Experience.* Continuum.

Van Lommel, Dr P. (2001) *Near-death experience in survivors of cardiac arrest: a prospective study in the Netherlands.* Find at http://profezie3m.altervista.org/archivio/TheLancet_NDE.htm [Accessed 16/03/2013].

Van Lommel, Dr P. (2006) *Near-Death Experience, Consciousness, and the Brain: A New Concept About the Continuity of Our Consciousness based on Recent Scientific Research on Near-Death Experience in Survivors of Cardiac Arrest.* World Futures, 62: pp134–151.

Websites/URLs visited

American Society for Psychical Research
http://aspr.com
Anthroposophy Group in the Philippines
http://anthrophils.wordpress.com/2013/04/02/the-four-ethers-a-summary/
BrainyQuote:
http://www.brainyquote.com/quotes/quotes/a/adamcaroll485689.html
http://www.brainyquote.com/quotes/quotes/f/friedrichd404245.html
http://www.brainyquote.com/quotes/quotes/t/tombrokaw108699.html
http://www.brainyquote.com/quotes/quotes/p/petersinge471299.html
Carol Bowman:
http://www.carolbowman.com/childrens-past-lives/

http://www.childpastlives.org/

Chadbad.org

http://www.chabad.org/library/article_cdo/aid/3194/jewish/What-is-a-Soul.htm

City of the Dead Tours

http://www.cityofthedeadtours.com/the-mackenzie-poltergeist/

Derek Acorah, psychic medium

http://freespirit-tv.com/2011/09/derek-acorah/

Diane Goble NDE experiencer

http://www.beyondtheveil.net/nde.html

Dr Chris Henshilwood

http://www.bradshawfoundation.com/africa/oldest_art/index.php

Dr Ian Stevenson

http://www.iisis.net/index.php?page=semkiw-ian-stevenson-xenglossy-reincarnation-past-lives

http://www.iisis.net/index.php?page=semkiw-ian-stevenson-xenoglossy-reincarnation-past-lives-gretchen&hl=en_US

http://www.medicine.virginia.edu/clinical/departments/psychiatry/sections/cspp/dops/regression-page

Edgar Mitchell astronaut

https://www.youtube.com/watch?v=7AAJ34_NMcI#t=333

Elizabeth Kubler-Ross (Foundation)

http://www.ekrfoundation.org/quotes/

Fortean Times magazine

http://www.forteantimes.com

Gaiamlife

http://blog.gaiam.com/quotes/authors/ian-gardner

Goodreads

http://www.goodreads.com/author/quotes/102062.Carl_R_Rogers

http://www.goodreads.com/quotes/117915-there-are-no-mistakes-no-coincidences-all-events-are-blessings

http://www.goodreads.com/author/quotes/1505445.James_Dean

History.com

http://www.history.com/topics/halloween/historical-ghost-stories

Horizon Research Foundation | Nour Foundation (Human Consciousness Project)

http://www.horizonresearch.org

http://www.nourfoundation.com

International Association for Near Death Studies (IANDS)

http://iands.org/experiences/nde-accounts/922-my-awakening-with-the-angels.html

http://iands.org/home.html

http://iands.org/research/important-research-articles/698-greyson-nde-scale.html
Life and Death the book
http://lifeanddeaththebook.com/fringe-benefits/lucky-escapes-or-intervention/
National Geographic
http://news.nationalgeographic.com/news/2003/06/0611_030611_earliesthuman.html
Nature journal
http://www.nature.com/news/2011/110823/full/news.2011.498.html
Near-Death Experience and the Afterlife
http://www.near-death.com/experiences/research14.html
Planetary Collective (2012) *Overview* movie.
http://overviewthemovie.com
Plotinus.com
http://www.plotinus.com/subtle_bodies_copy.htm
Public Domain Poetry
http://www.public-domain-poetry.com/alfred-lord-tennyson/ring-685
Rachel Keene (medium)
http://rachelkeene.co.uk/faq-life-on-the-other-side/
Roman Catholic Church
http://www.vatican.va/archive/ccc_css/archive/catechism/p123a11.htm#990
http://www.vatican.va/archive/ccc_css/archive/catechism/p1s2c1p6.htm#364
http://www.vatican.va/archive/ENG0015/__P2G.HTM
Society for Psychical Research UK
http://spr.ac.uk
http://www.spr.ac.uk/publication/pitmilly-house-poltergeist-manor
Some Inspiration
http://someinspiration.com/bit-of-a-story/nde-story-paul-eicke/
The Bloxham Tapes Revisited
http://www.ianlawton.com/plr1.htm
The British Psychological Society
http://www.bps.org.uk/
The Earth Association for Regression Therapy
http://www.earth-association.org/
The Olduvai Gorge Research Project
http://www.olduvaiproject.org/
The Past Life Therapists Association
http://www.pastliferegression.co.uk/pltahome.html
The Reincarnation of James the Submarine Man
http://www.ial.goldthread.com/brown.html
The Science Times

http://www.sciencetimes.com/articles/3687/20150305/ancient-human-jaw-bone-evidence-earlier-evolution.htm

The Swedenborg Society
http://www.swedenborg.org.uk/emanuel_swedenborg

Time Magazine
http://content.time.com/time/specials/packages/article/0,28804,1855221_1855285_1855252,00.html

Wikipedia
http://en.wikipedia.org/wiki/Astral_body
http://en.wikipedia.org/wiki/Aura_(paranormal)
http://en.wikipedia.org/wiki/Aurignacian
http://en.wikipedia.org/wiki/Bardo#cite_ref-2
http://en.wikipedia.org/wiki/Burial
http://en.wikipedia.org/wiki/Cro-Magnon
http://en.wikipedia.org/wiki/Death_%26_Taxes
http://en.wikipedia.org/wiki/Enfield_Poltergeist
https://en.wikipedia.org/wiki/Homo_naledi
https://en.wikipedia.org/wiki/Human
http://en.wikipedia.org/wiki/Karma
http://en.wikipedia.org/wiki/Monothelitism
http://en.wikipedia.org/wiki/Neanderthal
http://en.wikipedia.org/wiki/Near-death_experience
http://en.wikipedia.org/wiki/Origen
https://en.wikipedia.org/wiki/Pascal's_Wager
http://en.wikipedia.org/wiki/Past_life_regression
http://en.wikipedia.org/wiki/Poveglia
http://en.wikipedia.org/wiki/Reincarnation
http://en.wikipedia.org/wiki/Remote_viewing
http://en.wikipedia.org/wiki/RMS_Queen_Mary
http://en.wikipedia.org/wiki/Soul_sleep
http://en.wikipedia.org/wiki/Synod_of_Constantinople_(543)
https://en.wikipedia.org/wiki/United_States_Navy_Marine_Mammal_Program
http://en.wikipedia.org/wiki/What_I_Believe

Wikiquote
http://en.wikiquote.org/wiki/Albert_Einstein
http://en.wikiquote.org/wiki/Talk:Bertrand_Russell

Your Ghost Stories
http://www.yourghoststories.com/real-ghost-story.php?story=16440

Index

A life/death learning curriculum, 295

A lion's viewpoint, 142

About the author, 317

Adam and Eve, 67, 145

Africa and homo sapiens, 152

Africa and rock art, 154

Afterlife, 49

Albert Einstein, 65, 140, 285

Alice Bailey theosophist, writer, 195, 201, 202, 204

Alzheimer's, 193

Andrea Grieveson medium, 184, 263, 266

Angels, 10, 178, 287

Angry with God, 6

Animal ghosts, 96

Animals and crime, 143

Assisted suicide comment, 254

Astral vehicle, 200

Astrology, 9, 61, 190, 237, 299

Atheist, 7, 25

Aurignacian culture, 152

Australopithecus, 149

Author's past lives, 184

AWARE Study, 102

Awe for life, 14, 41, 52

Bardos of Tibetan Buddhism, 290

Being agnostic, 38

Bloxham Tapes - PLR, 126

Bob Lazar, physicist, 160

Bonus online content, 90, 300

Brain-centricity, 37, 280

Bridey Murphy and PLR, 120

British Psychological Society, 128

Carl Jung, 7, 93, 201, 232

Carl Rogers psychologist, 21

Carl Sagan, 55

Carol Bowman past life therapist, 109, 111, 117, 229

Catechism, 5, 50

Cave paintings, 154, 156

Cells and life, 206

CG Jung - Memories, Dreams, Reflections, 8

Charles Fort, 80

Childhood and baggage, 39

Children and Father Christmas, 39

Children and paranormal, 74, 81, 85, 89, 92

Children and past lives, 109, 111, 113, 117

Children and wonderment, 51

Children learning of death, 30

Children on the Other Side, 259

Children, initiation, 156

Children's education, 294

Chris Henshilwood archaeologist, 154

Christian belief/faith, 113, 146, 176, 179

Christian Church, 180

Christian mortalism, 180

Christianity - body and Soul, 177, 184

Christianity and reincarnation, 182

Church of England, 6

Colin Fry medium, 129, 131, 269

Comment on 10 big questions, 284

Compassion – practice of, 299

Computer - Soul analogy, 193

Conscious life in cosmos, 292

Consciousness, 47, 62, 147, 158, 161, 163, 193, 203, 207, 228, 292

Contemplating death, 32

Cro-Magnon man, 151

Cult and magic in cave art, 156

Custodians of the Garden, 147

Dalai Lama, 291

David Blaine - magician, 73

Death, 32

Death and sleep, 204

Death and survival, 293

Death announcement, 29

Death following motor accident, 246

Derek Acorah psychic medium, 92, 129, 262, 272

Diane Goble NDE, 258

DJ, Gretchen Gottlieb - PLR, 124

Dolphins, 144

Dr Eben Alexander, 102, 228, 258

Dr Ian Stevenson psychiatrist, 111, 114, 119

Dr Kenneth Ring, 253

Dr Pim van Lommel – NDE researcher, 102

Dr Raymond Moody, 98

Dr Sam Parnia, 103, 105

Earthbound soul, 76

Effects on radio, 93

Elisabeth Kubler-Ross, 98, 255

Emperor Justinian, 183

Enfield poltergeist, 67, 74, 93

Etheric vehicle, 195

Etheric vehicle and aura, 199

Etheric vehicle and chakras, 197

European Early Modern Humans, 152

Eve's paranormal story, 67

Evolution, 27, 148, 155, 158, 167

Evolution and the ant, 205

Existentialist, 7, 25, 189

Father Christmas, 38

Frank White - Overview Effect, 53

Fringe interests, 10, 14

Funeral arrangements, 302

Galileo Galilei, 282

Garden of Eden, 145

Genetic code, 25

Get a Will, 301

Ghost in the machine, 95

Ghost tours, 79

Ghosts, 60, 67, 78, 82, 85, 91

Ghosts - author's stories, 83

Ghosts and poltergeists, 73

God, 27, 145, 191

Good ship Earth, 52

Grantham ghost cyclists, 85

Greyson NDE scale, 101

Guardian Angel, 10

Guy Lyon Playfair parapsychologist, 65, 69, 75

Handwriting and PLR, 124

Hauntings and causes, 93, 95

Hauntings and closure, 95

Heaven and Hell, 241

Herbert Kuhn prehistorian, 155

Herbert Wendt nature scientist, 156

Hominids, 149

Homo naledi, 150

Homo sapiens, 150

Human beings, 141

Humanist, 25

Hungry ghost state, 244

Hunter-gatherers, 152

I Ching, 9, 234, 299

IANDS, 101

Ice Age, 151, 153

Intelligence, 163

James Leininger past life recall, 112, 229

Janet Hodgson - Enfield Poltergeist, 69

Jesus, 177, 179, 181, 267, 278

Judgement Day, 180

Karma, 37, 49, 191, 213, 239

Karma examples of, 217

Keeping in touch, 302

Kimberlee's NDE, 287

Law of Attraction, 37, 41, 238

Leakey's Olduvai Gorge, 150

Leap in consciousness, 157

Life and abundance, 22

Life and afterlife linked, 1

Life and Death Questions, 44

Life meaningful, 48

Life review, 299

Light vehicle, 203

Love, 42, 100, 199, 202, 287, 289

Lyall Watson life scientist, 9

Mackenzie poltergeist, 74, 77

Maurice Grosse parapsychologist, 75

Max Heindel astrologer, mystic, 201

Meaningful world, 38, 189, 232, 292

Meaningless world, 7
Mechanistic paradigm, 280
Meditation, 298
Mediums, 61, 92, 128, 133, 184, 227, 242, 246, 260, 262, 269
Mental vehicle, 201
Merchant Navy, 4, 186
Multi-cellular organisms, 148
Music, 63, 96, 154, 166, 257, 259, 264, 299
Nature, 60, 141, 164
Nature group, 266
Nature walk, 51
NDE and research, 102
NDE and suicide, 253
NDE Being of light, 100
NDE Boundaries, 101
NDE Dark tunnel, 99
NDE Out-of-body, 100
NDE Paul Eicke, 99, 106
NDE possible stages, 99
Neale Donald Walsch author, 286
Neanderthals, 150, 152
Near-death experience, 34, 61, 98, 102, 211, 246, 258, 267, 272, 287
Non-spiritual belief, 25
Normality, 14, 63, 66, 70, 73
Numerology, 299
Of sludge and slime, 167
Origen and anathemas, 184
Origen early Christian, 182, 192
Original Sin, 146, 177
Origins of life, 148
Orthodox science, 25, 280
Our spiritual agenda, 229, 237
Out of Africa, 149
Pascal's wager, 34
Past life recall of children, 61
Past Life Regression, 118
Past lives, 120, 126, 185
Past lives as group, 236
Piers Beirne criminologist, 143
Planet Neptune, 55
Playback hauntings, 91

PLR – Past Life Regression, 61
PLR and past lives comment, 127
Poltergeist, 65, 74, 79, 81, 82, 92
Priest, 5
Proactive evolution, 158, 169
Psychic cleaners, 96
Psychics, 128, 242, 246, 260
Questioning Christian belief, 6
Rachel Keene medium, 244, 268
Random acts of kindness, 300
Raymond Dart anthropologist, 149
Recurring numbers, 234
Reincarnation, 46, 61, 109, 114, 181, 207, 210, 220
Reincarnation and karma, 213
Reincarnation East and West, 208
Reincarnation is logical, 212
Relationships and harmony, 300
Remembering past lives, 109
Remembering where we are, 51
Resurrection of the body, 180
Resuscitation, 34, 98, 101, 106, 107
Rite of passage, 38
RMS Queen Mary hauntings, 83, 86, 94
Robert Louis Stevenson, 78
Robin Hood, 240
Roman Catholic, 4, 50, 125
Santa Claus, 39
Sceptics, 69, 280
Secularist, 25
Service to others, 300
Seven Centres of Force, 197
Shades of Pascal's wager, 34
Shocking experience, 10
Sigmund Freud, 7
Single-celled organisms, 148
Six months to live, 298
Society for Psychical Research, 75, 128
Sogyal Rinpoche Tibetan Lama and author, 189, 290
Soul, 10, 26, 49, 174, 181, 182, 293
Soul - astral vehicle, 200
Soul - etheric vehicle, 195

Soul - light vehicle, 203
Soul - mental vehicle, 201
Soul - physical vehicle, 194
Soul and crime, 239
Soul and expected death, 255
Soul and its vehicles, 194
Soul and karma, 220
Soul and life review, 261
Soul and new incarnation, 272
Soul and Reincarnation, 207
Soul and sleep state, 204
Soul and suicide, 251
Soul and the ant, 205
Soul in limbo, 250
Soul in Nature, 192
Soul Journey Start, 42
Soul sleep, 180
Souls - earthbound state, 243
Souls – earthbound state, 242
Spirit guides, 235
Spiritual hints/clues, 232
Spiritual journey, 191, 192, 211
Spiritual malnutrition, 282
Spiritual progress, 230
Spiritual urgency – Buddhist
    perspective, 290
State of innocence, 142, 145, 146, 157,
    162, 192, 239
Subconscious, 43, 93, 203, 214, 286
Subconscious and PLR, 119
Sujith and Sammy past life, 114
Sylvia Browne medium, 227, 261, 269,
    272
TE and Jensen Jocoby - PLR, 122
Ten big questions, 45
Ten reasons for author's beliefs, 60
The Aura, 191
The Awakening, 153
The Betty Book, 288
The Book of the Damned, 80
The Dark Side, 238
The desire for a long life, 33
The Fringes, 59, 66

The good life, 16, 21, 52
The good life - children leaving, 18
The good life - dying, 20
The good life - family, 18
The good life - happiness, 22
The good life - health, 22
The good life - love, 22
The good life - marriage, 18
The good life - retirement, 19
The good life - retirement home, 20
The good life - road to success, 17
The good life - schooling, 17
The good life - service, 25
The good life - spirituality, 23
The good life - start, 17
The Gospels, 178
The Internet, 279
The Missing Link, 149
The Other Side, 1, 46, 61, 131, 134, 211,
    225, 257, 291
The Other Side - life review, 261
The Other Side - moving to, 246
The Other Side - music, 259
The Other Side - summary, 273
The Other Side and love, 261
The Other Side and mediums, 262
The Other Side and this side, 260
The Other Side FAQs, 263
The Other Side location, 269
The Paranormal, 47, 60, 63, 94, 167
The Paranormal - author's stories, 83
The paranormal - explanations, 90
The Skeptic magazine, 66, 69
The Soul – what it is, 191
The spiritual & evolution, 28
The Stag Hotel, 85
The Traveller, 192
The void state, 243
The Web, 279
This side, 226
Tibetan Bardos, 209
Tibetan Buddhism, 290
Time and the Other Side, 256

Two endings to life, 27
Upper Palaeolithic culture, 151
Vortices, 91
Walter Semkiw MD, 122, 124

What if, 294
Where to next, 27, 278
Wolves, 165
World religions, 62

About The Author

Francis O'Neill is Irish by birth and although he feels very much at
home in England, where he has lived for most of his life, he admits that a part of him still lives in a misty and magical world that he associates with his roots.

Having written articles and guides on topics, ranging from IT and archaeology to holistic, New Age and spiritual matters, he has now turned his hand to writing this his first book. As indicated, at the front of the book, he plans to write more on philosophical and spiritual matters very close to his heart.

He has a BA Hons (1st) in Humanistic and Transpersonal Psychology. He is also a practising and award winning astrologer, having studied with the Faculty of Astrological Studies, and the Mayo School of Astrology, in the UK. He has spent a good deal of his life as a field archaeologist, supervising rescue excavations on Roman and prehistoric sites, and also as a qualified lecturer in adult education. He lives in the Cotswolds (UK) with his partner, the composer/musician, Annie Locke.

You can find out more about the book, and other topics, by the author, by visiting LifeandDeaththeBook.com or, alternatively, the publisher website – SomeInspiration.com.

Lightning Source UK Ltd.
Milton Keynes UK
UKOW06f2249120416

272112UK00001B/16/P